S0-ADH-590

ROCKVILLE CAMPUS LIBRARY

WITHDRAWN FROM LIBRARY

David L. Dunlop, Ph.D., is an associate professor and chairman of the Education Department at the University of Pittsburgh at Johnstown.

Thomas F. Sigmund, Ph.D., is an associate professor of math and computer science at the University of Pittsburgh at Johnstown.

In addition, they both have extensive experience teaching, writing, making presentations, and conducting workshops on math-related topics.

Prentice-Hall International, Inc., *London*
Prentice-Hall of Australia Pty. Limited, *Sydney*
Prentice-Hall Canada Inc., *Toronto*
Prentice-Hall of India Private Limited, *New Delhi*
Prentice-Hall of Japan, Inc., *Tokyo*
Prentice-Hall of Southeast Asia Pte. Ltd., *Singapore*
Whitehall Books Limited, *Wellington, New Zealand*
Editora Prentice-Hall do Brasil Ltda., *Rio de Janerio*

Problem Solving with the Programmable Calculator

Puzzles, Games & Simulations
with Math & Science Applications

DAVID L. DUNLOP
THOMAS F. SIGMUND

PRENTICE-HALL, INC., Englewood Cliffs, N.J. 07632

A SPECTRUM BOOK

Library of Congress Cataloging in Publication Data

Dunlop, David L.
    Problem solving with the programmable calculator.

  "A Spectrum Book."
    1. Programmable calculators—Problems, exercises,
etc. 2. Problem solving—Data processing. I. Sigmund,
Thomas F. II. Title.
QA75.D84 1983   510'.28'54   82-12341
ISBN 0-13-721340-9
ISBN 0-13-721332-8 (pbk.)

This book can be made available to businesses and organizations
at a special discount when ordered in large quantities.
Contact: Prentice-Hall, Inc., General Publishing Division,
Special Sales, Englewood Cliffs, New Jersey 07632

© 1983 by Prentice-Hall, Inc., Englewood Cliffs, New Jersey 07632.
All rights reserved. No part of this book may be reproduced in any
form or by any means without permission in writing from the publisher.
A Spectrum Book. Printed in the United States of America.

10 9 8 7 6 5 4 3 2 1

ISBN 0-13-721340-9

ISBN 0-13-721332-8 (PBK.)

Editorial/production supervision by Carol Smith
Cover design/illustration by Judy Leeds
Manufacturing buyer: Barbara A. Frick

To Cathy and Marcy

Contents

Preface

Problem solving can be a very exciting, challenging, and educational adventure. This book offers you the opportunity to develop your problem-solving and programming skills in the solution of a wide variety of mathematical and scientific applications. The unique approach to problem solving offered here illustrates an alternative to traditional problem solving and demonstrates the tremendous capability of a programmable calculator in using repetitive processes to solve problems, play games, and simulate real world phenomena.

For convenience, the book is separated into three general categories: (1) challenges, (2) games, and (3) simulations. Chapter 1 presents a series of interesting puzzles that you are challenged to solve using a programmable calculator. If you need a clue, a flowchart is provided for each puzzle. In the unlikely event that you give up, a solution is provided in the form of a keystroke sequence and accompanying user instructions.

Chapter 2 consists of five exciting games designed to keep you (in some cases you and a friend) active for many hours. In addition to familiar games such as football, the chapter includes an original space war game, Calculaser, in which you and an opponent attempt to find and destroy each other's spaceships. A sample game plan and detailed user instructions are provided for each game. In addition, program notes explain the program sequence that accompanies each game. This gives you an opportunity to modify the program if you choose.

Chapter 3 provides a wide range of simulations that will allow you to do such things as determine your annual radiation dosage, manipulate the variables that affect your car's gasoline mileage, calculate the dollar savings possible through changes in your personal or home energy budgets, estimate the number of calories necessary to lose weight, and much, much more.

We made no deliberate attempt to write the programs in their most efficient, condensed form. Although that would be desirable from a technical point of view, efficient programs are frequently more difficult to understand because of the multiple roles assigned to specific data registers, counters, flags, and the like. If you like to write or edit programs, consider it a challenge to rewrite ours in a shorter format.

Although the keystroke sequence composing each program has been written specifically for the Texas Instruments TI–59 programmable calculator, most of the programs will work *without* modification on the TI–58. Furthermore, the TI–57 and its Radio Shack equivalent will accept many of these programs, with only minor modifications (see Appendix I). These programs can also be modified for use with several other models of programmable calculators or home computers. The flowcharts in Chapter 1 and the program comments in Chapters 2 and 3 will assist you in modifying the programs for your specific model.

When entering Chapter 1 programs into your calculator, simply follow the keystroke sequence accompanying the flowcharts for each program. These keystrokes will match the keys on the face of your calculator. When entering Chapter 2 or Chapter 3 programs into your calculator, follow the keystroke sequence listed in the printout of the program. In *most* instances the keystrokes will again match the calculator's keyboard; however, a few of the abbreviations listed in the printout need special attention. To assist you in entering these keystrokes, see Appendix II, which provides a list of these special abbreviations and their associated keyboard keys.

You do not have to be an expert in the use of a programmable calculator to enjoy the programs in this book; however, if you are a beginner, you should keep your owner's manual handy as a reference in case questions arise. Although no programming skill is necessary to use any of the programs in this book, the challenges in Chapter 1 require a basic knowledge of programming. The games and simulations may be used without any programming knowledge.

We hope you will find as much pleasure using this book as we did writing it. We also encourage you to make your own collection of challenges, games, and simulations for the programmable calculator.

Regardless of whether you are a beginner or an expert, this book will provide an opportunity for many hours of fun, learning, and relaxation. Enjoy!

Acknowledgments   We would like to thank Donna Crowell and Shirley Smigla for their assistance in typing the manuscript and its many drafts. We also extend a special thanks to our wives, Cathy and Marcy, for their input and assistance in preparing the final manuscript. We appreciate the help of the editorial staff at Prentice-Hall. Finally, we acknowledge our indebtedness to our families (Marcy, Tommy, Kevin, and Kristin Sigmund; and Cathy, David, and Lisa Dunlop), from whom we stole so much time during the preparation of this book.

Challenges 1

NUMBER CURIOSITIES

Through the ages human beings have shown an interest in puzzles, tricks, challenges, and problems involving number patterns. The following challenges for the programmable calculator are just a few of the many recreational problems that depend on number theory and number patterns. These, and challenges like them, are recreational, but they also have a useful aspect, for they often lead to the development of concepts and relationships in our number system.

Changing Operations — Many interesting number relationships occur by writing numbers in different ways. Look at the following patterns:

$$1 \times \frac{1}{2} = 1 - \frac{1}{2}$$

$$2 \times \frac{2}{3} = 2 - \frac{2}{3}$$

$$3 \times \frac{3}{4} = 3 - \frac{3}{4} \qquad n \times \frac{n}{n+1} = n - \frac{n}{n+1}$$

1

Use your programmable calculator to show that this relationship is true for all values of n where $n \leqslant 15$, and a positive integer. Use your program to complete Table 1-1.

TABLE 1-1   Changing Operations

n	$n \times \dfrac{n}{n+1}$	$n - \dfrac{n}{n+1}$
1	0.5	0.5
2	$1.\overline{3}$	$1.\overline{3}$
3	2.25	2.25
4		
5		
6		
7		
8		
9		
10		
11		
12		
13		
14		
15		

User Instructions

Step	Procedure	Enter	Display
1.	Enter program		
2.	Initialize	RST	
3.	Run program	R/S	n
			$n \times \dfrac{n}{n+1}$
			$n - \dfrac{n}{n+1}$

Data Register
01   Initial value of n

Changing Operations

Flow Diagram   **Program**

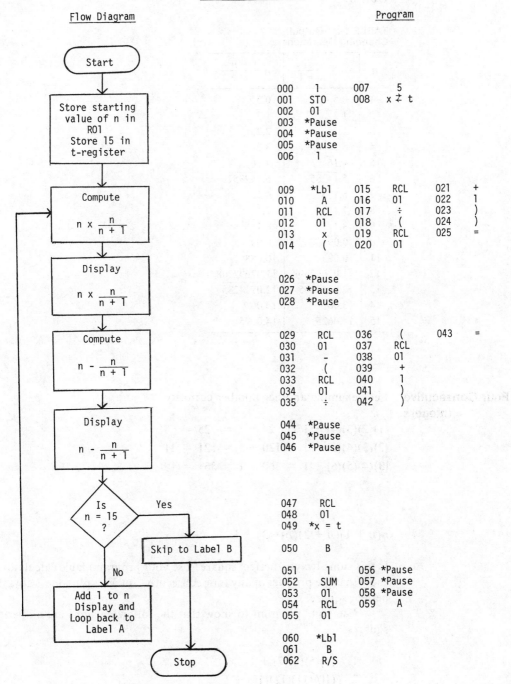

Start

Store starting value of n in R01
Store 15 in t-register

000	1	007	5
001	STO	008	x ⇄ t
002	01		
003	*Pause		
004	*Pause		
005	*Pause		
006	1		

Compute

$$n \times \frac{n}{n+1}$$

009	*Lbl	015	RCL	021	+
010	A	016	01	022	1
011	RCL	017	÷	023	)
012	01	018	(	024	)
013	x	019	RCL	025	=
014	(	020	01		

Display

$$n \times \frac{n}{n+1}$$

026	*Pause
027	*Pause
028	*Pause

Compute

$$n - \frac{n}{n+1}$$

029	RCL	036	(	043	=
030	01	037	RCL		
031	–	038	01		
032	(	039	+		
033	RCL	040	1		
034	01	041	)		
035	÷	042	)		

Display

$$n - \frac{n}{n+1}$$

044	*Pause
045	*Pause
046	*Pause

Is n = 15 ?   Yes

047	RCL
048	01
049	*x = t

Skip to Label B

| 050 | B |

No

Add 1 to n
Display and
Loop back to
Label A

051	1	056	*Pause
052	SUM	057	*Pause
053	01	058	*Pause
054	RCL	059	A
055	01		

060	*Lbl
061	B
062	R/S

Stop

3

Output

TABLE 1-2 Output:
Changing Operations

n	$n \times \dfrac{n}{n+1}$	$n - \dfrac{n}{n+1}$
1	0.5	0.5
2	$1.\overline{3}$	$1.\overline{3}$
3	2.25	2.25
4	3.2	3.2
5	$4.1\overline{6}$	$4.1\overline{6}$
6	$5.\overline{142857}$	$5.\overline{142857}$
7	6.125	6.125
8	$7.\overline{1}$	$7.\overline{1}$
9	8.1	8.1
10	$9.\overline{09}$	$9.\overline{09}$
11	$10.08\overline{3}$	$10.08\overline{3}$
12	11.07692308	11.07692308
13	$12.0\overline{714285}$	$12.0\overline{714285}$
14	$13.0\overline{6}$	$13.0\overline{6}$
15	14.0625	14.0625

Four Consecutive Integers

Let's examine another number curiosity.

$$(1)(2)(3)(4) + 1 = 24 + 1 = 25 = 5^2$$
$$(2)(3)(4)(5) + 1 = 120 + 1 = 121 = 11^2.$$
$$(3)(4)(5)(6) + 1 = 360 + 1 = 361 = 19^2$$

$$.$$
$$.$$
$$.$$

$$n(n + 1)(n + 2)(n + 3) + 1 = x^2$$

Is this sum always a perfect square? Use your programmable calculator to show that the product of any four consecutive integers plus one is always a perfect square.

Use your program to show that the following sums are all perfect squares:

1. $(4)(5)(6)(7) + 1$
2. $(10)(11)(12)(13) + 1$
3. $(15)(16)(17)(18) + 1$
4. $(29)(30)(31)(32) + 1$

4

Four Consecutive Integers

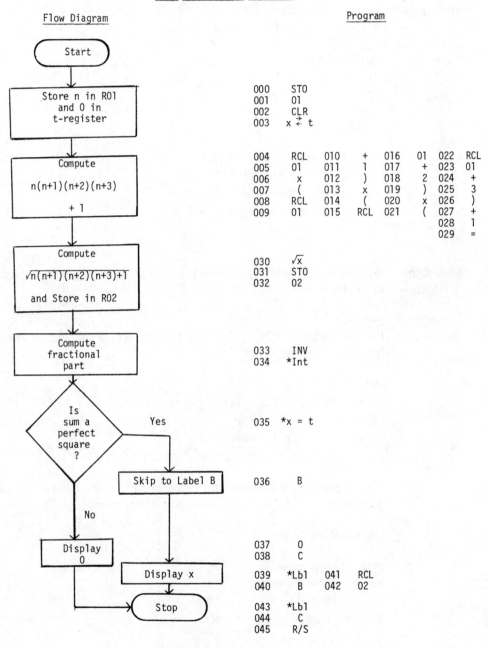

Flow Diagram		Program							

Start

Store n in R01 and 0 in t-register	000	STO
	001	01
	002	CLR
	003	x ⇄ t

Compute

n(n+1)(n+2)(n+3) + 1

004	RCL	010	+	016	01	022	RCL
005	01	011	1	017	+	023	01
006	x	012	)	018	2	024	+
007	(	013	x	019	)	025	3
008	RCL	014	(	020	x	026	)
009	01	015	RCL	021	(	027	+
						028	1
						029	=

Compute

√n(n+1)(n+2)(n+3)+1

and Store in R02

030	√x
031	STO
032	02

Compute fractional part

| 033 | INV |
| 034 | *Int |

Is sum a perfect square ?   Yes

| 035 | *x = t |

Skip to Label B   036   B

No

Display 0

| 037 | 0 |
| 038 | C |

Display x

| 039 | *Lbl | 041 | RCL |
| 040 | B | 042 | 02 |

Stop

043	*Lbl
044	C
045	R/S

User Instructions

	Step	Procedure	Enter	Display
	1.	Enter program		
5	2.	Initialize	*CMs RST	

3.	Enter n	n	
4.	Run program	R/S	x
5.	For a new case, go to step 2		

Data Registers
01   n
02   x

Output

1. $(4)(5)(6)(7) + 1 = 29^2$
2. $(10)(11)(12)(13) + 1 = 131^2$
3. $(15)(16)(17)(18) + 1 = 271^2$
4. $(29)(30)(31)(32) + 1 = 929^2$

Three-Digit Number

What three-digit number is eleven times the sum of its digits? Assume that the digits are nonzero.

Solution
Let the number be $100a + 10b + c$ where a, b, and c are nonnegative integers less than or equal to nine. Then:

$$100a + 10b + c = 11(a + b + c)$$
$$100a + 10b + c = 11a + 11b + 11c$$
$$89a = b + 10c$$
$$a = \frac{b + 10c}{89}$$

Write a program to determine the nonnegative integers, b and c, that make a a positive integer. a, b, $c \neq 0$. Display the number.

User Instructions

Step	Procedure	Press	Display
1.	Enter program		
2.	Initialize	*CMs RST	
3.	Run program	R/S	n

Data Registers
01   b
02   c

Output
$n = 198$

Three-Digit Number

Flow Diagram   Program

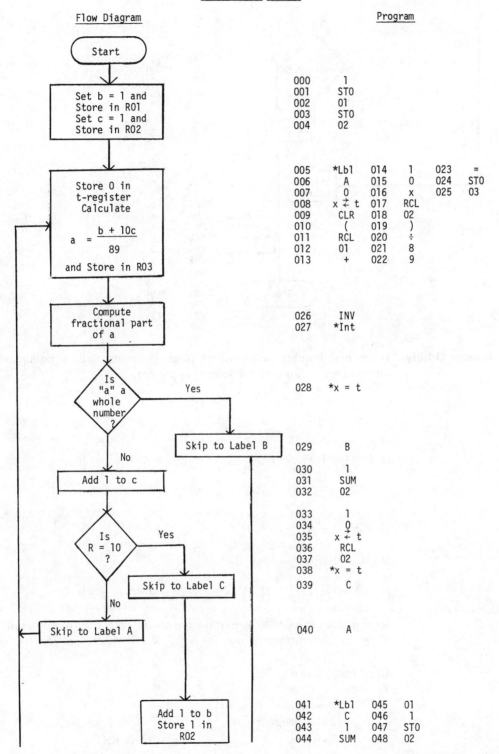

(continued on page 8)

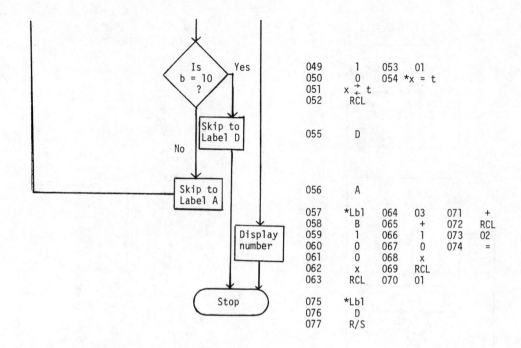

049	1	053	01
050	0	054	*x = t
051	x $\rightleftarrows$ t		
052	RCL		

| 055 | D |

| 056 | A |

057	*Lbl	064	03	071	+
058	B	065	+	072	RCL
059	1	066	1	073	02
060	0	067	0	074	=
061	0	068	x		
062	x	069	RCL		
063	RCL	070	01		

075	*Lbl
076	D
077	R/S

Integer Oddity

Interesting number relationships often occur by writing numbers in different ways. Observe the following pattern:

$$1^2 = 1 \qquad\qquad 1^3 = 1$$
$$(1 + 2)^2 = 9 \qquad\qquad 1^3 + 2^3 = 9$$
$$(1 + 2 + 3)^2 = 36 \qquad\qquad 1^3 + 2^3 + 3^3 = 36$$
$$(1 + 2 + 3 + 4)^2 = 100 \qquad\qquad 1^3 + 2^3 + 3^3 + 4^3 = 100$$

$$\vdots \qquad\qquad\qquad \vdots$$

$$(1 + 2 + 3 + 4 + \ldots + n)^2 \qquad 1^3 + 2^3 + 3^3 + \ldots + n^3$$

Write a program to show that:

$$(1 + 2 + 3 + 4 + \ldots + n)^2 = 1^3 + 2^3 + 3^3 + \ldots + n^3$$

for any given value of n, when n is a positive integer. Use your program to show that this formula is true for $n = 2, 4, 10, 15, 25,$ and 35.

User Instructions

Step	Procedure	Press	Display
1.	Enter program		
2.	Initialize	*CMs RST	
3.	Enter n	n	

8

Integer Oddity

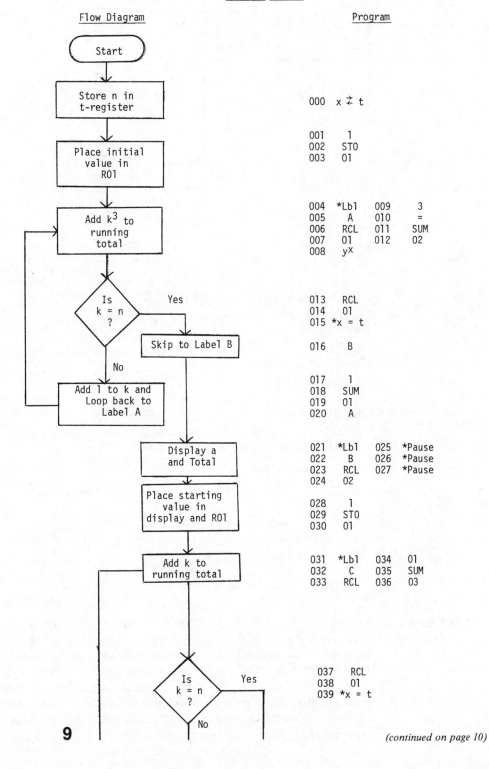

Flow Diagram

Program

Start

Store n in t-register

000 x ⇄ t

Place initial value in R01

001 1
002 STO
003 01

Add k^3 to running total

004 *Lbl   009 3
005 A   010 =
006 RCL   011 SUM
007 01   012 02
008 y^x

Is k = n ?

013 RCL
014 01
015 *x = t

Yes

Skip to Label B

016 B

No

Add 1 to k and Loop back to Label A

017 1
018 SUM
019 01
020 A

Display a and Total

021 *Lbl   025 *Pause
022 B   026 *Pause
023 RCL   027 *Pause
024 02

Place starting value in display and R01

028 1
029 STO
030 01

Add k to running total

031 *Lbl   034 01
032 C   035 SUM
033 RCL   036 03

Is k = n ?

Yes

037 RCL
038 01
039 *x = t

No

9

(continued on page 10)

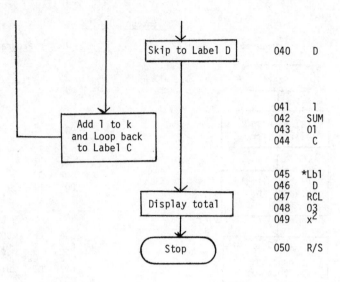

Skip to Label D	040 D
Add 1 to k and Loop back to Label C	041 1 042 SUM 043 01 044 C
	045 *Lbl 046 D 047 RCL 048 03 049 x^2
Display total	
Stop	050 R/S

4.   Run program   R/S   Sum of cubes
                                                              Square of sum

5.   For a new case, go to step 2.

Data Registers
01   *n*
02   Running total
03   Running total

Output

TABLE 1-3   Output: Integer Oddity

n	Square of Sum	Sum of Cubes
2	9	9
4	100	100
10	3025	3025
15	14,400	14,400
25	105,625	105,625
35	396,900	396,900

The Fibonacci Sequence

The sequence 1, 1, 2, 3, 5, 8, 13, 21, 34, . . . , where each succeeding number in the list is the sum of the two preceding numbers, is called the *Fibonacci sequence*. This sequence of numbers was named after the Italian monk Leonardo of Pisa (1170–1250), who was also called Fibonacci. Fibonacci discussed this sequence of numbers when he worked on the following problem: How many pairs of rabbits will be produced at the end of one year starting with one pair of rabbits, if each pair produces one pair each month starting the second month after birth?

The Fibonacci sequence occurs in nature in a variety of unexpected ways. The spiral pattern of the seeds of a sunflower, the scale patterns of pinecones and pineapples, and the shells of some mollusks display patterns given by the Fibonacci numbers. It is defined as:

$$f(1) = 1$$
$$f(2) = 1$$
$$f(k + 2) = f(k) + f(k + 1)$$

where k is an element of the set of natural numbers. An interesting relationship occurs when we form the ratio of consecutive Fibonacci numbers.

Write a program for your programmable calculator that takes as data the number of terms and displays the Fibonacci sequence. Also, display the ratios of consecutive Fibonacci numbers. Use your program to determine the first ten Fibonacci numbers.

User Instructions

Step	Procedure	Press	Display
1.	Enter program		
2.	Initialize	*CMs RST	
3.	Enter n	n	

The Fibonacci Sequence

Flow Diagram   Program

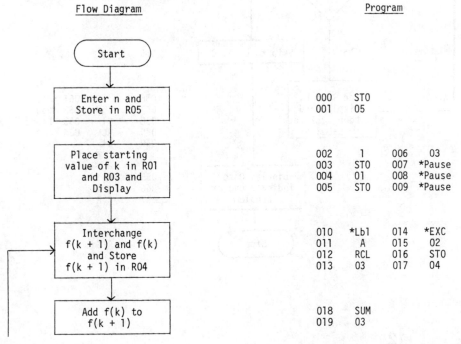

Start			
Enter n and Store in R05	000 STO		
	001 05		
Place starting value of k in R01 and R03 and Display	002 1	006 03	
	003 STO	007 *Pause	
	004 01	008 *Pause	
	005 STO	009 *Pause	
Interchange f(k + 1) and f(k) and Store f(k + 1) in R04	010 *Lb1	014 *EXC	
	011 A	015 02	
	012 RCL	016 STO	
	013 03	017 04	
Add f(k) to f(k + 1)	018 SUM		
	019 03		

(continued on page 12)

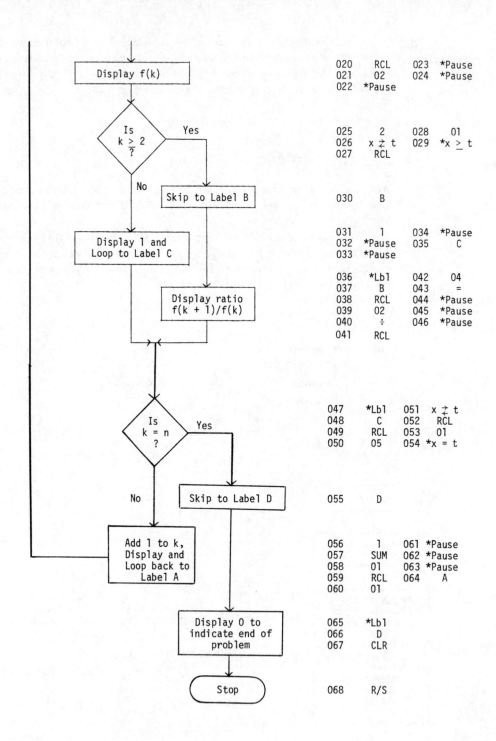

020	RCL	023	*Pause
021	02	024	*Pause
022	*Pause		

025	2	028	01
026	x ⇄ t	029	*x ≥ t
027	RCL		

030	B

031	1	034	*Pause
032	*Pause	035	C
033	*Pause		

036	*Lbl	042	04
037	B	043	=
038	RCL	044	*Pause
039	02	045	*Pause
040	÷	046	*Pause
041	RCL		

047	*Lbl	051	x ⇄ t
048	C	052	RCL
049	RCL	053	01
050	05	054	*x = t

055	D

056	1	061	*Pause
057	SUM	062	*Pause
058	01	063	*Pause
059	RCL	064	A
060	01		

065	*Lbl
066	D
067	CLR

068	R/S

12

4.	Run program	R/S	n
			$f(n)$
			$\dfrac{f(n+1)}{f(n)}$

5.   For a new case, go to step 2.

Data Registers
01   k
02   $f(k)$
03   $f(k+1)$
04   $f(k+1)$
05   n

Output

TABLE 1-4 Output:
The Fibonacci Sequence

n	$f(n)$	$\dfrac{f(n+1)}{f(n)}$
1	1	1
2	1	1
3	2	2
4	3	1.5
5	5	1.666666667
6	8	1.6
7	13	1.625
8	21	1.615384615
9	34	1.619047619
10	55	1.617647059

Comments

The successive ratios of Fibonacci numbers approach the golden ratio:

$$\tau = \frac{(\sqrt{5}+1)}{\sqrt{2}} \approx 1.618033989 \ldots$$

The golden ratio has been a guide to proportion since the time of the ancient Greeks. A rectangle with sides approximately in this ratio, called the golden rectangle, was discovered by the ancient Greeks. The golden rectangle is constructed by taking a square and dividing it into two equal regions, as shown in Figure 1-1. An arc of a circle is then constructed with center 0, and the base of the square is extended to meet the arc.

The ratio of length to width of this rectangle is the golden ratio.

$$\tau = \frac{L}{w}$$

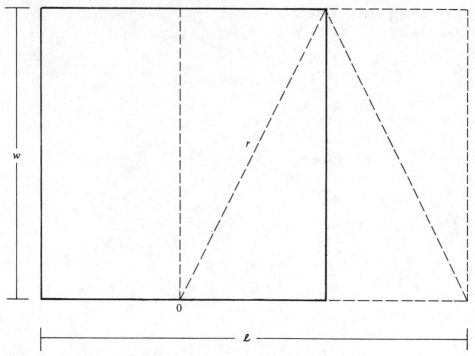

FIGURE 1-1   Golden Rectangle

Evidence of the use of the golden ratio and the golden rectangle can be found in ancient Greek art and architecture. The Parthenon of Athens fits almost exactly into a golden rectangle.

Fibonacci Number Patterns   Mathematicians and scientists often search for patterns and relationships in the numerical results of problems and experiments. The Fibonacci numbers provide many interesting relationships and patterns. These relationships are so fascinating that the *Fibonacci Quarterly*, a mathematics journal, is published to study them. The following challenges provide a starting point on the many patterns and relationships involving these numbers:

1.   Sum of Squares of Two Successive Fibonacci Numbers

$$1^2 + 1^2 = 2$$
$$1^2 + 2^2 = 5$$
$$2^2 + 3^2 =$$
$$3^2 + 5^2 =$$
$$5^2 + 8^2 =$$
$$8^2 + 13^2 =$$
$$13^2 + 21^2 =$$

14

$$21^2 + 34^2 =$$
$$34^2 + 55^2 =$$
$$55^2 + 89^2 =$$

Write a program to find the sum of squares of two successive Fibonacci numbers. Use your program to complete the pattern. What patterns do you observe?

2. Sum of Squares of Fibonacci Numbers

$$1^2 + 1^2 = 2 = 1 \times 2$$
$$1^2 + 1^2 + 2^2 = 6 = 2 \times 3$$
$$1^2 + 1^2 + 2^2 + 3^2 =$$
$$1^2 + 1^2 + 2^2 + 3^2 + 5^2 =$$
$$1^2 + 1^2 + 2^2 + 3^2 + 5^2 + 8^2 =$$
$$1^2 + 1^2 + 2^2 + 3^2 + 5^2 + 8^2 + 13^2 =$$
$$1^2 + 1^2 + 2^2 + 3^2 + 5^2 + 8^2 + 13^2 + 21^2 =$$
$$1^2 + 1^2 + 2^2 + 3^2 + 5^2 + 8^2 + 13^2 + 21^2 + 34^2 =$$

Write a program to find the sum of the squares of the Fibonacci numbers. Use your program to complete the pattern. What pattern do you observe?

User Instructions

Step	Procedure	Press	Display
1.	Enter program		
2.	Initialize	*CMs RST	
3.	Enter n (number of Fibonacci numbers)	n	
4.	Run program	R/S	Sum of squares of two successive Fibonacci numbers
5.	For a new case, go to step 2.		

Data Registers
01 k
02 $f(k)$
03 $f(k + 1)$

User Instructions

Step	Procedure	Press	Display
1.	Enter program		
2.	Initialize	*CMs RST	

Sum of Squares of Two Successive Fibonacci Numbers

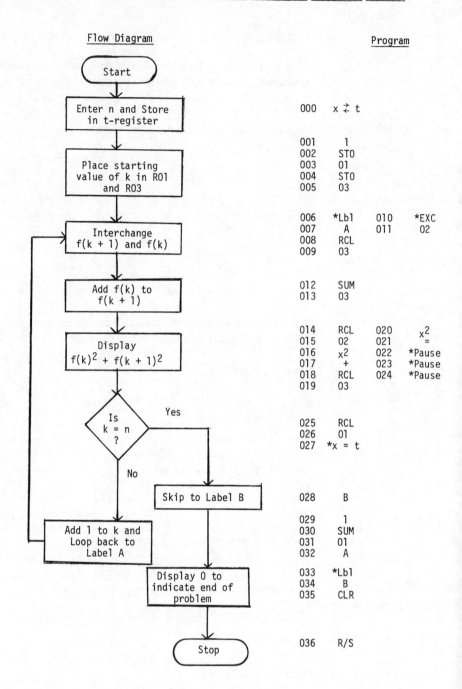

Flow Diagram

Start

Enter n and Store
in t-register

Place starting
value of k in R01
and R03

Interchange
f(k + 1) and f(k)

Add f(k) to
f(k + 1)

Display
$f(k)^2 + f(k + 1)^2$

Is
k = n
?

Yes

No

Skip to Label B

Add 1 to k and
Loop back to
Label A

Display 0 to
indicate end of
problem

Stop

Program

000	x ⇄ t		
001	1		
002	STO		
003	01		
004	STO		
005	03		
006	*Lbl	010	*EXC
007	A	011	02
008	RCL		
009	03		
012	SUM		
013	03		
014	RCL	020	x^2
015	02	021	=
016	x^2	022	*Pause
017	+	023	*Pause
018	RCL	024	*Pause
019	03		
025	RCL		
026	01		
027	*x = t		
028	B		
029	1		
030	SUM		
031	01		
032	A		
033	*Lbl		
034	B		
035	CLR		
036	R/S		

16

Sum of Squares of Fibonacci Numbers

Flow Diagram	Program

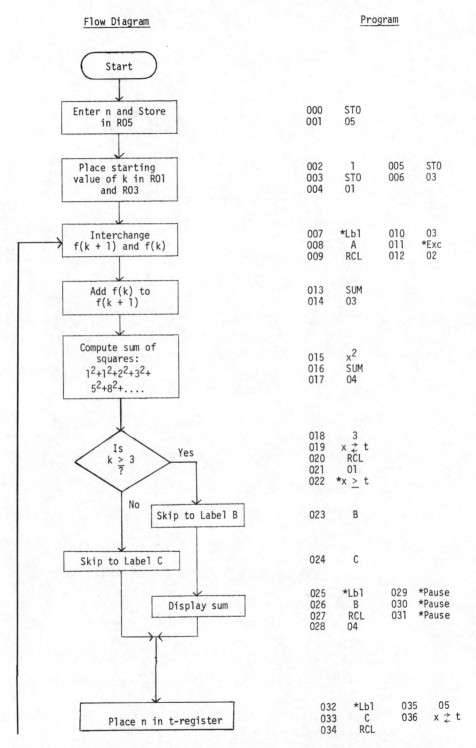

000	STO		
001	05		
002	1	005	STO
003	STO	006	03
004	01		
007	*Lbl	010	03
008	A	011	*Exc
009	RCL	012	02
013	SUM		
014	03		
015	x^2		
016	SUM		
017	04		
018	3		
019	$x \underset{\leftarrow}{\rightarrow}$ t		
020	RCL		
021	01		
022	*x $\geq$ t		
023	B		
024	C		
025	*Lbl	029	*Pause
026	B	030	*Pause
027	RCL	031	*Pause
028	04		
032	*Lbl	035	05
033	C	036	$x \underset{\leftarrow}{\rightarrow}$ t
034	RCL		

(continued on page 18)

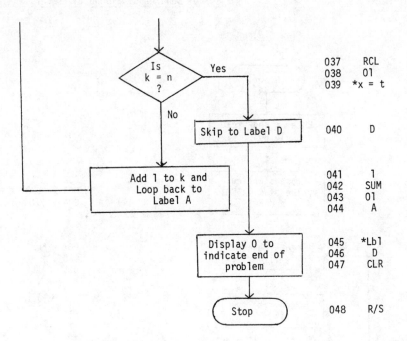

Is k = n ?	037 RCL 038 01 039 *x = t
Skip to Label D	040 D
Add 1 to k and Loop back to Label A	041 1 042 SUM 043 01 044 A
Display 0 to indicate end of problem	045 *Lbl 046 D 047 CLR
Stop	048 R/S

3.   Enter *n* (number of   *n*
     Fibonacci numbers)

4.   Run program   R/S   Sum of squares

5.   For a new case, go to
     step 2.

Data Registers
01   *k*
02   *f(k)*
03   *f(k + 1)*
04   Sum
05   *n*

Output
1. Sum of Squares of Two Successive Fibonacci Numbers

$$1^2 + 1^2 = 2$$
$$1^2 + 2^2 = 5$$
$$2^2 + 3^2 = 13$$
$$3^2 + 5^2 = 34$$
$$5^2 + 8^2 = 89$$
$$8^2 + 13^2 = 233$$
$$13^2 + 21^2 = 610$$
$$21^2 + 34^2 = 1597$$

18

$34^2 + 55^2 = 4181$

$55^2 + 89^2 = 10{,}946$

The sums of the squares of two successive Fibonacci numbers are alternate Fibonacci numbers.

2. Sum of Squares of Fibonacci Numbers

$$1^2 + 1^2 = 2 = 1 \times 2$$
$$1^2 + 1^2 + 2^2 = 6 = 2 \times 3$$
$$1^2 + 1^2 + 2^2 + 3^2 = 15 = 3 \times 5$$
$$1^2 + 1^2 + 2^2 + 3^2 + 5^2 = 40 = 5 \times 8$$
$$1^2 + 1^2 + 2^2 + 3^2 + 5^2 + 8^2 = 104 = 8 \times 13$$
$$1^2 + 1^2 + 2^2 + 3^2 + 5^2 + 8^2 + 13^2 = 273 = 13 \times 21$$
$$1^2 + 1^2 + 2^2 + 3^2 + 5^2 + 8^2 + 13^2 + 21^2 = 714 = 21 \times 34$$
$$1^2 + 1^2 + 2^2 + 3^2 + 5^2 + 8^2 + 13^2 + 21^2 + 34^2 = 1870 = 34 \times 55$$

The sum of the squares of the Fibonacci numbers is the product of successive Fibonacci numbers.

The number of output values is equal to $(n - 2)$ where n is the number of Fibonacci numbers.

When Will We Meet Again?

Starting from the same point and at the same time, three women driving electric cars travel in the same direction around a circular track 80 yards in circumference. If the three electrical cars move at respective average rates of 12 yards, 20 yards, and 28 yards a second, when will they first be together again?[1]

Solution

The key to solving this problem is determining at what time all three drivers would be at the same distance from the starting line.

  Let x = time in seconds
    y = distance from starting point in seconds
Then: $y = 12x \pmod{80}$
    $y = 20x \pmod{80}$
    $y = 28x \pmod{80}$

Write a program using your programmable calculator to solve this problem.

[1] Jim Metz, "When Will We Meet Again? A Modified Answer," *Mathematics Teacher,* 70, no. 1 (January 1977), 41–45, by permission of the publisher.

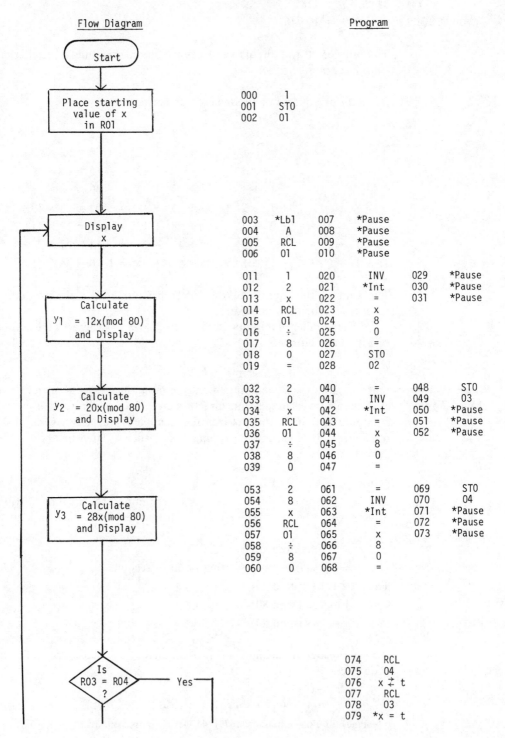

Flow Diagram

Start

Place starting
value of x
in R01

Display
x

Calculate
y_1 = 12x(mod 80)
and Display

Calculate
y_2 = 20x(mod 80)
and Display

Calculate
y_3 = 28x(mod 80)
and Display

Is
R03 = R04
?

Yes

Program

000	1
001	STO
002	01

003	*Lbl	007	*Pause
004	A	008	*Pause
005	RCL	009	*Pause
006	01	010	*Pause

011	1	020	INV	029	*Pause
012	2	021	*Int	030	*Pause
013	x	022	=	031	*Pause
014	RCL	023	x		
015	01	024	8		
016	÷	025	0		
017	8	026	=		
018	0	027	STO		
019	=	028	02		

032	2	040	=	048	STO
033	0	041	INV	049	03
034	x	042	*Int	050	*Pause
035	RCL	043	=	051	*Pause
036	01	044	x	052	*Pause
037	÷	045	8		
038	8	046	0		
039	0	047	=		

053	2	061	=	069	STO
054	8	062	INV	070	04
055	x	063	*Int	071	*Pause
056	RCL	064	=	072	*Pause
057	01	065	x	073	*Pause
058	÷	066	8		
059	8	067	0		
060	0	068	=		

074	RCL
075	04
076	x ⇄ t
077	RCL
078	03
079	*x = t

(continued on page 21)

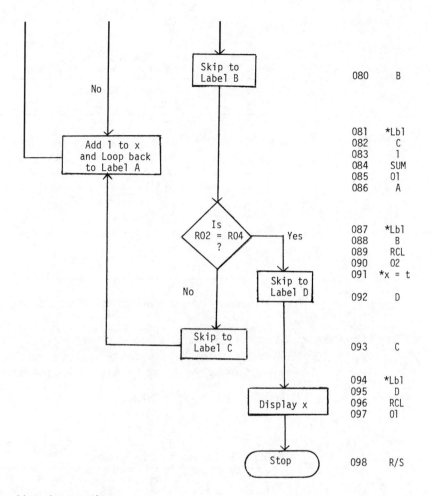

	080	B
	081	*Lbl
	082	C
	083	1
	084	SUM
	085	01
	086	A
	087	*Lbl
	088	B
	089	RCL
	090	02
	091	*x = t
	092	D
	093	C
	094	*Lbl
	095	D
	096	RCL
	097	01
	098	R/S

User Instructions

Step	Procedure	Press	Display
1.	Enter program		
2.	Initialize	*CMs RST	
3.	Run program	R/S	t
			y_1
			y_2
			y_3

Data Registers
01 Time in seconds
02 $y_1 = 12x \pmod{80}$
03 $y_2 = 20x \pmod{80}$
04 $y_3 = 28x \pmod{80}$

21

Output

TABLE 1-5 The Time and Distance from the
Starting Point for Three Drivers on an 80 Yard Track

	Distance (yd.)		
Time (sec.)	Driver A	Driver B	Driver C
1	12	20	28
2	24	40	56
3	36	60	4
4	48	0	32
5	60	20	60
6	72	40	8
7	4	60	36
8	16	0	64
9	28	20	12
10	40	40	40

After ten seconds each driver was 40 yards from the starting point.

Day of the Week On which day were you born? On what day did July 4, 1776 occur? The answers to these questions can be found by using the following formula. It will determine the day of the week, given the month, date, and year.[2]

$$D = [7.1(x - [x])] = [7.1 \text{ frac } x]$$

$$x = \frac{1.25\,Y + d + n}{7}$$

TABLE 1-6 Correction Factor for Month

	Correction Factor (n)	
Month	Not Leap Year	Leap Year (divisible by 4)
Jan.	6	5
Feb.	2	1
Mar.	2	2
Apr.	5	5
May	0	0
June	3	3
July	5	5
Aug.	1	1
Sept.	4	4
Oct.	6	6
Nov.	2	2
Dec.	4	4

[2] Michigan Council of Teachers of Mathematics, *Use of the Calculator in School Mathematics, K-12,* Monograph No. 12 (Lansing, Michigan: Michigan Council of Teachers of Mathematics, 1977), p. 48, by permission of the Michigan Council of Teachers of Mathematics.

Y = year

d = date of the month

n = correction factor for month according to Table 1-6

[ ] represents greatest integer function

TABLE 1-7   Numerical Substitute for
Day of the Week

Day of the Week	Numerical Substitute (D)
Sun.	1
Mon.	2
Tues.	3
Wed.	4
Thurs.	5
Fri.	6
Sat.	0

Day of the Week

Flow Diagram   Program

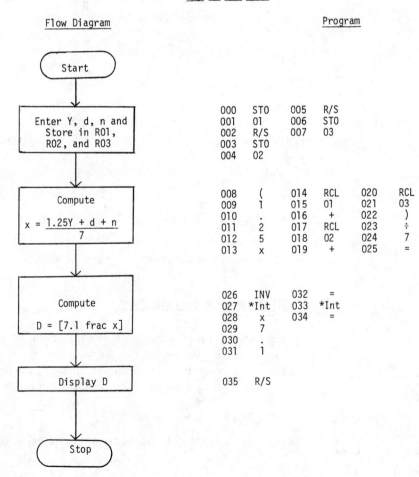

Start

Enter Y, d, n and
Store in R01,
R02, and R03

000	STO	005	R/S
001	01	006	STO
002	R/S	007	03
003	STO		
004	02		

Compute

$$x = \frac{1.25Y + d + n}{7}$$

008	(	014	RCL	020	RCL
009	1	015	01	021	03
010	.	016	+	022	)
011	2	017	RCL	023	÷
012	5	018	02	024	7
013	x	019	+	025	=

Compute

$D = [7.1 \text{ frac } x]$

026	INV	032	=
027	*Int	033	*Int
028	x	034	=
029	7		
030	.		
031	1		

Display D

035   R/S

Stop

Write a program for the programmable calculator to find the day of the week given the month, date, and year. Use your program to determine the day of week on which the following dates occur.

1. July 4, 1776, $y = 1776$, $d = 4$, $n = 5$
2. February 29, 1980
3. January 1, 2050
4. The day you were born

User Instructions

Step	Procedure		Press		Display
1.	Enter program				
2.	Initialize		*CMs RST		
3.	Enter				
	a. year $= Y$		Y	R/S	Y
	b. date of the month $= d$		d	R/S	d
	c. correction factor $= n$		n		
4.	Run program		R/S		D
5.	For a new case, go to step 2.				

Data Registers
01 Y
02 d
03 n

Output

1.	July 4, 1776	Tuesday
2.	February 29, 1980	Friday
3.	January 1, 2050	Saturday
4.	The day you were born	variable answers

FIGURATE NUMBERS

Figurate numbers have long been a popular recreational topic in mathematics. The ancient Greeks were very interested in geometry, and they used geometric representation to study the properties of numbers. Figurate numbers are obtained from certain geometric patterns.

The numbers 1, 3, 6, 10, . . . , $\dfrac{n(n + 1)}{2}$, . . . are called triangular numbers, since they form the triangular patterns shown in Figure 1-2.

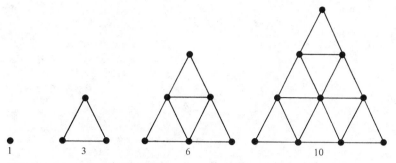

FIGURE 1-2   Triangular Numbers

The numbers $1, 4, 9, 16, \ldots, n^2, \ldots$ are called square numbers, since they form the square pattern shown in Figure 1-3.

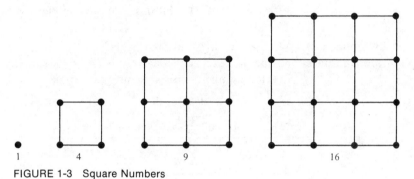

FIGURE 1-3   Square Numbers

The numbers $1, 5, 12, 22, \ldots, \dfrac{n(3n-1)}{2}, \ldots$ are called pentagonal numbers, since they form the pentagonal patterns shown in Figure 1-4.

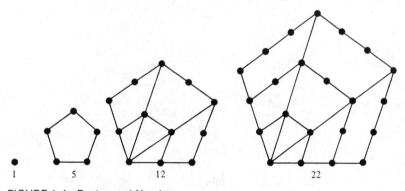

FIGURE 1-4   Pentagonal Numbers

25   The numbers $1, 6, 15, 28, \ldots, n(2n-1), \ldots$ are called hexagonal numbers, since they form the hexagonal pattern shown in Figure 1-5.

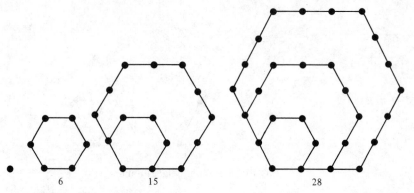

6   15   28

FIGURE 1-5 Hexagonal Numbers

Looking for patterns and relationships in sequences of numbers may often help us find solutions to more complex problems.

Sequences of Figurate Numbers

Write four programs to display the sequences of triangular, square, pentagonal, and hexagonal numbers and the sum, S_n, of these sequences of figurate numbers. Use your program to determine the nth term, a_n and S_n, for $n = 1, 2, 3, \ldots, 9, 10$.

TABLE 1-8 Sequences of Figurate Numbers

Figure	Figurate Numbers						kth Term a_k
Triangular	1	3	6	10	15	...	$\dfrac{k(k + 1)}{2}$
Square	1	4	9	16	25	...	k^2
Pentagonal	1	5	12	22	35	...	$\dfrac{k(3k - 1)}{2}$
Hexagonal	1	6	15	28	45	...	$k(2k - 1)$

Solution
Triangular Numbers

$$a_k = \frac{k(k + 1)}{2} \qquad k\text{th term}$$

$$S_n = \sum_{k=1}^{n} \frac{k(k + 1)}{2} \qquad \text{sum of first } n\text{-terms}$$

Square Numbers

$$a_k = k^2 \qquad k\text{th term}$$

$$S_n = \sum_{k=1}^{n} k^2 \qquad \text{sum of first } n\text{-terms}$$

Sequences of Figurate Numbers:

Flow Diagram   Program

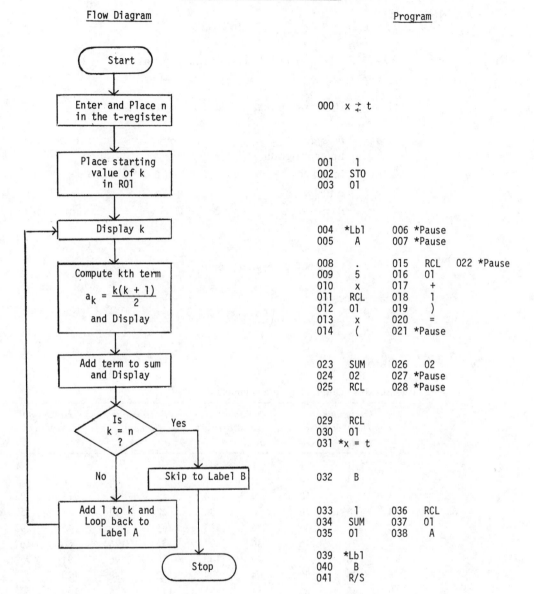

Start		
Enter and Place n in the t-register	000	x ⇄ t
Place starting value of k in R01	001 002 003	1 STO 01
Display k	004 005	*Lbl A	006 *Pause 007 *Pause
Compute kth term $a_k = \dfrac{k(k+1)}{2}$ and Display	008 009 010 011 012 013 014	. 5 x RCL 01 x (| 015 RCL 016 01 017 + 018 1 019) 020 = 021 *Pause	022 *Pause
Add term to sum and Display	023 024 025	SUM 02 RCL	026 02 027 *Pause 028 *Pause
Is k = n ?	029 030 031	RCL 01 *x = t
Skip to Label B	032	B
Add 1 to k and Loop back to Label A	033 034 035	1 SUM 01	036 RCL 037 01 038 A
Stop	039 040 041	*Lbl B R/S

Pentagonal Numbers

$$a_k = \frac{k(3k-1)}{2} \qquad k\text{th term}$$

$$S_n = \sum_{k=1}^{n} \frac{k(3k-1)}{2} \qquad \text{sum of first } n\text{-terms}$$

27

Hexagonal Numbers

$$a_k = k(2k - 1) \qquad k\text{th term}$$

$$S_n = \sum_{k=1}^{n} k(2k - 1) \qquad \text{sum of first } n\text{-terms}$$

User Instructions

Step	Procedure	Press	Display
1.	Enter program		
2.	Initialize	*CMs RST	
3.	Enter n	n	
4.	Run program	R/S	Number of term
			a_k
			S_n
5.	For a new case, go to step 2.		

Data Registers
01 n
02 S_n

Output

TABLE 1-9   Output: Figurate Numbers

	Triangular Numbers		Square Numbers		Pentagonal Numbers		Hexagonal Numbers	
n	a_n	S_n	a_n	S_n	a_n	S_n	a_n	S_n
1	1	1	1	1	1	1	1	1
2	3	4	4	5	5	6	6	7
3	6	10	9	14	12	18	15	22
4	10	20	16	30	22	40	28	50
5	15	35	25	55	35	75	45	95
6	21	56	36	91	51	126	66	161
7	28	84	49	140	70	196	91	252
8	36	120	64	204	92	288	120	372
9	45	165	81	285	117	405	153	525
10	55	220	100	385	145	550	190	715

Comments

The flow diagram for triangular numbers may be used for square, pentagonal, and hexagonal numbers, but you must modify the formula for the kth term.

The successive sums of the terms of the plane figurate numbers are the pyramidal figurate numbers or figurate numbers of the third dimension.

TABLE 1-10 Pyramidal Figurate Numbers

Pyramidal Figurate Numbers	General Term
1 4 10 20 35 ...	$\dfrac{n(n + 1)(n + 2)}{6}$
1 5 14 30 55 ...	$\dfrac{n(n + 1)(2n + 1)}{6}$
1 6 18 40 75 ...	$\dfrac{n^2(n + 1)}{6}$
1 7 22 50 95 ...	$\dfrac{n(n + 1)(4n - 1)}{6}$

The Twelve Days of Christmas

On the twelfth day of Christmas, my true love gave to me: twelve drummers drumming, eleven pipers piping, ten lords a-leaping, nine ladies dancing, eight maids a-milking, seven swans a-swimming, six geese a-laying, five gold rings, four calling birds, three French hens, two turtledoves, and a partridge in a pear tree.[3]

Determine how long it would take to return all the gifts, at the rate of one per day.

Solution
Method 1: Find the number of gifts given each day.

Day	Gifts Given	Number of Gifts
1	1 partridge	1
2	2 turtledoves, 1 partridge	3
3	3 French hens, 2 turtledoves, 1 partridge	6
4	4 calling birds, 3 French hens, 2 turtledoves, 1 partridge	10
.		
.		
.		
12	12 drummers, 11 pipers, 10 lords, 9 ladies, 8 maids, 7 swans,	78

[3] Robert A. Newell, "The Twelve Days of Christmas," *Mathematics Teacher,* 66, no. 8 (December 1973), 707, by permission of the publisher.

6 geese,
5 gold rings,
4 calling birds,
3 French hens,
2 turtledoves,
1 partridge

The number of gifts is the first twelve triangular numbers. Write a program to find the sum of the first twelve triangular numbers.

$$S_{12} = \sum_{k=1}^{12} \frac{k(k+1)}{2} = 1 + 3 + 6 + 10 + \ldots + 78$$

User Instructions

Step	Procedure	Press	Display
1.	Enter program		
2.	Initialize	*CMs RST	
3.	Enter number of days	12	
4.	Run program	R/S	k
			a_k

Note: After the sequence is completed, the sum, S_{12}, will be displayed.

Data Registers
01 k
02 Running total

Output
The last gift is returned 364 days after Christmas, that is, the day before Christmas of the next year.

Method 2: Add the total number of partridges, turtledoves, French hens, and other gifts.

	Number Given per Day	*Number of Days Given*	*Total Number Given*
Partridge	1	12	1×12
Turtledoves	2	11	2×11
French hens	3	10	3×10
Calling birds	4	9	4×9
Gold rings	5	8	5×8
Geese	6	7	6×7
Swans	7	6	7×6
Maids	8	5	8×5

The Twelve Days of Christmas

(Method 1)

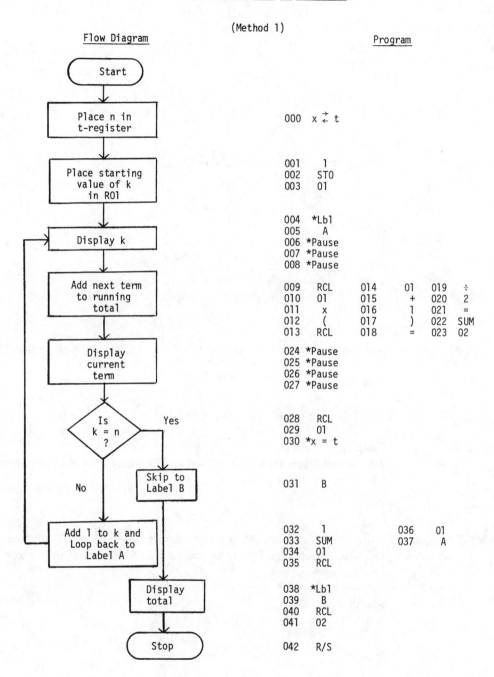

Flow Diagram   Program

| Start |

| Place n in t-register |
000   x ⇄ t

| Place starting value of k in RO1 |
001   1
002   STO
003   01

| Display k |
004   *Lbl
005   A
006   *Pause
007   *Pause
008   *Pause

| Add next term to running total |
009   RCL   014   01   019   ÷
010   01   015   +   020   2
011   x   016   1   021   =
012   (017   )   022   SUM
013   RCL   018   =   023   02

| Display current term |
024   *Pause
025   *Pause
026   *Pause
027   *Pause

| Is k = n ? | Yes
028   RCL
029   01
030   *x = t

| Skip to Label B |
031   B

No

| Add 1 to k and Loop back to Label A |
032   1   036   01
033   SUM   037   A
034   01
035   RCL

| Display total |
038   *Lbl
039   B
040   RCL
041   02

| Stop |
042   R/S

31

	Number Given per Day	Number of Days Given	Total Number Given
Ladies	9	4	9×4
Lords	10	3	10×3
Pipers	11	2	11×2
Drummers	12	1	12×1

$$S_{12} = \sum_{k=1}^{12} k(13 - k) = 1 \times 12 + 2 \times 11 + 3 \times 10 + \ldots + 12 \times 1$$

Write a program to calculate this finite sum.

User Instructions

Step	Procedure	Press	Display
1.	Enter program		
2.	Initialize	*CMs RST	
3.	Enter number of days	12	
4.	Run program	R/S	k
			a_k

Note: After the sequence is completed the sum, S_{12}, will be displayed.

Data Registers
01 k
02 Running total

Output
The last gift is returned 364 days after Christmas, that is, the day before Christmas of the next year.

Square-Triangular Numbers

Write a program to test n triangular numbers to identify which of them are also square numbers. Use your program to test the first 100 triangular numbers.

Solution
A triangular number is of the form

$$\frac{n(n + 1)}{2}$$

and a square number is of the form

32 y^2

The Twelve Days of Christmas

(Method 2)

Flow Diagram   Program

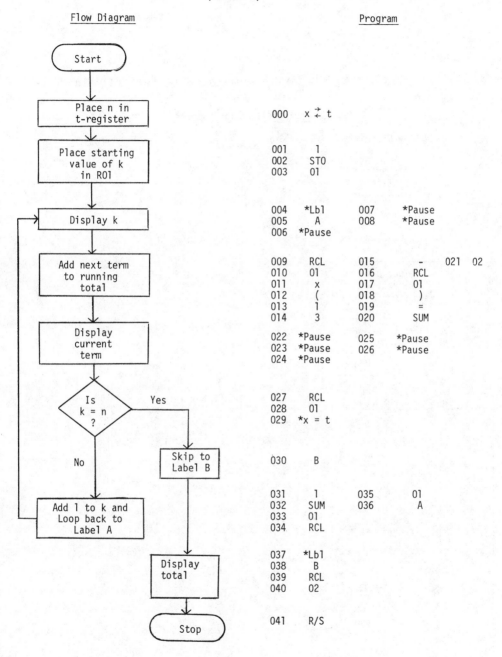

000	x ⇄ t				
001	1				
002	STO				
003	01				
004	*Lbl	007	*Pause		
005	A	008	*Pause		
006	*Pause				
009	RCL	015	−	021	02
010	01	016	RCL		
011	x	017	01		
012	(	018	)		
013	1	019	=		
014	3	020	SUM		
022	*Pause	025	*Pause		
023	*Pause	026	*Pause		
024	*Pause				
027	RCL				
028	01				
029	*x = t				
030	B				
031	1	035	01		
032	SUM	036	A		
033	01				
034	RCL				
037	*Lbl				
038	B				
039	RCL				
040	02				
041	R/S				

33

where n and y are positive integers. Thus:

$$y^2 = \frac{n(n + 1)}{2}$$

$$y = \sqrt{\frac{n(n + 1)}{2}}$$

Determine the positive integer n that makes y a positive integer.

Square-Triangular Numbers

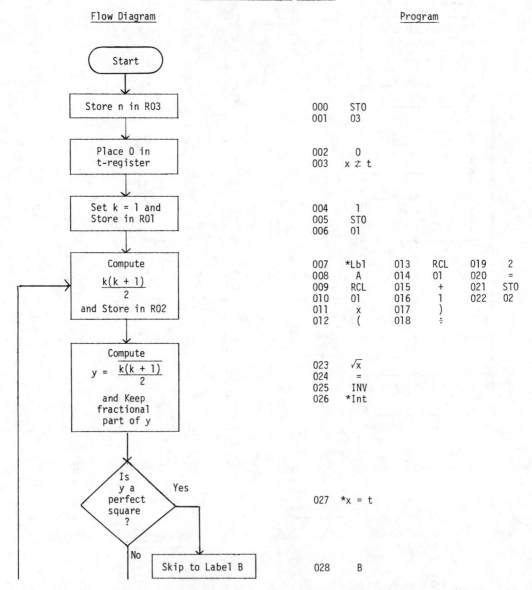

Flow Diagram

Program

Start

Store n in R03	000	STO		
	001	03		

Place 0 in t-register	002	0	
	003	x ⇄ t	

Set k = 1 and Store in R01	004	1
	005	STO
	006	01

Compute $\dfrac{k(k + 1)}{2}$ and Store in R02

007	*Lbl	013	RCL	019	2
008	A	014	01	020	=
009	RCL	015	+	021	STO
010	01	016	1	022	02
011	x	017	)		
012	(	018	÷		

Compute $y = \dfrac{k(k + 1)}{2}$ and Keep fractional part of y

023	√x
024	=
025	INV
026	*Int

Is y a perfect square ?   Yes

027   *x = t

No

Skip to Label B   028   B

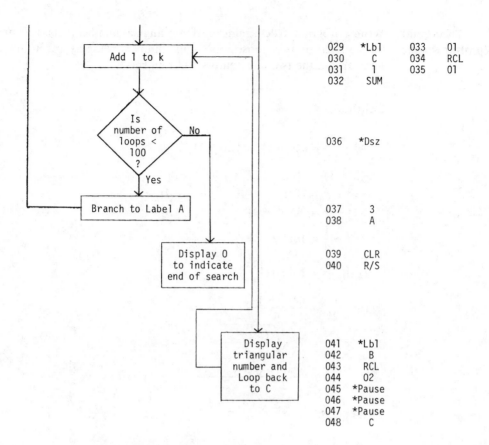

029	*Lbl	033	01
030	C	034	RCL
031	1	035	01
032	SUM		

036	*Dsz

037	3
038	A

039	CLR
040	R/S

041	*Lbl
042	B
043	RCL
044	02
045	*Pause
046	*Pause
047	*Pause
048	C

User Instructions

Step	Procedure	Press	Display
1.	Enter program		
2.	Initialize	*CMs RST	
3.	Enter *n*	*n*	
4.	Run program	R/S	Triangular numbers that are also square numbers

5.   For a new case, go to step 2.

Data Registers
01   k
02   y
03   n

Output

If $n = 100$, then the triangular numbers that are also perfect squares are 1, 36, and 1225.

Triangular Number Puzzle Write a program to determine the first triangular number that is the sum of the squares of two consecutive odd numbers. Display the triangular number and the two consecutive odd numbers.

Solution

$$\frac{x(x + 1)}{2} = (2y - 1)^2 + (2y + 1)^2$$

$$x(x + 1) = 2[(2y - 1)^2 + (2y + 1)^2]$$

$$x^2 + x = 2[4y^2 - 4y + 1 + 4y^2 + 4y + 1]$$

$$x^2 + x = 2[8y^2 + 2]$$

$$x^2 + x + \frac{1}{4} = 16y^2 + 4 + \frac{1}{4}$$

$$(x + \frac{1}{2})^2 = 16y^2 + \frac{17}{4}$$

$$(x + \frac{1}{2})^2 = \frac{64y^2 + 17}{4}$$

$$x + \frac{1}{2} = \pm \sqrt{\frac{64^2 + 17}{4}}$$

$$x = -\frac{1}{2} \pm \frac{\sqrt{64y^2 + 17}}{2}$$

$$x = \frac{-1 \pm \sqrt{64y^2 + 17}}{2}$$

Triangular Number Puzzle

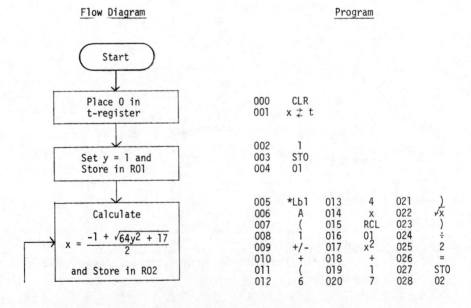

Flow Diagram

Start	

Place 0 in t-register	000 CLR 001 x ⇄ t
Set y = 1 and Store in R01	002 1 003 STO 004 01
Calculate $x = \frac{-1 + \sqrt{64y^2 + 17}}{2}$ and Store in R02	

Program

005	*Lb1	013	4	021	)
006	A	014	x	022	√x
007	(	015	RCL	023	)
008	1	016	01	024	÷
009	+/-	017	x²	025	2
010	+	018	+	026	=
011	(	019	1	027	STO
012	6	020	7	028	02

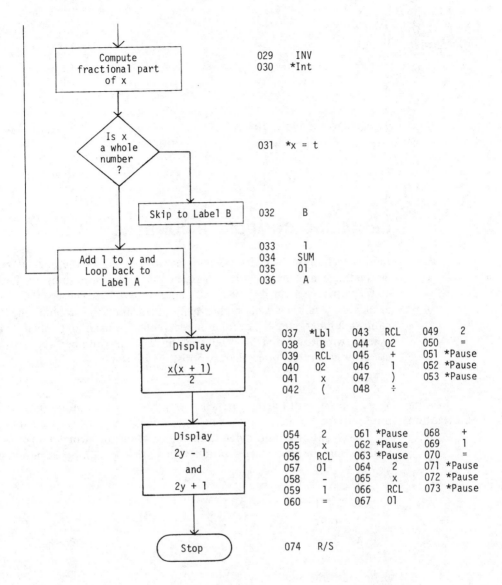

Compute fractional part of x	029 030	INV *Int					

Is x a whole number ? — 031 *x = t

Skip to Label B — 032 B

033	1
034	SUM
035	01
036	A

Add 1 to y and Loop back to Label A

Display $\frac{x(x + 1)}{2}$

037	*Lbl	043	RCL	049	2
038	B	044	02	050	=
039	RCL	045	+	051	*Pause
040	02	046	1	052	*Pause
041	x	047	)	053	*Pause
042	(	048	÷		

Display 2y − 1 and 2y + 1

054	2	061	*Pause	068	+
055	x	062	*Pause	069	1
056	RCL	063	*Pause	070	=
057	01	064	2	071	*Pause
058	−	065	x	072	*Pause
059	1	066	RCL	073	*Pause
060	=	067	01		

Stop — 074 R/S

Since x is a positive integer, $x = \dfrac{-1 + \sqrt{64y^2 + 17}}{2}$

User Instructions

Step	Procedure	Press	Display
1.	Enter program		
2.	Initialize	*CMs RST	
3.	Run program	R/S	Triangular number
			Odd number
			Odd number

Data Registers

01 *y*

02 *x*

Output

Triangular number $= 10$

$$2y - 1 = 1$$
$$2y + 1 = 3$$
$$10 = 1^2 + 3^2$$

PRIME AND COMPOSITE NUMBERS

In this section we will discuss and investigate one of the ancient and fascinating mathematical topics—prime and composite numbers. Early mathematicians divided the natural numbers into three subsets: the set of prime numbers, the set of composite numbers, and the set containing the natural number one. A natural number is called prime if and only if it has exactly two distinct divisors, itself and one. A natural number is composite if and only if it has more than two distinct divisors.

Prime Factorization

Write a program to determine whether a positive odd natural number is prime. If the number is not prime, determine its prime factorization.

Use your program to determine which of the following numbers are primes. Find the prime factorization of those that are composite numbers.

1. 697
2. 3481
3. 1697
4. 4199

User Instructions

Step	Procedure	Press	Display
1.	Enter program		
2.	Initialize	*CMs RST	
3.	Enter number	*n* R/S	Program displays prime factors of *n* and displays a 1 to indicate end of program. If the number is a prime number, the program will display the number.
4.	For a new case, go to step 2.		

Prime Factorization

Flow Diagram

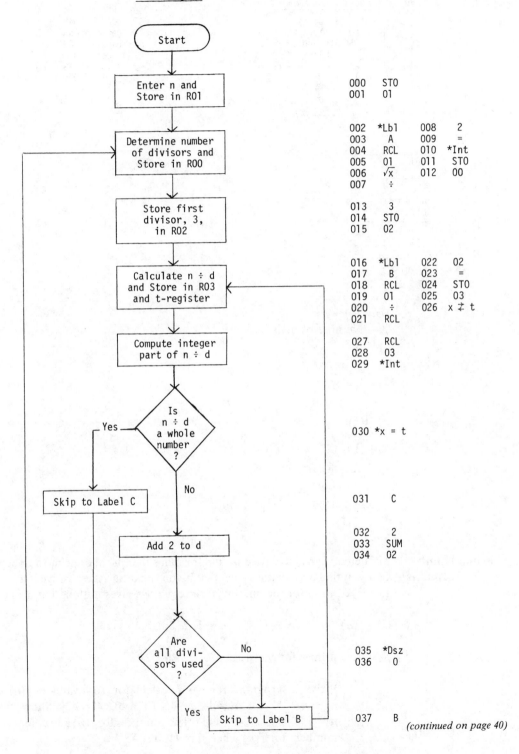

Start

Enter n and Store in R01	000 STO	
	001 01	

	002 *Lbl	008 2
Determine number of divisors and Store in R00	003 A	009 =
	004 RCL	010 *Int
	005 01	011 STO
	006 √x	012 00
	007 ÷	

Store first divisor, 3, in R02	013 3	
	014 STO	
	015 02	

	016 *Lbl	022 02
Calculate n ÷ d and Store in R03 and t-register	017 B	023 =
	018 RCL	024 STO
	019 01	025 03
	020 ÷	026 x ⇄ t
	021 RCL	

Compute integer part of n ÷ d	027 RCL	
	028 03	
	029 *Int	

Is n ÷ d a whole number ?

030 *x = t

Yes

Skip to Label C

031 C

No

Add 2 to d	032 2	
	033 SUM	
	034 02	

Are all divi-sors used ?

No

035 *Dsz
036 0

Yes

Skip to Label B

037 B

(continued on page 40)

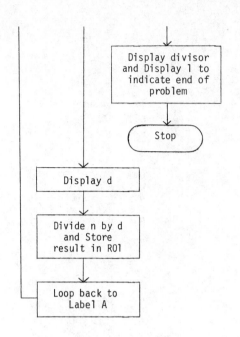

Display divisor
and Display 1 to
indicate end of
problem

Stop

Display d

Divide n by d
and Store
result in R01

Loop back to
Label A

038	RCL	044	1
039	01	045	*x = t
040	*Pause	046	D
041	*Pause	047	1
042	*Pause	048	R/S
043	x ⇄ t	049	*Lbl
		050	D
051	R/S		
052	*Lbl	056	*Pause
053	C	057	*Pause
054	RCL	058	*Pause
055	02		
059	RCL	063	02
060	01	064	=
061	÷	065	STO
062	RCL	066	01
067	A		

Data Registers
00   Number of divisors
01   n
02   d
03   $n \div d$

Output

1. $697 = 17 \times 41$
2. $3481 = 59 \times 59$
3. 1697
4. $4199 = 13 \times 17 \times 19$

Prime Number Formulas   Mathematicians have tried to find formulas that produce prime numbers. Can you find an equation such that if you substitute the positive integers, 1, 2, 3, . . . , n, for the unknown, the equation gives nothing but primes?

(1) $f(n) = n^2 - n + 41$ $n = 1, 2, 3, \ldots$

produces primes for $n = 1, 2, 3, \ldots, 40$.

1.   Write a program for your calculator to evaluate $f(n) = n^2 - n + 41$ for $n = 1, 2, 3, \ldots, 40, 41, 42$. Show that $n = 1, 2, 3, \ldots, 40$ yield prime numbers for $f(n)$ and composite numbers for $f(n)$ when $n = 41$ and 42.

40

The equation (2) $g(n) = \sqrt{1 + 24n}$ $n = 1, 2, 3, \ldots$

produces every prime number except 2 and 3.

2. Write a program for your calculator to evaluate $g(n) = \sqrt{1 + 24n}$ for $n = 1, 2, 3, \ldots, 150$. Determine the values of n that yield prime numbers for $g(n)$.

Prime Number Formulas

$f(n) = n^2 - n + 41$

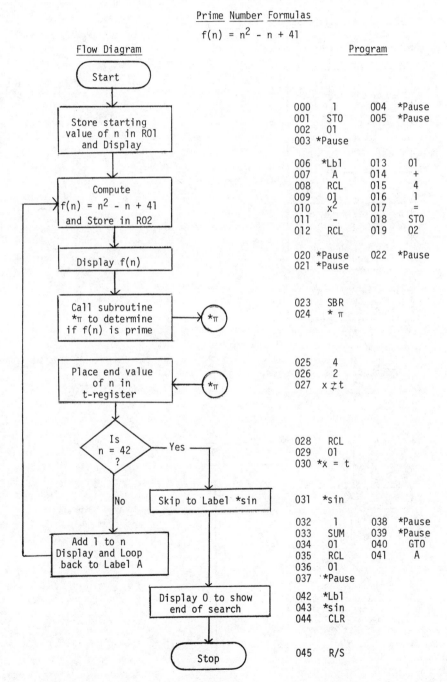

Flow Diagram

Program

Start

Store starting value of n in R01 and Display

```
000    1        004  *Pause
001    STO      005  *Pause
002    01
003  *Pause
```

Compute $f(n) = n^2 - n + 41$ and Store in R02

```
006  *Lbl      013    01
007    A       014    +
008   RCL      015    4
009    01      016    1
010   x²       017    =
011    -       018   STO
012   RCL      019    02
```

Display f(n)

```
020  *Pause   022  *Pause
021  *Pause
```

Call subroutine *π to determine if f(n) is prime

*π

```
023   SBR
024   * π
```

Place end value of n in t-register

*π

```
025    4
026    2
027   x ⇄ t
```

Is n = 42 ? — Yes

```
028   RCL
029    01
030  *x = t
```

No   Skip to Label *sin

```
031  *sin
```

Add 1 to n Display and Loop back to Label A

```
032    1       038  *Pause
033   SUM      039  *Pause
034    01      040   GTO
035   RCL      041    A
036    01
037  *Pause
```

Display 0 to show end of search

```
042  *Lbl
043  *sin
044   CLR
```

Stop

```
045   R/S
```

Subroutine *π

Flow Diagram	Prime Number	Program

```
        ( *π )
          │
          ▼
┌──────────────────────┐        046   *Lbl    048   STO
│  Store f(n) in R03   │        047   *π      049   03
└──────────────────────┘
          │
          ▼
┌──────────────────────┐        050   √x      054   *Int
│  Determine number    │        051   ÷       055   STO
│  of divisors and     │        052   2       056   00
│  Store in R00        │        053   =
└──────────────────────┘
          │
          ▼
┌──────────────────────┐        057   3
│  Store first         │        058   STO
│  divisor in R04      │        059   04
└──────────────────────┘
          │
          ▼
┌──────────────────────┐        060   *Lbl    066   04
│  Determine           │        061   C       067   =
│  quotient of         │        062   RCL     068   STO
│  f(n) ÷ d and        │        063   03      069   05
│  Store in R05 and    │        064   ÷       070   x ⇄ t
│  t-register          │        065   RCL
└──────────────────────┘
          │
          ▼
┌──────────────────────┐        071   RCL
│  Determine integer   │        072   05
│  part of quotient    │        073   *Int
└──────────────────────┘
          │
          ▼
        ╱ Is ╲
       ╱ quotient a ╲     Yes
      ╱  whole        ╲─────────         074   *x = t
       ╲  number     ╱
        ╲    ?      ╱
          │
         No
          │           ┌────────────────────┐
          │           │  Skip to Label D   │   075   D
          │           └────────────────────┘
          ▼
┌──────────────────────┐        076   2
│    Add 2 to d        │        077   SUM
└──────────────────────┘        078   04
          │
          ▼
        ╱ Are ╲
       ╱ all divi- ╲    Yes
      ╱  sors used   ╲───────             079   *Dsz
       ╲    ?       ╱                     080   0
          │
         No
          ▼
```

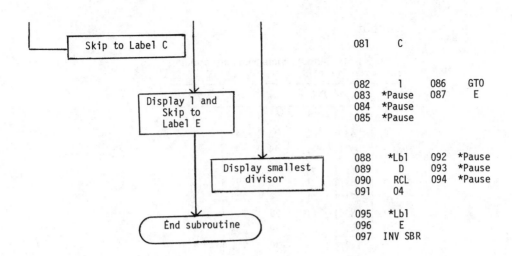

081	C		
082	1	086	GTO
083	*Pause	087	E
084	*Pause		
085	*Pause		
088	*Lbl	092	*Pause
089	D	093	*Pause
090	RCL	094	*Pause
091	04		
095	*Lbl		
096	E		
097	INV SBR		

User Instructions

Step	Procedure	Press	Display
1.	Enter program		
2.	Initialize	*CMs RST	
3.	Run program	R/S	n
			$f(n)$
			1 if $f(n)$ is prime, divisor if $f(n)$ is composite

Data Registers
00 Number of divisors
01 n
02 $f(n)$
03 $f(n)$
04 d
05 $f(n) \div d$

The number 1 indicates $f(n)$ is prime, any other number is the smallest divisor of $f(n)$.

User Instructions

Step	Procedure	Press	Display
1.	Enter program		
2.	Initialize	*CMs RST	
3.	Run program	R/S	n
			$g(n)$
			1 if $g(n)$ is prime, smallest divisor if $g(n)$ is composite

Output

TABLE 1-11   Output: Prime Number Formula
$f(n) = n^2 - n + 41$

n	f(n)	Prime?	n	f(n)	Prime?
1	41	1	22	503	1
2	43	1	23	547	1
3	47	1	24	593	1
4	53	1	25	641	1
5	61	1	26	691	1
6	71	1	27	743	1
7	83	1	28	797	1
8	97	1	29	853	1
9	113	1	30	911	1
10	131	1	31	971	1
11	151	1	32	1033	1
12	173	1	33	1097	1
13	197	1	34	1163	1
14	223	1	35	1231	1
15	251	1	36	1301	1
16	281	1	37	1373	1
17	313	1	38	1447	1
18	347	1	39	1523	1
19	383	1	40	1601	1
20	421	1	41	1681	41
21	461	1	42	1763	41

Prime Number Formulas

$$g(n) = \sqrt{1 + 24n}$$

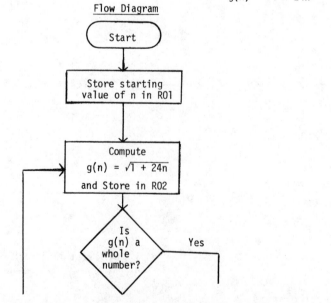

Flow Diagram

Start

Store starting
value of n in R01

Compute
$g(n) = \sqrt{1 + 24n}$
and Store in R02

Is
g(n) a
whole
number?   Yes

Program

000	1
001	STO
002	01

003	*Lbl	011	RCL
004	A	012	01
005	(	013	)
006	1	014	√x
007	+	015	=
008	2	016	STO
009	4	017	02
010	x		

018	0	022	INV
019	x ⇄ t	023	*Int
020	RCL	024	*x = t
021	02		

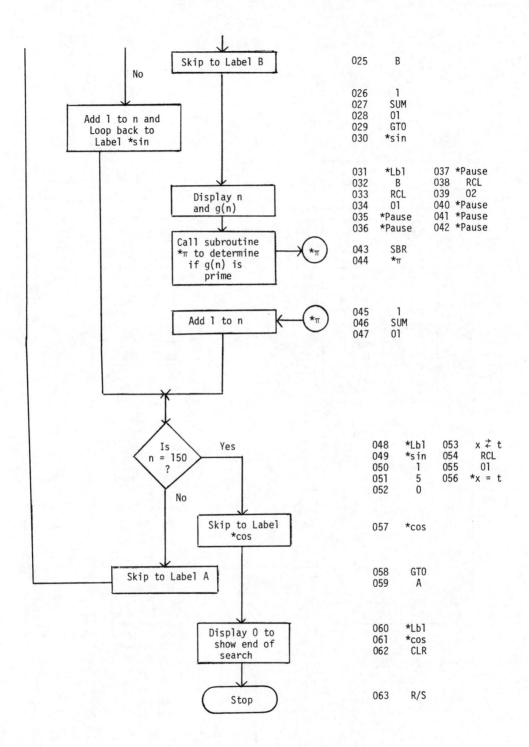

Skip to Label B	025 B

Add 1 to n and Loop back to Label *sin	026 1
	027 SUM
	028 01
	029 GTO
	030 *sin

No

Display n and g(n)	031 *Lbl	037 *Pause
	032 B	038 RCL
	033 RCL	039 02
	034 01	040 *Pause
	035 *Pause	041 *Pause
	036 *Pause	042 *Pause

Call subroutine *π to determine if g(n) is prime	043 SBR
	044 *π

*π

Add 1 to n	045 1
	046 SUM
	047 01

*π

Is n = 150 ?	048 *Lbl	053 x ⇄ t
	049 *sin	054 RCL
	050 1	055 01
	051 5	056 *x = t
	052 0	

Yes

No

Skip to Label *cos	057 *cos

Skip to Label A	058 GTO
	059 A

Display 0 to show end of search	060 *Lbl
	061 *cos
	062 CLR

Stop	063 R/S

45

Flow Diagram		Program

```
    ( *π )
      |
```

| Store f(n) in R03 | 064 *Lbl   066 STO |
| | 065 *π   067 03 |

Determine number of divisors and Store in R00	068 √x 072 *Int
	069 ÷ 073 STO
	070 2 074 00
	071 =

Store first divisor in R04	075 3
	076 STO
	077 04

Determine quotient of g(n) ÷ d and Store in R05 and t-register	078 *Lbl 084 04
	079 C 085 =
	080 RCL 086 STO
	081 03 087 05
	082 ÷ 088 x ⇄ t
	083 RCL

Determine integer part of quotient	089 RCL
	090 05
	091 *Int

Is quotient a whole number ? —— Yes   092 *x = t

No

| Skip to Label D | 093 D |

Add 2 to d	094 2
	095 SUM
	096 04

Are all divisors used ? —— Yes   097 *Dsz
                                   098 0

No

| Skip to Label C | 099 C |

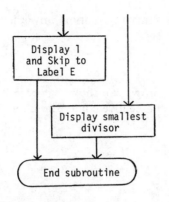

100	1	103	*Pause
101	*Pause	104	GTO
102	*Pause	105	E
106	*Lbl	110	*Pause
107	D	111	*Pause
108	RCL	112	*Pause
109	04		
113	*Lbl		
114	E		
115	INV SBR		

Data Registers

00   Number of divisors
01   n
02   $g(n)$
03   $g(n)$
04   d
05   $g(n) \div d$

Output

TABLE 1-12   Output: Prime
Number <u>Formula</u>.
$g(n) = \sqrt{1 + 24n}$

n	$g(n)$	*Prime or Composite*
1	5	1
2	7	1
5	11	1
7	13	1
12	17	1
15	19	1
22	23	1
26	25	5
35	29	1
40	31	1
51	35	5
57	37	1
70	41	1
77	43	1
92	47	1
100	49	7
117	53	1
126	55	5
145	59	1

The number 1 indicates that $g(n)$ is prime, any other number is the smallest divisor of $g(n)$.

If n is a positive integer, we can show that $n! + 2, n! + 3, n! + 4, \ldots,$ $n! + n$ gives $(n - 1)$ consecutive composite numbers. For example, if:

$$n = 3: \quad 3! + 2 = 3 \times 2 \times 1 + 2 = 6 + 2 = 8$$
$$3! + 3 = 3 \times 2 \times 1 + 3 = 6 + 3 = 9$$
$$n = 4: \quad 4! + 2 = 4 \times 3 \times 2 \times 1 + 2 = 24 + 2 = 26$$
$$4! + 3 = 4 \times 3 \times 2 \times 1 + 3 = 24 + 3 = 27$$
$$4! + 4 = 4 \times 3 \times 2 \times 1 + 4 = 24 + 4 = 28$$

We can use our programmable calculator to find n consecutive numbers that are composite numbers. Write a program to determine n consecutive numbers that are composite numbers.

Use your program to find:

1. five consecutive composite numbers
2. six consecutive composite numbers
3. ten consecutive composite numbers

We can use this approach to produce larger and larger gaps between primes.

User Instructions

Step	Procedure	Press	Display
1.	Enter program		
2.	Initialize	*CMs RST	
3.	Enter n	n	
4.	Run program	R/S	Consecutive composite numbers, then program halts on n.
5.	For a new case, go to step 2.		

Data Registers
00   x
01   $(n + 1)$
02   Initial value
03   $(n + 1)!$
04   $x!$

48

How Far Apart Are Adjacent Primes?

Flow Diagram   Program

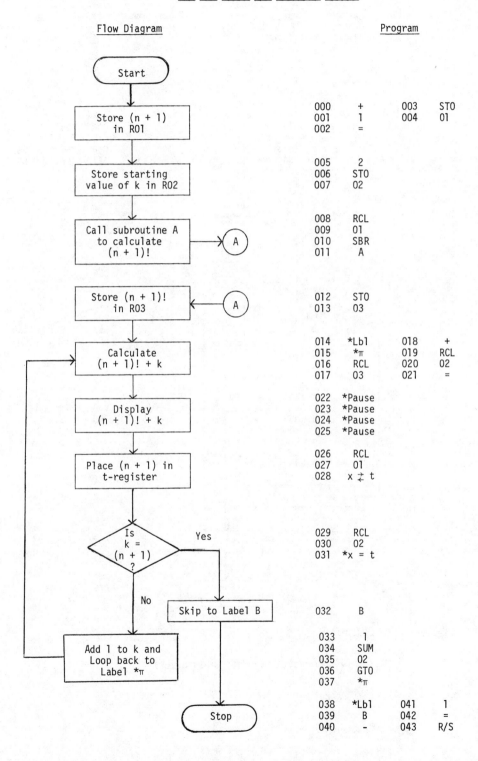

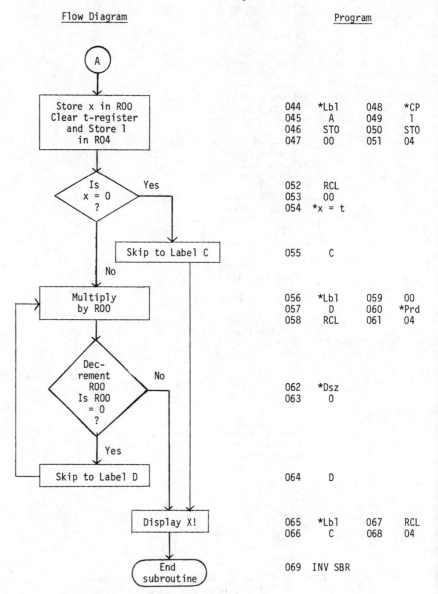

Subroutine A

X! Program

Flow Diagram

Program

044	*Lbl	048	*CP
045	A	049	1
046	STO	050	STO
047	00	051	04

052	RCL
053	00
054	*x = t

| 055 | C |

056	*Lbl	059	00
057	D	060	*Prd
058	RCL	061	04

| 062 | *Dsz |
| 063 | 0 |

| 064 | D |

| 065 | *Lbl | 067 | RCL |
| 066 | C | 068 | 04 |

| 069 | INV SBR |

Output

1. Five consecutive composite numbers

722
723

50   724

725
726
5

2. Six consecutive composite numbers

5042
5043
5044
5045
5046
5047
6

3. Ten consecutive composite numbers

39916802
39916803
39916804
39916805
39916806
39916807
39916808
39916809
39916810
39916811
10

DIOPHANTINE EQUATIONS

Diophantine equations are those in which the solutions must be integers. For example, the equation $x^2 + y^2 = z^3$ has an infinite number of solutions when x, y, and z are real numbers. But, if we restrict x, y, and z to the set of positive integers, the only solutions are:

$x = 2$, $y = 2$, and $z = 2$ or $x = 2$, $y = 11$, and $z = 5$

Since: $2^2 + 2^2 = 2^3$ $2^2 + 11^2 = 5^3$

$4 + 4 = 8$ $4 + 121 = 125$

$8 = 8$ $125 = 125$

The Monkey and the Coconuts "The Monkey and the Coconuts" is probably the most famous and most worked-on problem of all the Diophantine brainteasers. It appears in many puzzle and problem-solving books in a variety of forms.

Four shipwrecked pirates, A, B, C, and D, collect a great pile of coconuts for food. They gather them together and agree to divide them equally on the following day. They have a pet monkey. In the middle of the night, one of the pirates gets up secretly. To make sure he won't be cheated, he divides the coconuts into four equal piles, and, finding an extra one left, gives it to the pet monkey. Then, hiding his pile, he gathers the rest of the coconuts into one pile and goes back to sleep. Each of the other pirates goes through the same process sequentially; waking up, dividing the pile of coconuts into four equal piles, finding an extra coconut and giving it to the monkey, and hiding his fourth of the coconuts. In the morning the pirates do as they planned, and this time the coconuts come out even, in four equal shares with no extra coconut for the monkey. How many coconuts did the pirates have in the beginning?

Solution

Assume initially that there are z coconuts and that A took u coconuts, B took v coconuts, C took w coconuts, and D took x coconuts, leaving equal shares of y coconuts in the morning.

A's four piles contained $4u$ coconuts, B's contained $4v$ coconuts, C's contained $4w$ coconuts, and D's contained $4x$ coconuts. Adding the extras given to the monkey, we arrive at the following equations:

$$z = 4u + 1$$
$$3u = 4v + 1$$
$$3v = 4w + 1$$
$$3w = 4x + 1$$

and the four equal shares of coconuts that were divided in the morning result in the equation

$$3x = 4y$$

Using algebraic substitution, these equations simplify to

$$z = \frac{1024y + 525}{81}$$

Use your programmable calculator to solve this problem.

User Instructions

Step	Procedure	Press	Display
1.	Enter program		
2.	Initialize	*CMs RST	
3.	Run program	R/S	z

The Monkey and the Coconuts

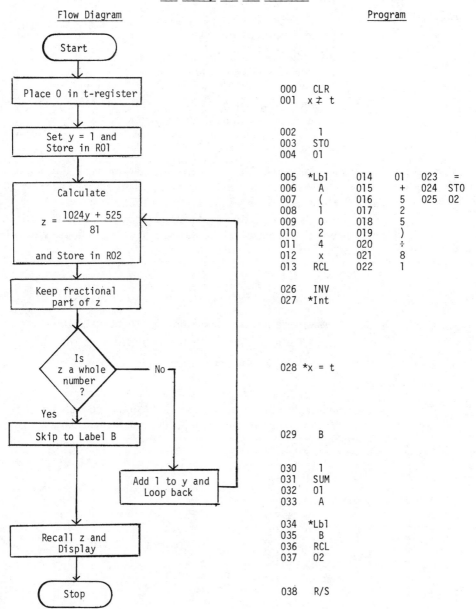

Flow Diagram

Start

Place 0 in t-register

Set y = 1 and Store in R01

Calculate

$$z = \frac{1024y + 525}{81}$$

and Store in R02

Keep fractional part of z

Is z a whole number ?

No

Yes

Skip to Label B

Add 1 to y and Loop back

Recall z and Display

Stop

Program

000	CLR					
001	x ⇄ t					
002	1					
003	STO					
004	01					
005	*Lbl	014	01	023	=	
006	A	015	+	024	STO	
007	(	016	5	025	02	
008	1	017	2			
009	0	018	5			
010	2	019	)			
011	4	020	÷			
012	x	021	8			
013	RCL	022	1			
026	INV					
027	*Int					
028	*x = t					
029	B					
030	1					
031	SUM					
032	01					
033	A					
034	*Lbl					
035	B					
036	RCL					
037	02					
038	R/S					

Data Registers

01 y

02 z

Output

Running the program gives $z = 765$, $y = 60$. To determine y, press RCL 01.

53

Total Number of Coconuts: 765
First Pirate Leaves: 573
Second Pirate Leaves: 429
Third Pirate Leaves: 321
Fourth Pirate Leaves: 240

This program can be adapted to find solutions when the number of pirates and the number of coconuts given to the monkey changes.

The Book Problem

Four men, Peter and Paul and their sons Tom and Dick, buy books. When their purchases are completed, it turns out that each man has paid for each of his books a number of dollars equal to the number of books he has bought. Each family (father and son) has spent $65. Peter has bought one more book than Tom, and Dick has bought only one book. Who is Dick's father?[4]

Solution

Let x = number and price of the books bought by a father
y = number and price of the books bought by a son
Then: $x^2 + y^2 = 65$ or $y = \sqrt{65 - x^2}$

since each father who bought x books paid x dollars per book, and each son who bought y books paid y dollars per book and each family paid $65.
Write a program for your programmable calculator to solve this problem.

User Instructions

Step	Procedure	Press	Display
1.	Enter program		
2.	Initialize	*CMs RST	
3.	Run program	R/S	x
			y

Data Registers
01 x
02 $65 - x^2$
03 y

---

[4] Maurice Kraitchik, *Mathematical Recreations* (New York: Dover Publications, Inc., 1953), p. 37, by permission of the publisher.

The Book Problem

Program

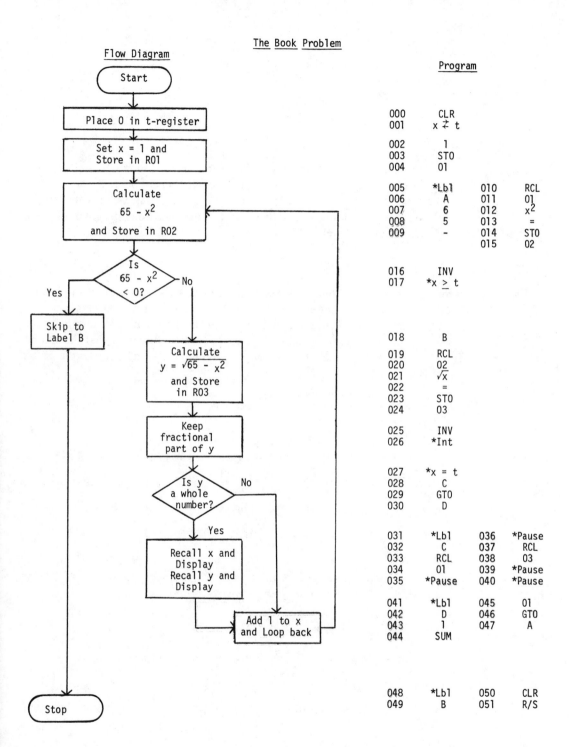

55

Output

$$x = 1, \ y = 8$$
$$x = 4, \ y = 7$$
$$x = 7, \ y = 4$$
$$x = 8, \ y = 1$$

Since Dick bought one book, Dick's father is the man who bought eight books. This same man who bought eight books obviously bought one more book than whoever bought seven books. Peter, we are told, bought one more book than Tom; so it must be Peter who bought eight books, and accordingly, Peter is Dick's father.

The Carpenter's Error A carpenter is told to saw a board x meters and y centimeters in length; however, he makes an error and interchanges the original dimensions into y meters and x centimeters. After he cuts the board, he saws another piece of lumber that is 85 centimeters long. He then discovers that the second board is twice the length of the original board. What is the length of the original board?

Solution

Let x = number of meters, $\qquad 0 \leqslant x < 100$
$\quad y$ = number of centimeters, $\quad 0 \leqslant y < 100$
Then: $100y + x - 85 = 2(100x + y)$
$$100y + x - 85 = 200x + 2y$$
$$98y = 85 + 199x$$
$$y = \frac{85 + 199x}{98}$$

Write a program to determine the positive integers x, $0 \leqslant x < 100$, for which y is a positive integer.

User Instructions

Step	Procedure	Press	Display
1.	Enter program		
2.	Initialize	*CMs RST	
3.	Run program	R/S	x
			y
			$x.y$
			x = Number of meters
			y = Number of centimeters

The Carpenter's Error

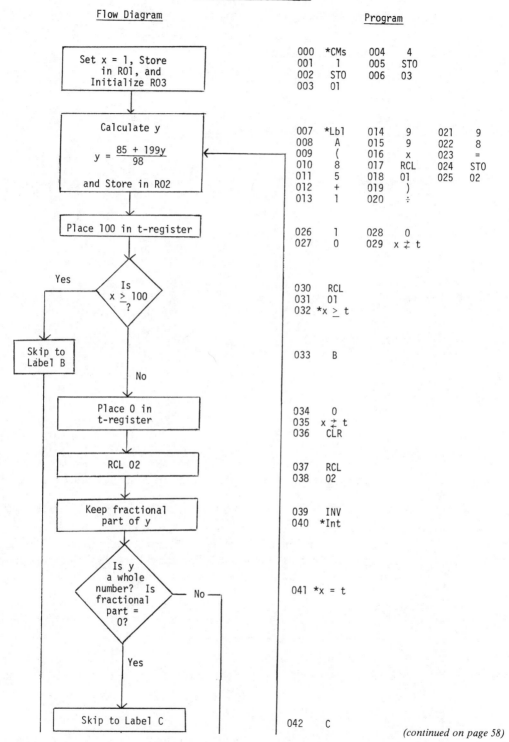

Flow Diagram

Set x = 1, Store in R01, and Initialize R03	

Calculate y

$$y = \frac{85 + 199y}{98}$$

and Store in R02

Place 100 in t-register

Yes

Is x ≥ 100 ?

Skip to Label B

No

Place 0 in t-register

RCL 02

Keep fractional part of y

Is y a whole number? Is fractional part = 0?

No

Yes

Skip to Label C

Program

000	*CMs	004	4
001	1	005	STO
002	STO	006	03
003	01		

007	*Lbl	014	9	021	9
008	A	015	9	022	8
009	(	016	x	023	=
010	8	017	RCL	024	STO
011	5	018	01	025	02
012	+	019	)		
013	1	020	÷		

| 026 | 1 | 028 | 0 |
| 027 | 0 | 029 | x ⇄ t |

030	RCL
031	01
032	*x ≥ t

| 033 | B |

034	0
035	x ⇄ t
036	CLR

| 037 | RCL |
| 038 | 02 |

| 039 | INV |
| 040 | *Int |

| 041 | *x = t |

| 042 | C |

(continued on page 58)

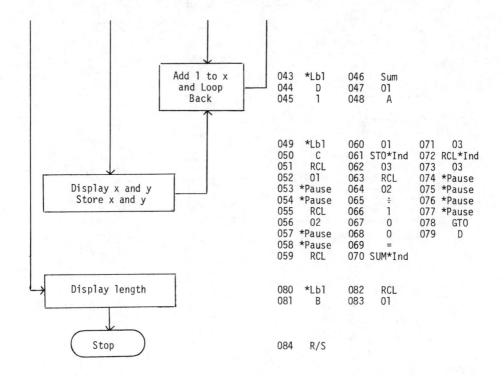

043	*Lbl	046	Sum		
044	D	047	01		
045	1	048	A		

049	*Lbl	060	01	071	03
050	C	061	STO*Ind	072	RCL*Ind
051	RCL	062	03	073	03
052	01	063	RCL	074	*Pause
053	*Pause	064	02	075	*Pause
054	*Pause	065	÷	076	*Pause
055	RCL	066	1	077	*Pause
056	02	067	0	078	GTO
057	*Pause	068	0	079	D
058	*Pause	069	=		
059	RCL	070	SUM*Ind		

080	*Lbl	082	RCL
081	B	083	01

084	R/S

Data Registers

01   x

02   y

03   Indirect counter

Output

37.76 (The length of the original board is 37 meters and 76 centimeters.)

My Apartment   My apartment is in a building where the floors run 1, 2, 3, 4, . . . consecutively. The sum of all the floor numbers greater than mine is twice the sum of all the floor numbers less than mine. How many floors are there in my apartment building, and on what floor do I live?

Solution

Let x = number of my floor

     y = number of floors

Then: $1 + 2 + 3 + \ldots + (x - 1) = 2[(x + 1) + (x + 2) + \ldots + y]$

Using the identity,

58 $1 + 2 + 3 + \ldots + n = \dfrac{n(n + 1)}{2}$

we obtain the equation:

$$\frac{x(x-1)}{2} = 2\left[\frac{y(y+1)}{2} - \frac{x(x+1)}{2}\right]$$
$$x(x-1) = 2[y(y+1) - x(x+1)]$$
$$x^2 - x = 2[y^2 + y - x^2 - x]$$
$$x^2 - x = 2y^2 + 2y - 2x^2 - 2x$$
$$0 = 2y^2 + 2y - 3x^2 - x$$

Using the quadratic equation we obtain:

$$y = \frac{-2 \pm \sqrt{4 - 4(2)(-3x^2 - x)}}{4}$$

$$y = \frac{-2 \pm \sqrt{4 + 24x^2 + 8x}}{4}$$

$$y = \frac{-1 \pm \sqrt{1 + 6x^2 + 2x}}{2}$$

since y is a positive integer, $y = \dfrac{-1 + \sqrt{1 + 6x^2 + 2x}}{2}$

Write a program to determine the positive integer y when $x = 2, 3, \ldots,$ 100.

My Apartment

Flow Diagram

Program

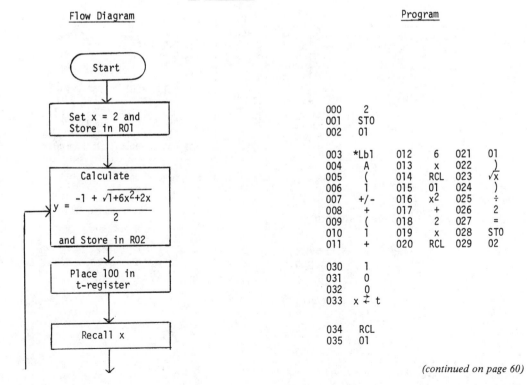

000	2	
001	STO	
002	01	

003	*Lb1	012	6	021	01
004	A	013	x	022	)
005	(	014	RCL	023	√x
006	1	015	01	024	)
007	+/-	016	x2	025	÷
008	+	017	+	026	2
009	(	018	2	027	=
010	1	019	x	028	STO
011	+	020	RCL	029	02

030	1
031	0
032	0
033	x ⇄ t

034	RCL
035	01

(continued on page 60)

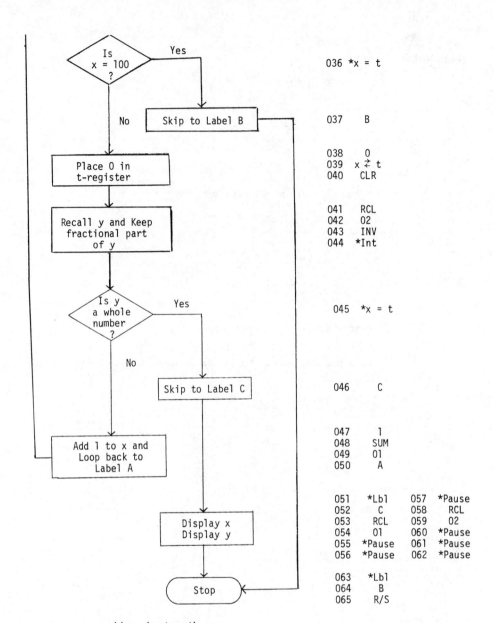

Is x = 100 ? Yes	036 *x = t
No → Skip to Label B	037 B
	038 0
Place 0 in t-register	039 x ⇄ t
	040 CLR
	041 RCL
Recall y and Keep fractional part of y	042 02
	043 INV
	044 *Int
Is y a whole number ? Yes	045 *x = t
No	
Skip to Label C	046 C
	047 1
Add 1 to x and Loop back to Label A	048 SUM
	049 01
	050 A

	051	*Lbl	057 *Pause
Display x Display y	052	C	058 RCL
	053	RCL	059 02
	054	01	060 *Pause
	055	*Pause	061 *Pause
	056	*Pause	062 *Pause
Stop	063	*Lbl	
	064	B	
	065	R/S	

User Instructions

Step	Procedure	Press	Display
1.	Enter program		
2.	Initialize	*CMs RST	
3.	Run program	R/S	*x*
			y

Data Registers
01 *x*

60 02 *y*

Output

$$x = \text{number of my floor} = 28$$
$$y = \text{number of floors} = 34$$

PROBABILITY

The concepts and ideas of probability appear frequently in everyday life. We often hear statements such as:

"There is a 70% chance of snow tomorrow."
"What odds will you give me on the Steelers–Cowboys game?"
"I have a 50-50 chance of passing this test."

This section of challenges contains problems that illustrate the many ways probability and statistics influence our lives.

The Birthday Problem In a group of n people, what is the probability that at least two of them will have the same birthday; that is, the same day and the same month of birth, but not necessarily the same year?

Solution
Let p_n be the probability that, of n persons, at least two were born on the same day of the year. The simplest method of determining p_n is to determine q_n, the probability that no two persons have the same birthday. Then $p_n = 1 - q_n$. We will assume that a year has 365 days and that it is equally likely for a person to be born on each of these days. The probability that two persons will have different birthdays is:

$$q_2 = \frac{364}{365}$$

Thus: $p_2 = 1 - \dfrac{364}{365}$

The probability that three persons will have different birthdays is:

$$q_3 = \frac{364}{365} \times \frac{363}{365}$$

Thus: $p_3 = 1 - \dfrac{364}{365} \times \dfrac{363}{365}$

$$p_4 = 1 - q_4 = 1 - \frac{364}{365} \times \frac{363}{365} \times \frac{362}{365}$$

.
.
.

$$p_n = 1 - q_n = 1 - \underbrace{\frac{364}{365} \times \frac{363}{365} \times \frac{362}{365} \times \ldots \times \frac{[365 - (n-1)]}{365}}_{(n-1) \text{ terms}}$$

$$= 1 - \underbrace{\frac{364}{365} \times \frac{363}{365} \times \frac{362}{365} \times \ldots \times \frac{(365 - n + 1)}{365}}_{(n-1) \text{ terms}}$$

Write a program for your programmable calculator to evaluate p_n. Obtain a table of values starting at $n = 5$ and ending at any value of n in intervals of 5 units. The display should alternate between the values of n and p_n. Use your program to complete Table 1-13.

TABLE 1-13   The Birthday Problem

Number of People n	Probability of at Least Two with the Same Birthday p_n
5	
10	
15	
20	
25	
30	
35	
40	
45	
50	
55	
60	

The Birthday Problem

Flow Diagram   Program

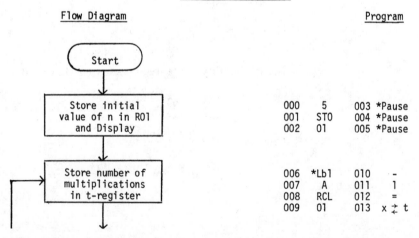

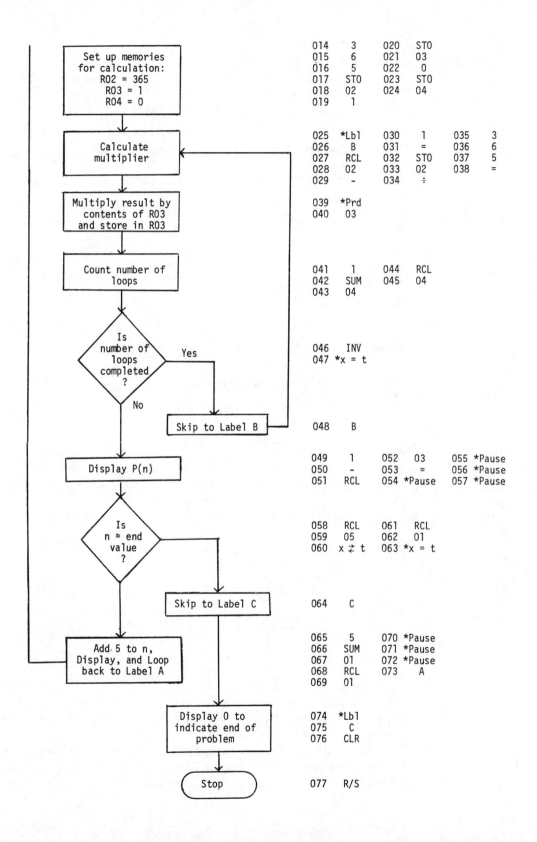

Set up memories for calculation: R02 = 365, R03 = 1, R04 = 0	014 3	020 STO			
	015 6	021 03			
	016 5	022 0			
	017 STO	023 STO			
	018 02	024 04			
	019 1				

Set up memories
for calculation:
RO2 = 365
RO3 = 1
RO4 = 0

```
014    3      020    STO
015    6      021    03
016    5      022    0
017    STO    023    STO
018    02     024    04
019    1
```

Calculate
multiplier

```
025    *Lbl   030    1      035    3
026    B      031    =      036    6
027    RCL    032    STO    037    5
028    02     033    02     038    =
029    -      034    ÷
```

Multiply result by
contents of R03
and store in R03

```
039    *Prd
040    03
```

Count number of
loops

```
041    1      044    RCL
042    SUM    045    04
043    04
```

Is
number of
loops
completed
?   Yes

```
046    INV
047    *x = t
```

No

Skip to Label B

```
048    B
```

Display P(n)

```
049    1      052    03     055    *Pause
050    -      053    =      056    *Pause
051    RCL    054    *Pause 057    *Pause
```

Is
n = end
value
?

```
058    RCL    061    RCL
059    05     062    01
060    x ⇄ t  063    *x = t
```

Skip to Label C

```
064    C
```

Add 5 to n,
Display, and Loop
back to Label A

```
065    5      070    *Pause
066    SUM    071    *Pause
067    01     072    *Pause
068    RCL    073    A
069    01
```

Display 0 to
indicate end of
problem

```
074    *Lbl
075    C
076    CLR
```

Stop

```
077    R/S
```

User Instructions

Step	Procedure	Press	Display
1.	Enter program		
2.	Initialize	*CMs *Fix 5 RST	
3.	Store n in R05	n STO 05	
4.	Run program	R/S	$n : p_n$

Note: The program will display a 0 to indicate the end of the problem.

Data Registers
01 n
02 365
03 q_n
04 Number of loops
05 End value

Output

TABLE 1-14   Output: The Birthday Problem

Number of People n	Probability of at Least Two with the Same Birthday p_n
5	0.02714
10	0.11695
15	0.25290
20	0.41144
25	0.56870
30	0.70632
35	0.81438
40	0.89123
45	0.94098
50	0.97037
55	0.98626
60	0.99412

Comments

From our table we see that the probability is better than one-half that at least two persons will have the same birthday if $n = 25$. The chances are better than 99 out of 100 if $n = 60$.

Two of our presidents—James Polk and Warren Harding—had the same birthday, and John Adams and Thomas Jefferson had the same date of death, a real-life illustration of this problem.

Bubble Gum Cards   There are 28 National Football League teams. Each team is represented by a team photo in each of the Whammie Whopper Bubble Gum packs. If there is one card in each bubble gum pack and these cards are distributed randomly among the packs so that each pack is equally likely to contain any particular one of the cards, how many packs of Whammie Whopper Bubble Gum, on the average, would you have to buy to get a complete set of team photos?

The following year the Whammie Whopper Bubble Gum Company decides to feature individual NFL player photos in their bubble gum packs. Each team is asked to select ten players whose photos will appear on the bubble gum cards. If you wanted to collect the entire set of 280 individual player photos, how many packs of bubble gum, on the average, would you have to buy to get a complete set?

Solution

The expected number of bubble gum packs is obtained by using the rule that if an event has probability p, on the average, it will take $1/p$ trials for it to occur.

The probability of getting a team photo from the first pack of bubble gum is 1. The probability that the second pack will contain a different team photo from the first is $27/28$. Once two different team photos have been obtained, the probability of a bubble gum pack having a team photo different from both is $26/28$. Therefore, the expected number of bubble gum packs needed to obtain 28 cards is:

$$E(n) = 1 + \frac{1}{27/28} + \frac{1}{26/28} + \frac{1}{25/28} + \ldots + \frac{1}{2/28} + \frac{1}{1/28}$$

$$= \frac{28}{28} + \frac{28}{27} + \frac{28}{26} + \frac{28}{25} + \ldots + \frac{28}{2} + \frac{28}{1}$$

$$= 28\left(\frac{1}{28} + \frac{1}{27} + \frac{1}{26} + \frac{1}{25} + \ldots + \frac{1}{2} + 1\right)$$

$$= 28\left(1 + \frac{1}{2} + \frac{1}{3} + \ldots + \frac{1}{26} + \frac{1}{27} + \frac{1}{28}\right)$$

$$= 28 \sum_{k=1}^{28} \frac{1}{k}$$

In a similar manner, the expected number of bubble gum packs needed to obtain $28(10) = 280$ individual players is:

$$E(n) = 1 + \frac{1}{279/280} + \frac{1}{278/280} + \ldots + \frac{1}{2/280} + \frac{1}{1/280}$$

$$= 280\left(\frac{1}{280} + \frac{1}{279} + \ldots + \frac{1}{2} + 1\right)$$

$$= 280\left(1 + \frac{1}{2} + \frac{1}{3} + \ldots + \frac{1}{279} + \frac{1}{280}\right)$$

65

$$= 280 \sum_{k=1}^{280} \frac{1}{k}$$

Write a program for your programmable calculator to evaluate:

$$Sn = n \sum_{k=1}^{n} \frac{1}{k} = n(1 + \frac{1}{2} + \frac{1}{3} + \ldots + \frac{1}{n})$$

Use your program to evaluate Sn when $n = 28$ and $n = 280$.

User Instructions

Step	Procedure	Press	Display
1.	Enter program		
2.	Initialize	*CMs RST	
3.	Enter number of cards, n, and run program.	n R/S	Number of term Running total Total
4.	For a new case, go to step 2.		

Data Registers
01 Initial value of n
02 Running total
03 n

Output
The output from this program gives us the following results:
1. You must purchase 110 bubble gum packs, on the average, to obtain one complete set of team photos of the 28 National Football League teams.

$$E(n) = 28 \sum_{k=1}^{28} \frac{1}{k} = 109.9607891$$

2. You must purchase 1740 bubble gum packs, on the average, to obtain one complete set of the 280 player photos.

$$E(n) = 280 \sum_{k=1}^{280} \frac{1}{k} = 1739.861177$$

The Wine Taster A wine taster claims that he can distinguish between domestic and imported wines. He estimates that he is right two out of three times. As a

Bubble Gum Cards

Flow Diagram   Program

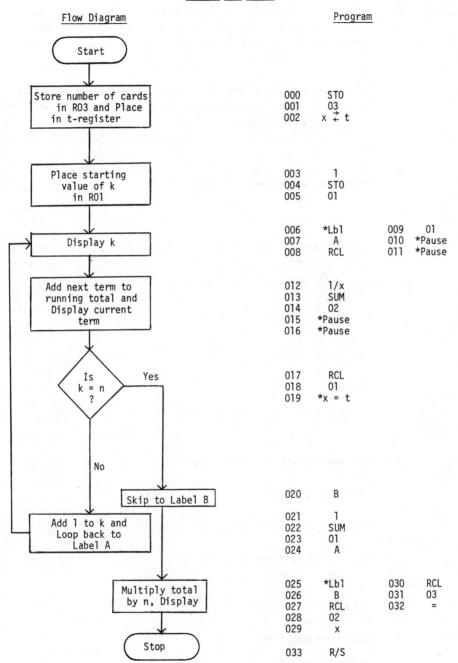

Start

Store number of cards   000   STO
in R03 and Place   001   03
in t-register   002   x ⇄ t

Place starting   003   1
value of k   004   STO
in R01   005   01

Display k   006   *Lbl   009   01
                               007   A   010   *Pause
                               008   RCL   011   *Pause

Add next term to   012   1/x
running total and   013   SUM
Display current   014   02
term   015   *Pause
                               016   *Pause

Is   017   RCL
k = n   018   01
?   019   *x = t

Yes

No

Skip to Label B   020   B

                               021   1
Add 1 to k and   022   SUM
Loop back to   023   01
Label A   024   A

Multiply total   025   *Lbl   030   RCL
by n, Display   026   B   031   03
                               027   RCL   032   =
                               028   02
                               029   x

Stop   033   R/S

67

test he is given ten wines to taste and determine whether they are domestic or imported. What is the probability that he will have exactly k correct choices, where $k = 0, 1, 2, 3, \ldots, 10$? What is the probability that he will have at most k correct choices, where $k = 0, 1, 2, 3, \ldots, 10$?

Solution

The probability of any specific sequence of ten trials having k successes can be computed as follows. Assume the first k trials are successes and the last $10 - k$ trials are failures. These trials are independent of one another, thus, the probability of k successes followed by $10 - k$ failures is given by:

$$\underbrace{p \times p \times p \times \ldots \times p}_{k \text{ times}} \times \underbrace{q \times q \times \ldots \times q}_{\substack{10 - k \\ \text{times}}}$$

The number of different sequences having k successes is the number of combinations of 10 items taken k at a time. Therefore, the probability of k successes in ten trials is:

$$p(k) = \binom{10}{k} p^k q^{10-k}$$

$$p = \frac{2}{3}, \quad q = \frac{1}{3}$$

Therefore: $p(k) = \binom{10}{k} \left(\frac{2}{3}\right)^k \left(\frac{1}{3}\right)^{10-k}$

$$= \binom{10}{k} \frac{2^k}{3^{10}}$$

The probability of at most k correct choices in ten trials is given by:

$$p(\text{at most } k) = p(1) + p(2) + \ldots + p(k)$$

Write a program to compute the probability of:

1. k successes in ten trials
2. at most k successes in ten trials

where $k = 0, 1, 2, 3, \ldots, 10$.

User Instructions

Step	Procedure	Press	Display
1.	Enter program		
2.	Initialize	*CMs *Fix 5 RST	
3.	Run program	R/S	k
			$p(k)$
			Sum

The Wine-Taster

Flow Diagram

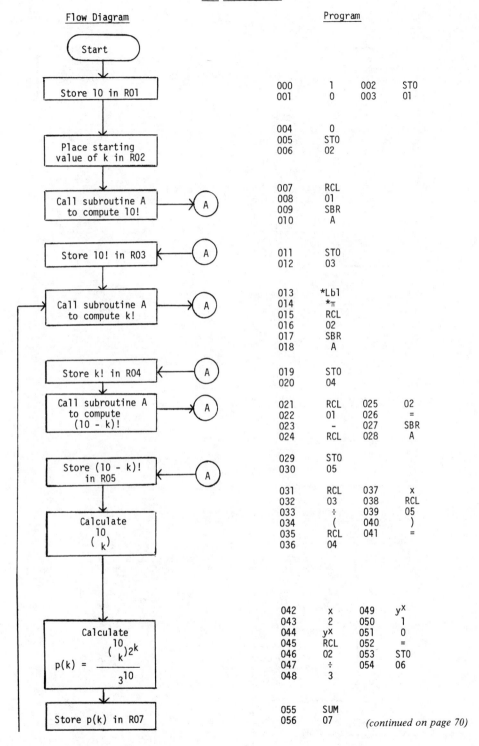

Start

Store 10 in R01

Place starting
value of k in R02

Call subroutine A
to compute 10! → A

Store 10! in R03 ← A

Call subroutine A
to compute k! → A

Store k! in R04 ← A

Call subroutine A
to compute
(10 − k)! → A

Store (10 − k)!
in R05 ← A

Calculate
$\binom{10}{k}$

Calculate
$$p(k) = \frac{\binom{10}{k}2^k}{3^{10}}$$

Store p(k) in R07

Program

000	1	002	STO
001	0	003	01

004	0
005	STO
006	02

007	RCL
008	01
009	SBR
010	A

011	STO
012	03

013	*Lbl
014	*π
015	RCL
016	02
017	SBR
018	A

019	STO
020	04

021	RCL	025	02
022	01	026	=
023	−	027	SBR
024	RCL	028	A

029	STO
030	05

031	RCL	037	x
032	03	038	RCL
033	÷	039	05
034	(	040	)
035	RCL	041	=
036	04		

042	x	049	y^x
043	2	050	1
044	y^x	051	0
045	RCL	052	=
046	02	053	STO
047	÷	054	06
048	3		

055	SUM
056	07

(continued on page 70)

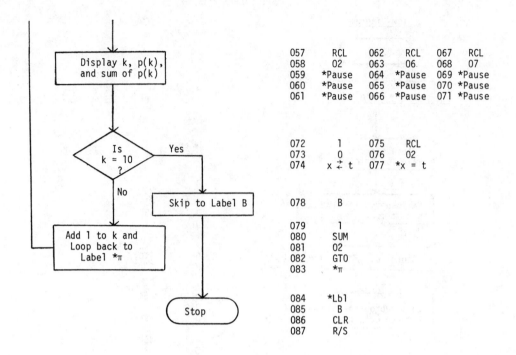

057	RCL	062	RCL	067	RCL
058	02	063	06	068	07
059	*Pause	064	*Pause	069	*Pause
060	*Pause	065	*Pause	070	*Pause
061	*Pause	066	*Pause	071	*Pause

072	1	075	RCL
073	0	076	02
074	x ⇄ t	077	*x = t

078	B

079	1
080	SUM
081	02
082	GTO
083	*π

084	*Lbl
085	B
086	CLR
087	R/S

Subroutine A

X! Program

Flow Diagram   Program

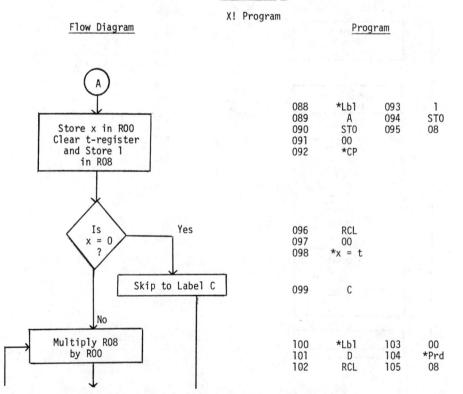

088	*Lbl	093	1
089	A	094	STO
090	STO	095	08
091	00		
092	*CP		

096	RCL
097	00
098	*x = t

099	C

100	*Lbl	103	00
101	D	104	*Prd
102	RCL	105	08

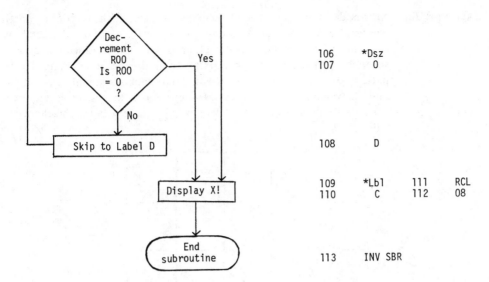

| 106 | *Dsz | | |
| 107 | 0 | | |

| 108 | D | | |

| 109 | *Lbl | 111 | RCL |
| 110 | C | 112 | 08 |

| 113 | INV SBR | | |

Data Registers

00	x
01	10
02	k
03	10!
04	$k!$
05	$(10 - k)!$
06	$p(k)$
07	Sum
08	Counter

Output

TABLE 1-15   Output: The Wine Taster

k	$p(k)$	$p(\text{at most } k)$
0	0.00002	0.00002
1	0.00034	0.00036
2	0.00305	0.00340
3	0.01626	0.01966
4	0.05690	0.07656
5	0.13656	0.21313
6	0.22761	0.44074
7	0.26012	0.70086
8	0.19509	0.89595
9	0.08671	0.98266
10	0.01734	1.00000

Jack and Jill   Jack and Jill are good friends who live at the opposite ends of town. On a beautiful day they each decide to go for a walk. Suppose that Jack, who lives in the northernmost corner of town, and Jill, who lives in the southernmost corner, begin walking toward each other along the street pattern shown in Figure 1-6. Assume that Jack walks only west or south and Jill walks only north or east. If they choose their paths at random and are equally likely to go either way at any corner, what is the chance they will meet?

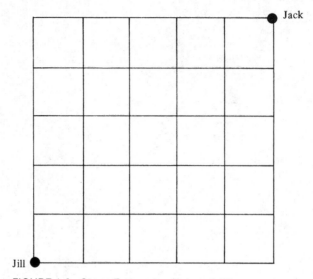

FIGURE 1-6   Street Pattern for Jack and Jill

Solution

One of the strategies used in solving a problem is to simplify it into special cases that are less complex than the original. We will use this approach to solve "Jack and Jill."

Consider a (1×1) grid. What is the probability that Jack and Jill will meet?

The probability that Jack will walk to point A = 1/2. The probability that Jill will walk to point A = 1/2.

Thus, the probability that they will meet at point A is:

$$p(\text{meet at A}) = \frac{1}{2} \times \frac{1}{2} = \frac{1}{2^2}$$

The probability that Jack will walk to point B = 1/2. The probability that Jill will walk to point B = 1/2.

Thus, the probability that they will meet at point B is:

72 $p(\text{meet at B}) = \frac{1}{2} \times \frac{1}{2} = \frac{1}{2^2}$

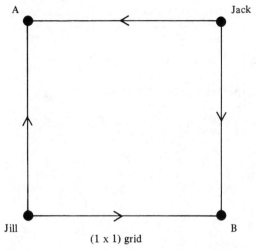

A   Jack

Jill   B

(1 x 1) grid

FIGURE 1-7   (1 $\times$ 1) Grid for Jack and Jill

Therefore, the probability that Jack and Jill will meet is:

$$p(\text{meet}) = \frac{1}{2^2} + \frac{1}{2^2} = \frac{2}{2^2} = 0.5000$$

Consider a (2 $\times$ 2) grid. What is the probability that Jack and Jill will meet?

The probability that Jack will walk to point A =

$$\frac{1}{2} \times \frac{1}{2} = \frac{1}{2^2}$$

FIGURE 1-8   (2 $\times$ 2) Grid for Jack and Jill

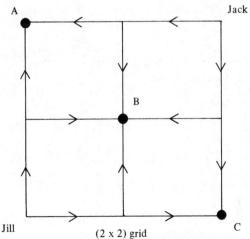

A   Jack

B

Jill   C

73   (2 x 2) grid

The probability that Jill will walk to point A =

$$\frac{1}{2} \times \frac{1}{2} = \frac{1}{2^2}$$

Thus, the probability that they will meet at point A is:

$$p(\text{meet at A}) = \frac{1}{2^2} \times \frac{1}{2^2} = \frac{1}{2^4}$$

The probability that Jack will walk to point B =

$$\frac{1}{2} \times \frac{1}{2} + \frac{1}{2} \times \frac{1}{2}$$

$$= \frac{1}{2^2} + \frac{1}{2^2}$$

$$= \frac{2}{2^2}$$

The probability that Jill will walk to point B =

$$\frac{1}{2} \times \frac{1}{2} + \frac{1}{2} \times \frac{1}{2}$$

$$= \frac{1}{2^2} + \frac{1}{2^2}$$

$$= \frac{2}{2^2}$$

Thus, the probability that they will meet at point B is:

$$p(\text{meet at B}) = \frac{2}{2^2} \times \frac{2}{2^2} = \frac{4}{2^4}$$

The probability that they will meet at C is the same as the probability that they will meet at A, thus:

$$p(\text{meet at C}) = \frac{1}{2^4}$$

Therefore, the probability that Jack and Jill will meet is:

$$p(\text{meet}) = \frac{1}{2^4} + \frac{4}{2^4} + \frac{1}{2^4}$$

$$= \frac{6}{2^4} = 0.3750$$

Consider a (3 × 3) grid. What is the probability that Jack and Jill will meet?

The probability that Jack will walk to point A =

$$\frac{1}{2} \times \frac{1}{2} \times \frac{1}{2} = \frac{1}{2^3}$$

The probability that Jill will walk to point A =

$$\frac{1}{2} \times \frac{1}{2} \times \frac{1}{2} = \frac{1}{2^3}$$

Thus, the probability that they will meet at point A is:

$$p(\text{meet at A}) = \frac{1}{2^3} \times \frac{1}{2^3} = \frac{1}{2^6}$$

The probability that Jack will walk to point B =

$$\frac{1}{2^3} + \frac{1}{2^3} + \frac{1}{2^3}$$

$$= \frac{3}{2^3}$$

FIGURE 1-9 (3 × 3) Grid for Jack and Jill

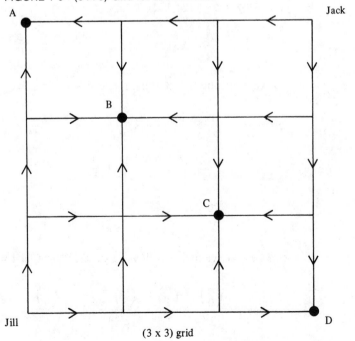

(3 x 3) grid

The probability that Jill will walk to point B =

$$\frac{1}{2^3} + \frac{1}{2^3} + \frac{1}{2^3}$$

$$= \frac{3}{2^3}$$

Thus, the probability that they will meet at point B is:

$$p(\text{meet at B}) = \frac{3}{2^3} \times \frac{3}{2^3} = \frac{9}{2^6}$$

The probability that they will meet at point C is:

$$p(\text{meet at C}) = \frac{9}{2^6}$$

The probability that they will meet at point D is:

$$p(\text{meet at D}) = \frac{1}{2^6}$$

Therefore, the probability that Jack and Jill will meet is:

$$p(\text{meet}) = \frac{1}{2^6} + \frac{9}{2^6} + \frac{9}{2^6} + \frac{1}{2^6}$$

$$= \frac{20}{26} = 0.3125$$

If we continue this pattern for a (4×4) grid, we find:

$$p(\text{meet}) = \frac{1}{2^4} \times \frac{1}{2^4} + \frac{4}{2^4} \times \frac{4}{2^4} + \frac{6}{2^4} \times \frac{6}{2^4} + \frac{4}{2^4} \times \frac{4}{2^4} + \frac{1}{2^4} \times \frac{1}{2^4}$$

$$= \frac{1}{2^8} + \frac{16}{2^8} + \frac{36}{2^8} + \frac{16}{2^8} + \frac{1}{2^8}$$

$$= \frac{70}{2^8} = 0.2734$$

and we arrive at the following general formula for an $(n \times n)$ grid:

$$p(\text{meet}) = \frac{\binom{n}{0}^2}{2^{2n}} + \frac{\binom{n}{1}^2}{2^{2n}} + \frac{\binom{n}{2}^2}{2^{2n}} + \ldots + \frac{\binom{n}{n}^2}{2^{2n}}$$

$$= \frac{2 \dbinom{2n-1}{n-1}}{2^{2n}}$$

Write a program to solve the problem. Use your program to determine the probability that Jack and Jill will meet when the street pattern is a (1×1) grid, (2×2) grid, (3×3) grid, (4×4) grid, (5×5) grid, (10×10) grid, (15×15) grid, (25×25) grid, (30×30) grid, and (35×35) grid.

<u>Jack</u> <u>and</u> <u>Jill</u>

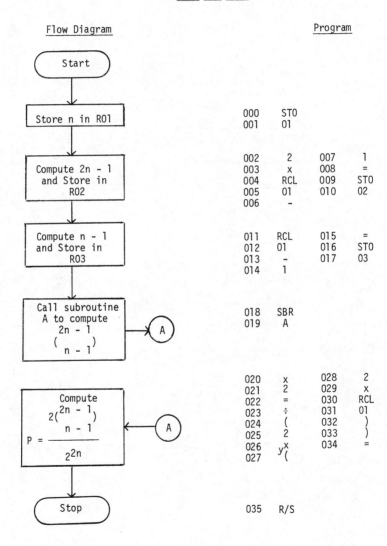

Flow Diagram

Start

Store n in R01

Compute 2n - 1 and Store in R02

Compute n - 1 and Store in R03

Call subroutine A to compute $2n - 1$ $\dbinom{}{n - 1}$ → A

Compute $P = \dfrac{2\dbinom{2n - 1}{n - 1}}{2^{2n}}$ ← A

Stop

Program

000	STO		
001	01		
002	2	007	1
003	x	008	=
004	RCL	009	STO
005	01	010	02
006	-		
011	RCL	015	=
012	01	016	STO
013	-	017	03
014	1		
018	SBR		
019	A		
020	x	028	2
021	2	029	x
022	=	030	RCL
023	÷	031	01
024	(	032	)
025	2	033	)
026	y^x	034	=
027	(		
035	R/S		

$$\text{Compute} \binom{2n-1}{n-1}$$

Flow Diagram   Program

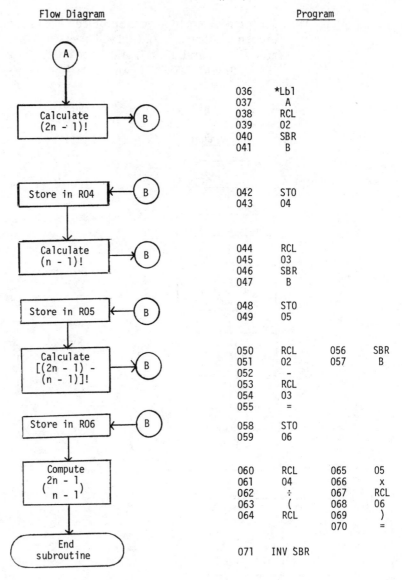

036	*Lbl	
037	A	
038	RCL	
039	02	
040	SBR	
041	B	
042	STO	
043	04	
044	RCL	
045	03	
046	SBR	
047	B	
048	STO	
049	05	
050	RCL	056 SBR
051	02	057 B
052	−	
053	RCL	
054	03	
055	=	
058	STO	
059	06	
060	RCL	065 05
061	04	066 x
062	÷	067 RCL
063	(	068 06
064	RCL	069)
		070 =
071	INV SBR	

Subroutine B

X! Program

Flow Diagram   Program

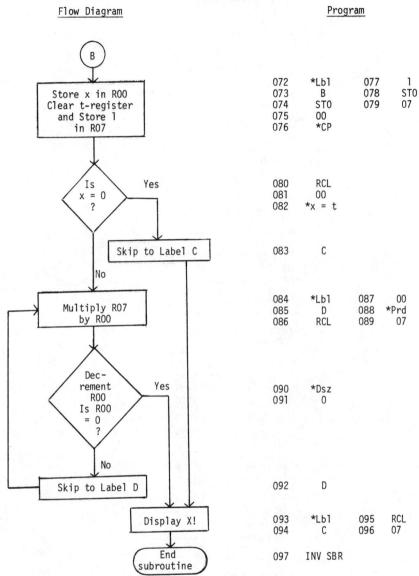

072	*Lbl	077	1
073	B	078	STO
074	STO	079	07
075	00		
076	*CP		

080	RCL	
081	00	
082	*x = t	

083	C

084	*Lbl	087	00
085	D	088	*Prd
086	RCL	089	07

090	*Dsz
091	0

092	D

093	*Lbl	095	RCL
094	C	096	07

097	INV SBR

79

User Instructions

Step	Procedure	Press	Display
1.	Enter program		
2.	Initialize	*CMs *FIX 4 RST	
3.	Enter n	n	
4.	Run program	R/S	p
5.	For a new case, go to step 2.		

Data Registers

00	x
01	n
02	$2n - 1$
03	$n - 1$
04	$(2n - 1)!$
05	$(n - 1)!$
06	$[(2n - 1) - (n - 1)]!$
07	$x!$

Output

TABLE 1-16   Output:
Jack and Jill

$(n \times n)$	$p(\text{meet})$
(1×1)	0.5000
(2×2)	0.3750
(3×3)	0.3125
(4×4)	0.2734
(5×5)	0.2461
(10×10)	0.1762
(15×15)	0.1445
(25×25)	0.1123
(30×30)	0.1026
(35×35)	0.0950

MAXIMUM AND MINIMUM

A programmable calculator is especially adapted to solve optimization problems, in which some quantity is to be maximized or minimized. The challenges in this section are just a sampling of many applications in all areas of mathematics, science, industry, agriculture, and business.

Jelly Beans   A child with a jar of jelly beans finds that if she removes the jelly beans either 2, 3, 4, 5, or 6 at a time there is always one jelly bean left; however, if she removes the jelly beans 7 at a time, there are no jelly beans left. If the jar holds up to 500 jelly beans, how many jelly beans does the child have?

Solution

Let n = the number of jelly beans. If n is divided by 2, the remainder is 1, thus $n - 1$ will be divisible by 2. In a similar manner, $n - 1$ will also be divisible by 3, 4, 5, and 6. Thus:

$$n - 1 = 2^2 \times 3 \times 5 \times k$$
$$n = 60k + 1$$

Write a program to find the smallest value of n less than 500 that is divisible by seven.

Jelly Beans

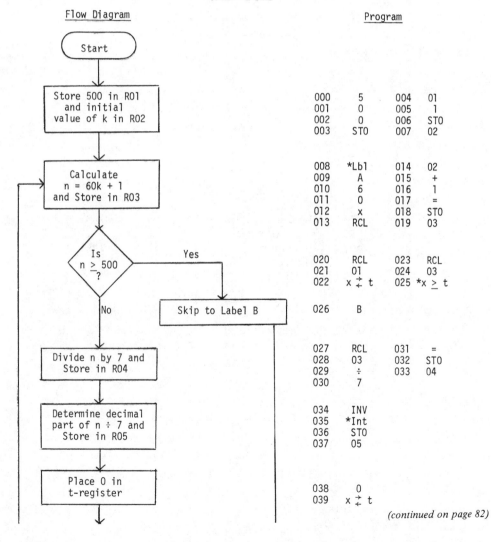

(continued on page 82)

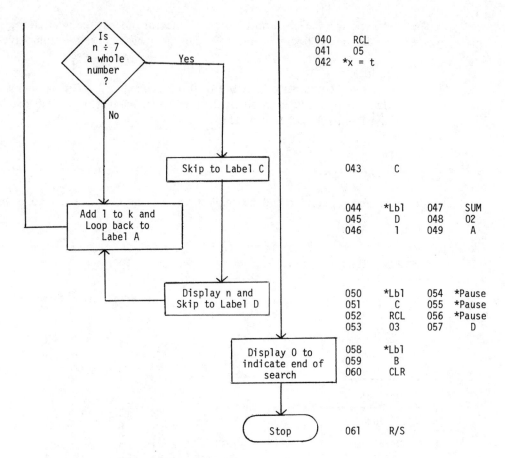

040	RCL
041	05
042	*x = t

Is
n ÷ 7
a whole
number
?

Yes

No

Skip to Label C   043   C

Add 1 to k and
Loop back to
Label A

044	*Lbl	047	SUM
045	D	048	02
046	1	049	A

Display n and
Skip to Label D

050	*Lbl	054	*Pause
051	C	055	*Pause
052	RCL	056	*Pause
053	03	057	D

Display 0 to
indicate end of
search

058	*Lbl
059	B
060	CLR

Stop   061   R/S

User Instructions

Step	Procedure	Press	Display
1.	Enter program		
2.	Initialize	*CMs RST	
3.	Run program	R/S	n

Note: Program will display 0 to indicate end of search.

Data Registers
01   500

02   k

03   n

04   $\dfrac{n}{7}$

05   Decimal part of $\dfrac{n}{7}$

Output
$n = 301$

82

The Arabian Prince An Arabian prince wants to divide his fortune among his heirs. He has 2000 bars of gold and wants to distribute them so that each son, eldest to youngest, will receive one bar more than his younger brother. None of the gold bars can be broken. If the prince divides his fortune so that the least number of sons will be involved, how many sons does the prince have, and how many bars of gold will the youngest son receive?

Solution

Let x = number of bars of gold received by youngest son

$x + 1$ = number of bars of gold received by second youngest son

$x + 2$ = number of bars of gold received by third youngest son

$\cdot$

$\cdot$

$\cdot$

$x + (k - 1)$ = number of bars of gold received by kth youngest son

Then: $\underbrace{x + (x + 1) + (x + 2) + \ldots + (x + k - 1)}_{k \text{ terms}} = 2000$

$kx + \underbrace{1 + 2 + 3 + \ldots + k - 1}_{(k-1) \text{ terms}} = 2000$

Given: $1 + 2 + 3 + \ldots + n = \dfrac{n(n + 1)}{2}$,

the following is true: $1 + 2 + 3 + \ldots + k - 1 = \dfrac{(k - 1)(k - 1 + 1)}{2}$

Thus: $kx + \dfrac{(k - 1)k}{2} = 2000$

$2kx + (k - 1)k = 4000$

$2kx + k^2 - k = 4000$

$2kx = 4000 - k^2 + k$

$x = \dfrac{4000 - k^2 + k}{2k}$

Write a program to determine the smallest positive integer, k, such that x is a positive integer.

User Instructions

Step	Procedure	Press	Display
1.	Enter program		
2.	Initialize	*CMs RST	
3.	Run program	R/S	k
			x

83

The Arabian Prince

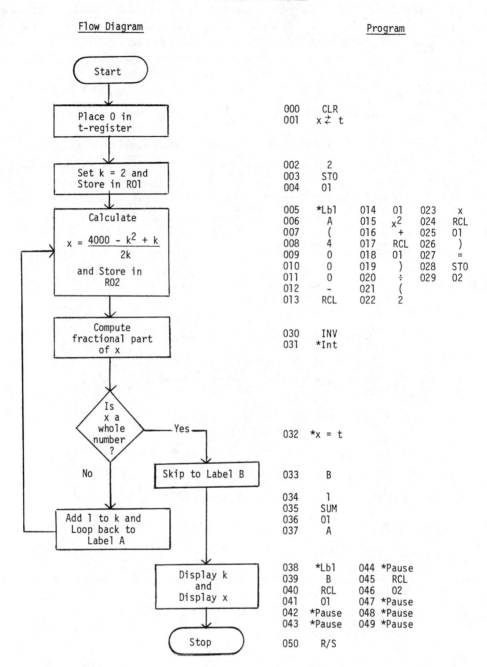

Flow Diagram

Program

Start

Place 0 in t-register	000 CLR 001 x ⇄ t

Set k = 2 and Store in R01	002 2 003 STO 004 01

Calculate

$$x = \frac{4000 - k^2 + k}{2k}$$

and Store in R02

005	*Lbl	014	01	023	x
006	A	015	x^2	024	RCL
007	(	016	+	025	01
008	4	017	RCL	026	)
009	0	018	01	027	=
010	0	019	)	028	STO
011	0	020	÷	029	02
012	–	021	(		
013	RCL	022	2		

Compute fractional part of x	030 INV 031 *Int

Is x a whole number ?

Yes ——

032 *x = t

No

Skip to Label B	033 B

Add 1 to k and Loop back to Label A	034 1 035 SUM 036 01 037 A

Display k and Display x	038 *Lbl	044	*Pause
	039 B	045	RCL
	040 RCL	046	02
	041 01	047	*Pause
	042 *Pause	048	*Pause
	043 *Pause	049	*Pause

Stop

050 R/S

84

Data Registers

01   *k*

02   *x*

Output

number of sons = 5

number of bars of gold received by youngest son = 398

Kristin's
Knockouts

Kristin played on the last-placed girls' softball team. At the end of the season the standings were such that the number of wins separating each team from the next was identical. There were twelve softball teams in Kristin's league. Each team played each of the other teams in the league sixteen times. What was the largest number of games Kristin's team could have won?

Solution

Let d = number of games separating each team

n = number of games Kristin's team won

Then: $n + \ \ d$ = number of wins of eleventh place team

$n + \ \ 2d$ = number of wins of tenth place team

$n + \ \ 3d$ = number of wins of ninth place team

.

.

.

$n + 11d$ = number of wins of first place team

$$\text{Number of games played} = 16\binom{12}{2}$$

$$= 16 \times 66$$

$$= 1056$$

Thus: $\underbrace{n + (n + d) + (n + 2d) + \ldots + (n + 11d)}_{12 \text{ terms}} = 1056$

$$12n + d + 2d + 3d + \ldots + 11d = 1056$$

$$12n + d(1 + 2 + 3 + \ldots + 11) = 1056$$

$$12n + d\,\frac{11(12)}{2} = 1056$$

$$12n + 66d = 1056$$

$$2n + 11d = 176$$

$$2n = 176 - 11d$$

$$n = \frac{176 - 11d}{2}$$

The maximum value of n will occur when d is a minimum. Write a program that determines the smallest positive integer value of d for which n is a positive integer.

<u>Kristin's Knockouts</u>

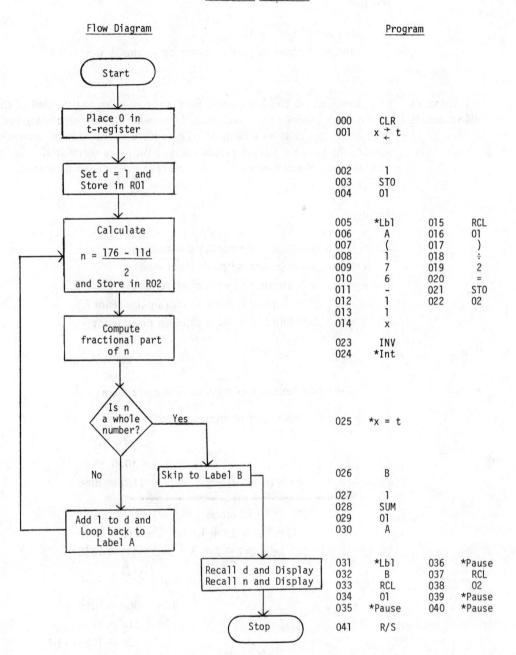

Flow Diagram

Start	

Place 0 in t-register

Set d = 1 and Store in R01

Calculate

$$n = \frac{176 - 11d}{2}$$

and Store in R02

Compute fractional part of n

Is n a whole number?   Yes

No

Skip to Label B

Add 1 to d and Loop back to Label A

Recall d and Display
Recall n and Display

Stop

Program

000	CLR		
001	x → t		
002	1		
003	STO		
004	01		
005	*Lbl	015	RCL
006	A	016	01
007	(	017	)
008	1	018	÷
009	7	019	2
010	6	020	=
011	-	021	STO
012	1	022	02
013	1		
014	x		
023	INV		
024	*Int		
025	*x = t		
026	B		
027	1		
028	SUM		
029	01		
030	A		
031	*Lbl	036	*Pause
032	B	037	RCL
033	RCL	038	02
034	01	039	*Pause
035	*Pause	040	*Pause
041	R/S		

User Instructions

Step	Procedure	Press	Display
1.	Enter program		
2.	Initialize	*CMs RST	
3.	Run program	R/S	d
			n

Data Registers
01 d
02 n

Output

$$d = 2$$
$$n = 77$$

Flight Fare   A travel agency offers a trip to Disney World in Florida. The charge is $799 if 100 people go on the flight. If more than 100 participate, the charge per person is reduced by $5 times the number of people above 100. Find the number of people that will result in maximum revenue for the airline. The plane holds 150 people.

Solution

Let x = number of people going on the trip
Then the price per person is:

$$P = 799 - 5(x - 100) \qquad 100 \leqslant x \leqslant 150$$
$$= 799 - 5x + 500$$
$$= 1299 - 5x \qquad 100 \leqslant x \leqslant 150$$

Total revenue = (number of people) × price
$$= x(1299 - 5x)$$
$$R = 1299x - 5x^2$$

Write a program to determine the number of people that will result in maximum revenue for the airline. The program should also display the flight fare per person.

User Instructions

Step	Procedure	Press	Display
1.	Enter program		
2.	Initialize	*CMs RST	
3.	Run program	R/S	Best x
			Flight fare

Flight Fare

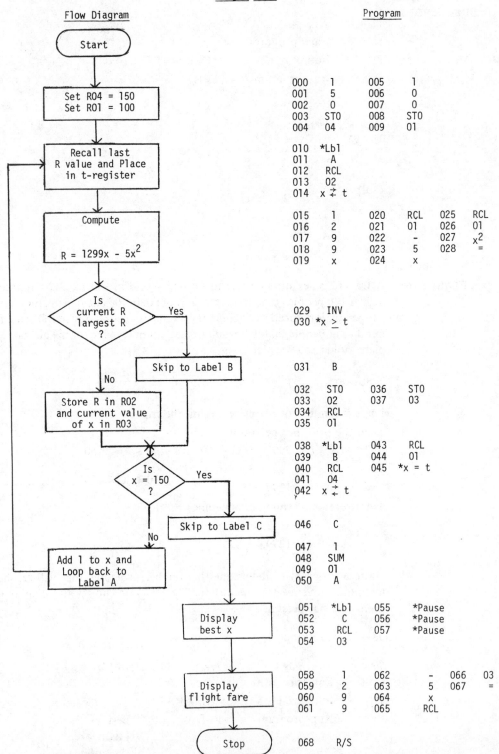

Flow Diagram

- Start
- Set RO4 = 150
  Set RO1 = 100
- Recall last R value and Place in t-register
- Compute
  $R = 1299x - 5x^2$
- Is current R largest R ? — Yes
- Skip to Label B
- No
- Store R in RO2 and current value of x in RO3
- Is x = 150 ? — Yes
- Skip to Label C
- No
- Add 1 to x and Loop back to Label A
- Display best x
- Display flight fare
- Stop

Program

000	1	005	1
001	5	006	0
002	0	007	0
003	STO	008	STO
004	04	009	01

010	*Lbl
011	A
012	RCL
013	02
014	x ⇄ t

015	1	020	RCL	025	RCL
016	2	021	01	026	01
017	9	022	−	027	x^2
018	9	023	5	028	=
019	x	024	x		

| 029 | INV |
| 030 | *x ≥ t |

| 031 | B |

032	STO	036	STO
033	02	037	03
034	RCL		
035	01		

038	*Lbl	043	RCL
039	B	044	01
040	RCL	045	*x = t
041	04		
042	x ⇄ t		

| 046 | C |

047	1
048	SUM
049	01
050	A

051	*Lbl	055	*Pause
052	C	056	*Pause
053	RCL	057	*Pause
054	03		

058	1	062	−	066	03
059	2	063	5	067	=
060	9	064	x		
061	9	065	RCL		

| 068 | R/S |

Data Registers

01	100
02	*R*
03	*x*
04	150

Output

$x = 130$

Flight fare $= \$649$

GEOMETRY

Everyone is familiar with some geometric concepts—our world is a geometric environment of objects having shape, size, and location. We are all naturally curious about shapes and their relationships and patterns. This section of challenges will explore several geometric concepts that are especially suitable for the programmable calculator.

Squares and Rectangles
How many different squares and how many different rectangles are there in an $(n \times n)$ grid?

Determine the number of different squares and different rectangles in a:

1. (5×5) grid
2. (10×10) grid
3. (25×25) grid
4. (50×50) grid

FIGURE 1-10 Squares and Rectangles

Solution

The strategy of reducing the problem to a simpler case will be used to solve these problems.

How many different squares are in a (1×1) grid, (2×2) grid, (3×3) grid, (4×4) grid, . . . , $(n \times n)$ grid?

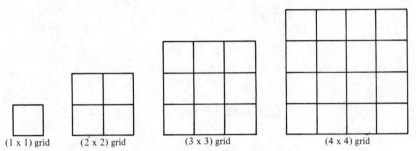

(1 x 1) grid   (2 x 2) grid   (3 x 3) grid   (4 x 4) grid

FIGURE 1-11   Squares and Rectangles: Graduated Grids

TABLE 1-17   Total Number of Squares

Size of Square	Size of Square				Total Number of Squares
	(1×1)	(2×2)	(3×3)	(4×4)	
(1×1)	1				1
(2×2)	4	1			5
(3×3)	9	4	1		14
(4×4)	16	9	4	1	30

Table 1-17 establishes the following pattern:

(1×1) square $T = 1^2$ $= 1$
(2×2) square $T = 1^2 + 2^2$ $= 5$
(3×3) square $T = 1^2 + 2^2 + 3^2$ $= 14$
(4×4) square $T = 1^2 + 2^2 + 3^2 + 4^2$ $= 30$

.
.
.

$(n \times n)$ square $T = 1^2 + 2^2 + 3^2 + \ldots + n^2 = \displaystyle\sum_{k=1}^{n} k^2$

How many different rectangles are there in a (1×1) grid, (2×2) grid, (3×3) grid, (4×4) grid, . . . , $(n \times n)$ grid?

TABLE 1-18 Total Number of Rectangles

Size of Rectangle	Size of Square			
	1×1	2×2	3×3	4×4
1×1	1	4 ⎫	9 ⎫	16 ⎫
1×2		4 ⎬ 8	12 ⎬ 27	24 ⎫
1×3			6 ⎭	16 ⎬ 64
1×4				8 ⎭
2×2		1	4 ⎫	9 ⎫
2×3			4 ⎬ 8	12 ⎬ 27
2×4				6 ⎭
3×3			1	4 ⎫
3×4				4 ⎬ 8
4×4				1
Total Number of Rectangles	1	9	36	100

Table 1-18 establishes the following pattern:

(1×1) square $T = 1^3$ = 1
(2×2) square $T = 1^3 + 2^3$ = 9
(3×3) square $T = 1^3 + 2^3 + 3^3$ = 36
(4×4) square $T = 1^3 + 2^3 + 3^3 + 4^3$ = 100

.
.
.

$(n \times n)$ square $T = 1^3 + 2^3 + 3^3 + 4^3 + \ldots + n^3 = \sum_{k=1}^{n} k^3$

The number of different rectangles in an $(n \times n)$ grid are the squares of the triangular numbers.

Write a program to evaluate the following series:

$$\sum_{k=1}^{n} k^2 = 1^2 + 2^2 + 3^2 + \ldots + n^2$$

and $$\sum_{k=1}^{n} k^3 = 1^3 + 2^3 + 3^3 + \ldots + n^3$$

for any value of *n*. Use your program to determine the number of different squares and the number of different rectangles in a:

1. (5 × 5) grid
2. (10 × 10) grid
3. (25 × 25) grid
4. (50 × 50) grid

<u>Squares</u> <u>and</u> <u>Rectangles</u>

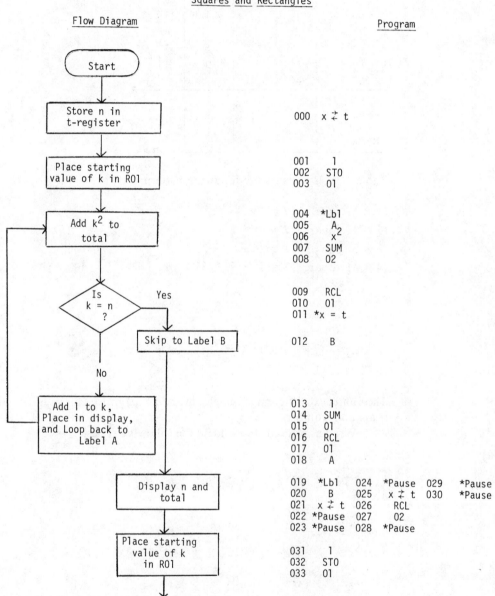

Flow Diagram

Program

Start		

Store n in t-register	000	x ⇄ t

Place starting value of k in R01	001	1
	002	STO
	003	01

Add k^2 to total	004	*Lbl
	005	A
	006	x^2
	007	SUM
	008	02

Is k = n ?	009	RCL
Yes	010	01
	011	*x = t

Skip to Label B	012	B

No

Add 1 to k, Place in display, and Loop back to Label A	013	1
	014	SUM
	015	01
	016	RCL
	017	01
	018	A

Display n and total	019	*Lbl	024	*Pause	029 *Pause
	020	B	025	x ⇄ t	030 *Pause
	021	x ⇄ t	026	RCL	
	022	*Pause	027	02	
	023	*Pause	028	*Pause	

Place starting value of k in R01	031	1
	032	STO
	033	01

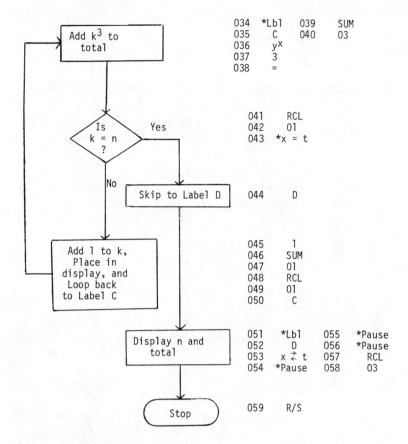

034	*Lbl	039	SUM
035	C	040	03
036	y^x		
037	3		
038	=		

041	RCL
042	01
043	*x = t

044	D

045	1
046	SUM
047	01
048	RCL
049	01
050	C

051	*Lbl	055	*Pause
052	D	056	*Pause
053	x ⇄ t	057	RCL
054	*Pause	058	03

059	R/S

User Instructions

Step	Procedure	Press	Display
1.	Enter program		
2.	Initialize	*CMs RST	
3.	Enter *n*	*n*	
4.	Run program	R/S	*n*
			Sum of squares
			n
			Sum of cubes

Data Registers
01 *k*
02 Sum of squares
03 Sum of cubes

Output

	Total Number of:	
	Squares	*Rectangles*
1. (5 × 5) grid	55	225
2. (10 × 10) grid	385	3,025

| 3. | (25 × 25) grid | 5,525 | 105,625 |
| 4. | (50 × 50) grid | 42,929 | 1,625,625 |

The Painted Box A rectangular box with a square base is painted red and then cut into one-inch subcubes. It is found that the number of cubes with no paint on them is equal to the number of cubes with some red paint on them. If the dimensions are positive integers x and y such that $3 \leqslant x \leqslant 20$ and $3 \leqslant y \leqslant 20$, what are the dimensions of the box?

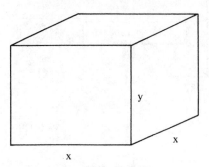

FIGURE 1-12 The Painted Box

Solution

$$\text{Let } x^2y = \text{number of unit cubes}$$
$$(x - 2)(x - 2)(y - 2) = \text{number of unit cubes with no paint on them}$$

Then:

Number of Unit Cubes	=	Number of Cubes with No Paint on Them	+	Number of Cubes with Some Paint on Them
x^2y	=	$(x - 2)^2(y - 2)$	+	$(x - 2)^2(y - 2)$
x^2y	=	$2(x - 2)^2(y - 2)$		

Write a program for your programmable calculator to determine the positive integers x and y that satisfy this equation where $3 \leqslant x \leqslant 20$ and $3 \leqslant y \leqslant 20$.

User Instructions

Step	Procedure	Press	Display
1.	Enter program		
2.	Initialize	*CMs RST	
3.	Run program	R/S	x
			y

Data Registers
01 x

02 y

The Painted Box

Flow Diagram

Program

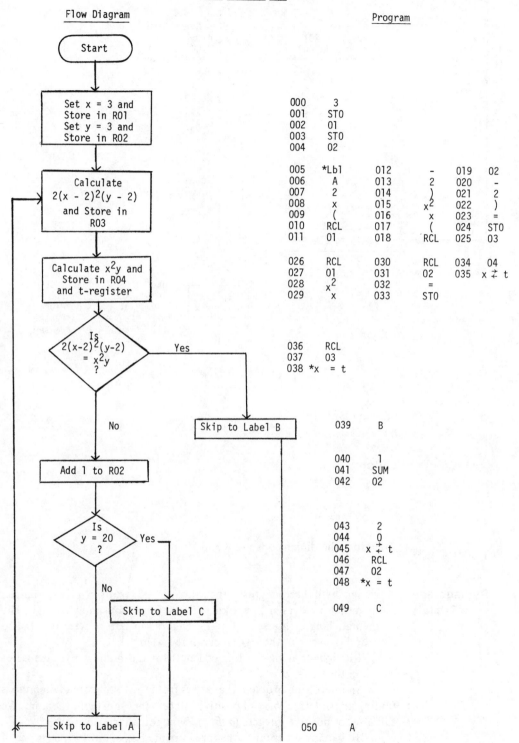

000	3	
001	STO	
002	01	
003	STO	
004	02	

005	*Lbl	012	–	019	02	
006	A	013	2	020	–	
007	2	014	)	021	2	
008	x	015	x^2	022	)	
009	(	016	x	023	=	
010	RCL	017	(	024	STO	
011	01	018	RCL	025	03	

026	RCL	030	RCL	034	04
027	01	031	02	035	x ⇄ t
028	x^2	032	=		
029	x	033	STO		

036	RCL
037	03
038	*x = t

039	B

040	1
041	SUM
042	02

043	2
044	0
045	x ⇄ t
046	RCL
047	02
048	*x = t

049	C

050	A

(continued on page 96)

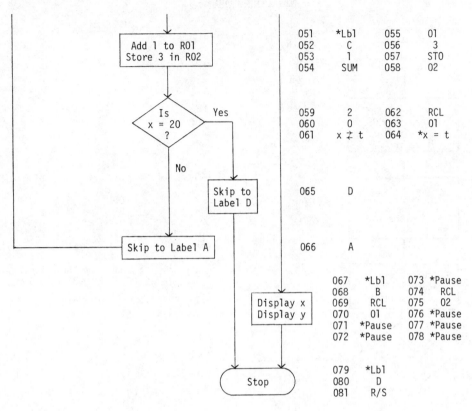

051	*Lbl	055	01		
052	C	056	3		
053	1	057	STO		
054	SUM	058	02		

059	2	062	RCL
060	0	063	01
061	x ⇄ t	064	*x = t

065   D

066   A

067	*Lbl	073	*Pause
068	B	074	RCL
069	RCL	075	02
070	01	076	*Pause
071	*Pause	077	*Pause
072	*Pause	078	*Pause

079	*Lbl
080	D
081	R/S

03    $2(x - 2)^2(y - 2)$

04    $x^2 y$

Output

$$x = 8$$
$$y = 18$$

Therefore the dimensions are $8 \times 8 \times 18$.

Pythagorean Triplets

A triangle with three lengths in the ratio of 3:4:5 results in a right triangle; the pyramid builders of Egypt knew this several thousand years ago. The mathematicians of the school of Pythagoras in Greece were the first to state and prove it in the Pythagorean theorem.

If a right triangle has legs of lengths a and b and a hypotenuse of length c, then $c^2 = a^2 + b^2$.

An interesting problem that arises from the Pythagorean theorem is finding all triplets (a, b, c) of positive integers that satisfy the theorem. We call a set of positive integers (a, b, c) Pythagorean triplets if $a^2 + b^2 = c^2$.

How many different Pythagorean triplets exist in which 60 is one of the two smaller integers?

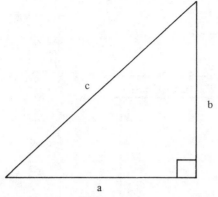

FIGURE 1-13 Pythagorean Triplets: Right
Triangle

Solution

$$c^2 = a^2 + b^2$$
$$c^2 = (60)^2 + b^2$$
$$c^2 = 3600 + b^2$$
$$c = \sqrt{3600 + b^2}$$

Write a program to determine all Pythagorean triplets where $a = 60$. Have
your program determine the values of b that produce integral values of c.
Have your program stop when c is less than or equal to some arbitrary
value. Use your program to find all Pythagorean triplets when c is less than
200.

Pythagorean Triplets

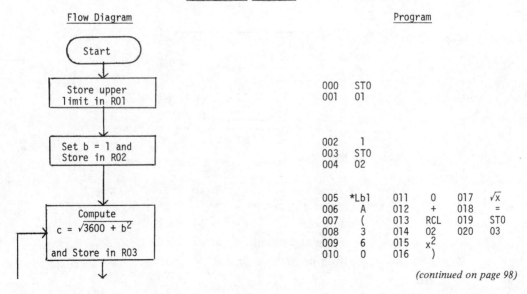

Flow Diagram		Program					
Start							
Store upper limit in R01		000	STO				
		001	01				
Set b = 1 and Store in R02		002	1				
		003	STO				
		004	02				
Compute $c = \sqrt{3600 + b^2}$ and Store in R03		005	*Lbl	011	0	017	√x
		006	A	012	+	018	=
		007	(	013	RCL	019	STO
		008	3	014	02	020	03
		009	6	015	x^2		
		010	0	016	)		

(continued on page 98)

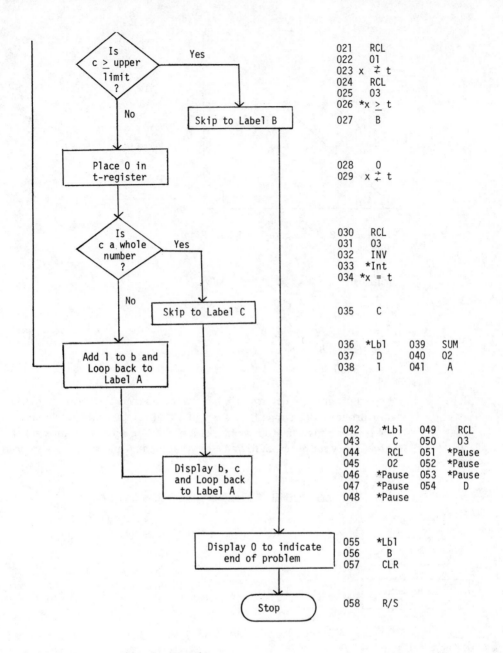

021	RCL
022	01
023	x ⇄ t
024	RCL
025	03
026	*x ≥ t
027	B

Is c ≥ upper limit ? — Yes → Skip to Label B

No

Place 0 in t-register

| 028 | 0 |
| 029 | x ⇄ t |

Is c a whole number ? — Yes → Skip to Label C

030	RCL
031	03
032	INV
033	*Int
034	*x = t

No

Skip to Label C

| 035 | C |

Add 1 to b and Loop back to Label A

036	*Lbl	039	SUM
037	D	040	02
038	1	041	A

Display b, c and Loop back to Label A

042	*Lbl	049	RCL
043	C	050	03
044	RCL	051	*Pause
045	02	052	*Pause
046	*Pause	053	*Pause
047	*Pause	054	D
048	*Pause		

Display 0 to indicate end of problem

055	*Lbl
056	B
057	CLR

Stop

| 058 | R/S |

User Instructions

Step	Procedure	Press	Display
1.	Enter program		
2.	Initialize	*CMs RST	
3.	Enter upper limit	ul	
4.	Run program	R/S	b
			c

98

Data Registers

01   Upper limit
02   *b*
03   *c*

Output

TABLE 1-19   Output:
Pythagorean Triplets

b	*c*
11	61
25	65
32	68
45	75
63	87
80	100
91	109
144	156
175	185

Integral 60° and
120° Triangles   A problem closely related to the Pythagorean triplets is that of finding triplets of positive integers that form 60° and 120° triangles.

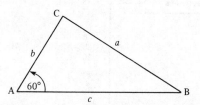 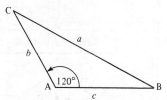

FIGURE 1-14   60° and 120° Triangles

Solution
Using the law of cosines for each triangle we find:

$$c^2 = a^2 + b^2 - 2ab \cos 60° \quad \text{or} \quad c^2 = a^2 + b^2 - 2ab \cos 120°$$

$$c^2 = a^2 + b^2 - 2ab\left(\tfrac{1}{2}\right) \quad \text{or} \quad c^2 = a^2 + b^2 - 2ab\left(-\tfrac{1}{2}\right)$$

$$c^2 = a^2 + b^2 - ab \quad \text{or} \quad c^2 = a^2 + b^2 + ab$$

Thus, we want to write a program to find positive integers (a, b, c) such that a, b, c form a 60° triangle or a 120° triangle. Use your program to find all triangles where $a < 20$ and $b < 20$.

Integral 60° Triangles

Flow Diagram

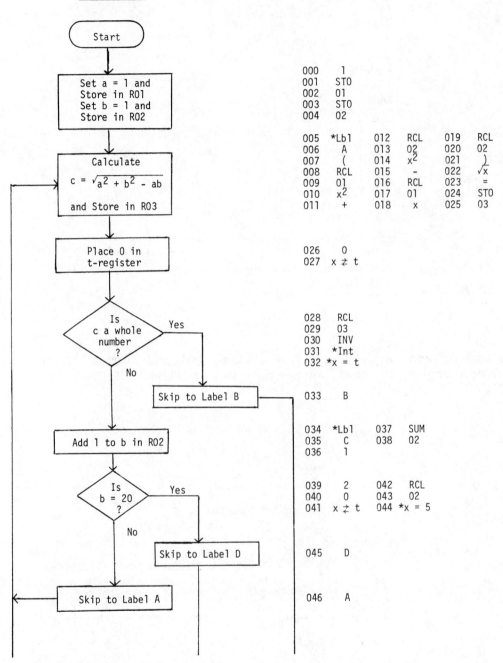

Start

Set a = 1 and
Store in R01
Set b = 1 and
Store in R02

000	1
001	STO
002	01
003	STO
004	02

Calculate

$$c = \sqrt{a^2 + b^2 - ab}$$

and Store in R03

005	*Lbl	012	RCL	019	RCL
006	A	013	02	020	02
007	(	014	x^2	021	)
008	RCL	015	-	022	$\sqrt{x}$
009	01	016	RCL	023	=
010	x^2	017	01	024	STO
011	+	018	x	025	03

Place 0 in
t-register

026	0
027	$x \gtrless t$

Is
c a whole
number
?

Yes

028	RCL
029	03
030	INV
031	*Int
032	*x = t

No

Skip to Label B

| 033 | B |

Add 1 to b in R02

034	*Lbl	037	SUM
035	C	038	02
036	1		

Is
b = 20
?

Yes

039	2	042	RCL
040	0	043	02
041	$x \gtrless t$	044	*x = 5

No

Skip to Label D

| 045 | D |

Skip to Label A

| 046 | A |

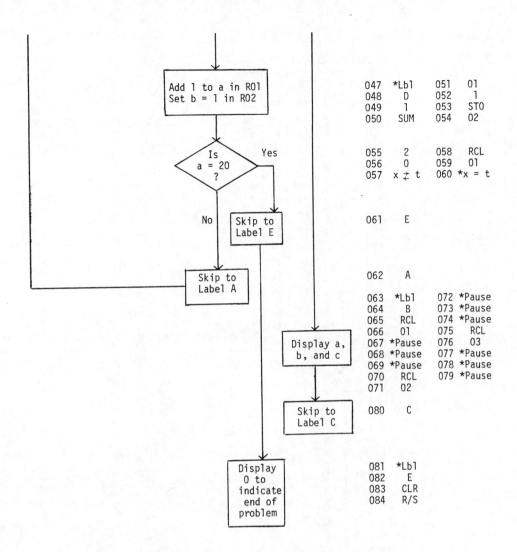

047	*Lbl	051	01
048	D	052	1
049	1	053	STO
050	SUM	054	02

055	2	058	RCL
056	0	059	01
057	x ⇄ t	060	*x = t

061   E

062   A

063	*Lbl	072	*Pause
064	B	073	*Pause
065	RCL	074	*Pause
066	01	075	RCL
067	*Pause	076	03
068	*Pause	077	*Pause
069	*Pause	078	*Pause
070	RCL	079	*Pause
071	02		

080   C

081	*Lbl
082	E
083	CLR
084	R/S

User Instructions

Step	Procedure	Press	Display
1.	Enter program		
2.	Initialize	*CMs RST	
3.	Run program	R/S	*a*
			b
			c

Data Registers

01   *a*

02   *b*

101   03   *c*

Output

TABLE 1-20   Output: 60° Triangle

a	b	c	a	b	c
1	1	1	10	10	10
2	2	2	10	16	14
3	3	3	11	11	11
3	8	7	12	12	12
4	4	4	13	13	13
5	5	5	14	14	14
5	8	7	15	7	13
6	6	6	15	8	13
6	16	14	15	15	15
7	7	7	16	6	14
7	15	13	16	10	14
8	3	7	16	16	16
8	5	7	17	17	17
8	8	8	18	18	18
8	15	13	19	19	19
9	9	9			

TABLE 1-21   Output:
120° Triangle

a	b	c
3	5	7
5	3	7
5	16	19
6	10	14
7	8	13
8	7	13
9	15	21
10	6	14
14	16	26
15	9	21
16	5	19
16	14	26

Comments

To use the program for integral 120° triangles, change the program for integral 60° triangles so that step 015 is a plus (+).

The Red Square   A unit square is divided into four equal squares, and the square in the upper left hand corner is painted red. The remaining three squares are then divided into four equal squares, and each square in the upper left hand corner is painted red. If we continue this procedure indefinitely, what is the area of the painted squares?

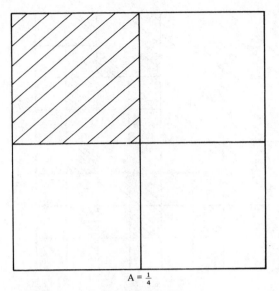

$$A = \tfrac{1}{4}$$

FIGURE 1-15   The Red Square (Part I)

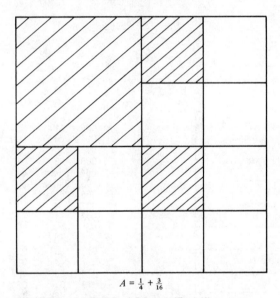

$$A = \tfrac{1}{4} + \tfrac{3}{16}$$

FIGURE 1-16   The Red Square (Part II)

Solution
The problem of the painted squares calls for the limit of the following series:

$$An = \frac{1}{4} + \frac{3}{16} + \frac{9}{64} + \frac{27}{256} + \ldots + \frac{3^{n-1}}{4^n} + \ldots$$

103   Write a program for your programmable calculator to evaluate this series.

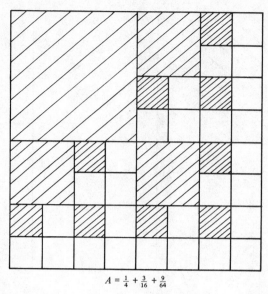

$$A = \tfrac{1}{4} + \tfrac{3}{16} + \tfrac{9}{64}$$

FIGURE 1-17   The Red Square (Part III)

The Red Square

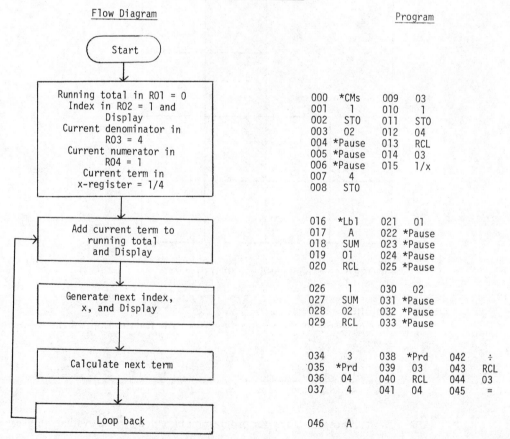

Flow Diagram

Program

Start

Running total in R01 = 0
Index in R02 = 1 and
Display
Current denominator in
R03 = 4
Current numerator in
R04 = 1
Current term in
x-register = 1/4

000	*CMs	009	03
001	1	010	1
002	STO	011	STO
003	02	012	04
004	*Pause	013	RCL
005	*Pause	014	03
006	*Pause	015	1/x
007	4		
008	STO		

Add current term to
running total
and Display

016	*Lbl	021	01
017	A	022	*Pause
018	SUM	023	*Pause
019	01	024	*Pause
020	RCL	025	*Pause

Generate next index,
x, and Display

026	1	030	02
027	SUM	031	*Pause
028	02	032	*Pause
029	RCL	033	*Pause

Calculate next term

034	3	038	*Prd	042	÷
035	*Prd	039	03	043	RCL
036	04	040	RCL	044	03
037	4	041	04	045	=

Loop back

| 046 | A | | |

User Instructions

Step	Procedure	Press	Display
1.	Enter program		
2.	Initialize	*FIX 5 RST	
3.	Run program	R/S	Index
			Running total

Data Registers

01 Running total
02 Index
03 Current denominator
04 Current numerator

Output

TABLE 1-22   Output: The Red Square

Term	Sn	Term	Sn
1	0.25000	23	0.99866
2	0.43750	24	0.99900
3	0.57813	25	0.99925
4	0.68359	26	0.99944
5	0.76270	27	0.99958
6	0.82202	28	0.99968
7	0.86652	29	0.99976
8	0.89989	30	0.99982
9	0.92492	31	0.99987
10	0.94369	32	0.99990
11	0.95776	33	0.99992
12	0.96832	34	0.99994
13	0.97624	35	0.99996
14	0.98218	36	0.99997
15	0.98664	37	0.99998
16	0.98998	38	0.99998
17	0.99248	39	0.99999
18	0.99436	40	0.99999
19	0.99577	41	0.99999
20	0.99683	42	0.99999
21	0.99762	43	1.00000
22	0.99822		

As the number of painting operations increases, the painted area of the unit square approaches the area of one. The limit is a fully painted square.

Games 2

Football   Materials

Programmable calculator

Sketch of football field

Marker

Object of the Game
To score more points than your opponent while playing this modified
game of football.

General Description
This program allows two people to play a modified game of football. Play
begins with Player A kicking off from the 40 yard line. The calculator will
briefly display the distance of the kick and halt with the line of scrimmage
in display. Since there are never any runbacks (returns), the line of
scrimmage will be the distance of the kick plus 40.

If a fumble occurs on the kickoff, as indicated by a flashing display,
the team with the fewest points recovers the ball. If the score is tied, the
kicking team recovers. The line of scrimmage after a fumble on the kickoff

is always 20 yards from the receiving team's goal. If no fumble occurs, the kicking team becomes the defense, and play from scrimmage begins.

On each play from scrimmage the defensive player decides to defend against a run or a pass. This is accomplished by selecting a decimal number from zero to one to use as the *defensive probability*. A probability of 1 is a total pass defense, while a defense of 0 is stacked against the run. A probability of 0.5 defends equally against the pass and run; however, this gain in flexibility is accompanied by a loss of defensive strength.

After the defense has selected and entered the secret probability, the calculator is given to the offensive player, who can select and enter any one of six plays (including punt and field goal attempts).

As in standard football, the offense has four downs to advance the ball ten yards. If this is not achieved, the defensive player gains possession of the ball with the line of scrimmage set at the yard line where the ball was located at the end of the fourth down play. Play then continues as described in step 8C of the user instructions.

If a score occurs, the appropriate number of points (touchdown = 6; field goal = 3; safety = 2) should be added to the team score (register 36 for Player A or register 37 for Player B), and play continues as described in step 8C of the user instructions.

Fumbles and interceptions from plays that begin at the line of scrimmage *always* result in the defense gaining possession of the ball. The new line of scrimmage will be the location of the previous one. (Just turn the marker arrow in the opposite direction.) Play continues as described in step 8C of the user instructions.

The game ends when the time allocated for play has expired. One hour is a good limit for most games. The team with the most points wins, and ties can occur.

Preliminaries

You should make a diagram of the field (Figure 2-1) and a line of scrimmage marker before starting the game. If you shape the marker as an arrow, it will help you remember in which direction the ball is moving.

Identify the participants as Player A and Player B. You should also agree on how long the game will last.

Sample Game

Use this sample game with the user instructions and the general description of the game. The procedure step numbers correspond with those of the user instructions.

Step	Procedure	Press	Display
1.	Repartition calculator	4 *Op 17	639.39
2.	Enter program		
3A.	Store seed	.3921 STO 10	Seed
3B.	Store generator number	147 STO 11	147
4.	Place ball for kickoff	40 *B′	40.

To see:

Current down	RCL	35
Current line of scrimmage	RCL	32
Original line of scrimmage	RCL	34
Player A's score	RCL	36
Player B's score	RCL	37
Offensive player number	RCL	33
Last gain or loss	RCL	30

Press:

A	for a dive	
B	for a sweep	
C	for a short pass	
D	for a long pass	
E	for a field goal	
*D'	for a punt	

Remember: 1 = maximum *pass* defense
2 = maximum *run* defense

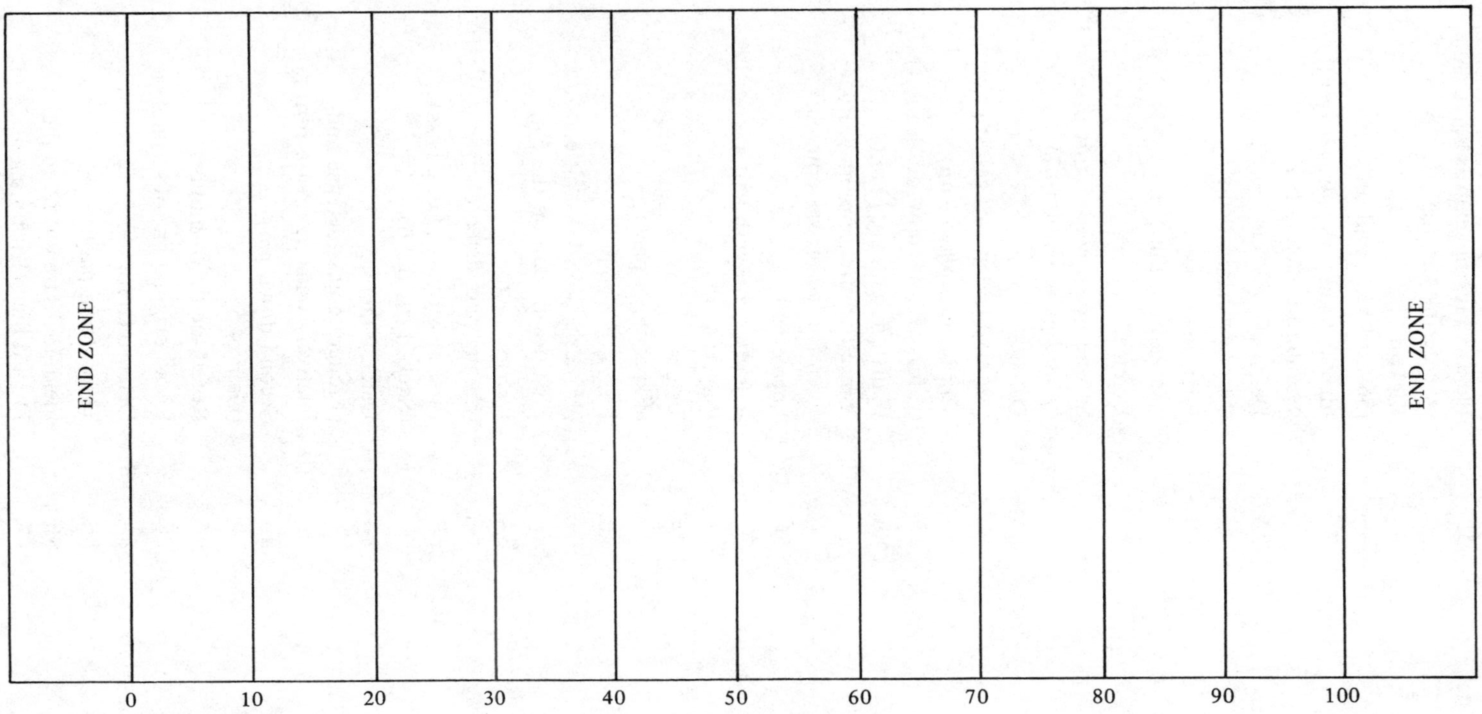

END ZONE

END ZONE

0 10 20 30 40 50 60 70 80 90 100

FIGURE 2-1 Football Field with Notes

5.	Identify kicking team as Player A by entering the digit, 1.	1 *A′	40.
6.	Kickoff (56 yard kick, ball on 96)	*D′	56; 96.
7.	Identify team with ball as Player B by entering the digit, 2.	2 *A′	96.
8A.	Defense (Stronger against run)	.3 *E′	0
8B.	First down play (No gain on this run)	A	0; 96.
8A.	Defense	.4 *E′	0
8B.	Second down play (Short pass) (9 yard gain, ball on 87)	C	9; 87.
8A.	Defense (Maximum defense against a run)	0 *E′	0
8B.	Third down play (Run) (A loss of 3; it is now fourth and 4)	A	−3; 90.
8B.	Fourth down play (Punt) (Since the offense punted, no defensive factor was entered.)	*D′	36; 54.
8C6.	Locate ball	54 *B′	54.
7.	Identify team with ball as Player A	1 *A′	54.
8A.	Defense (Expecting a pass)	.75 *E′	0
8B.	First down play (15 yards gained on this end run. First down. Ball on the 69.)	B	15.; 69.
8A.	Defense factor (Strong pass defense)	.95 *E′	0
8B.	First down play (Long pass) (Sack! Loss of 10)	D	−10.; 59.
8A.	Defense factor (Moderate pass defense and relatively weak against a run)	.7 *E′	0
8B.	Second down play (Gain of 8)	A	8.; 67.
9A.	Recall the down number	RCL 35	3.
9E.	Recall original line of scrimmage	RCL 34	69.
8A.	Defense factor	.8 *E′	0
8B.	Third down play	B	7.; 74.
8B.	Field goal attempt from the 74 yard line; (Kick must be 26 or more) (Too bad! Only a 15 yard kick.)	E	15; 89.

8C2.	Relocate ball to the last line of scrimmage	74 *B'	74.
7.	Identify team with ball as Player B (Line of scrimmage is the 74)	2 *A'	74.
8A.	Defense factor (Expecting a run)	0 *E'	0
8B.	First down play (Bomb) (Gain of 58!)	D	58.; 16
8A.	Defense factor (Still expecting a run)	0 *E'	0
8B.	First down play (Bomb) (TD! Ball crossed goal)	D	58.;−42
8C1a.	Add 6 points to Player B's score	6 sum 37	6.
8C1b.	Place ball for extra point	2 *B'	2.
8A.	Defense factor (He can't pass forever)	0 *E'	0
8B.	Extra point attempt (Loss of 3, no score)	A	−3.; 5
4.	Place ball for kickoff	60 *B'	60.
5.	Identify kicking team as Player B (Player B is going to kick from the 60)	2 *A'	60.
6.	Kickoff (35 yard kick. Ball on 25)	*D'	35.; 25
7.	Identify team with ball as Player A	1 *A'	25.
8A.	Defense factor (Maximum pass defense)	1 *E'	0
8B.	First down play (Long pass)	D	−10.; 15

Play continues in this manner until the time limit expires.

Program Notes

The "Spinner Simulation" in Chapter 3 is used as a subroutine (locations 000–075) to generate pseudorandom numbers. To use a generator other than the 147 generator, store the number of your choice in register 11. This occurs as step 3B of the user instructions.

The probability entered by the defense before each play from scrimmage is used in several program locations to modify the results of the random number generator. For example, assume that the offense has selected a running play and that the defense probability factor was entered as 0.85 (a weak defense against a running play). The offense will be "rewarded" by increasing the yards gained by the probability factor (0.85 in this case) times 10. Hence, the gain is 8.5 yards greater than it would have been if the probability factor had not been utilized. (See locations 335–346.)

The defensive probability factor has no effect on kickoffs, punts, and field goals.

User Instructions

Step	Procedure	Press	Display
1.	Repartition calculator	4 *Op 17	639.39
2.	Enter program		
3.	Initialize:		
	A. Enter seed, S, $(0 < S < 1)$	S STO 10	Seed
	B. Enter generator number	147 STO 11	Generator number
4.	Place ball on yard line, yard, kickoff (Yard = 40 or 60)	Yard *B′	Yard
5.	Identify the kicking team, K, as Player A or Player B. Use the digit 1 to indicate Player A and the digit 2 to indicate Player B. Hence, enter K as a 1 or a 2.	K *A′	Yard
6.	Kick (no runback)	*D′	*Distance* of kick and then the new yard line
	Note: If the ball is kicked farther than 60 yards, it will cross the goal line. You must then reposition the ball 20 yards from the goal by entering Yards (20 or 80): (Continue play at step 7)	Yards *B′	Yards
7.	Identify the team with the ball, T, as Player A or Player B. Enter 1 for Player A and 2 for Player B.	T *A′	New yard line
8.	Play from scrimmage		
	A. Defensive team selects probability factor, p, so that $0 \leqslant p \leqslant 1$	p *E′	0
	B. Offense selects one of the following plays from scrimmage, P_s		
	(1) If dive, press A		
	(2) If sweep, press B		
	(3) If short pass, press C		
	(4) If long pass, press D		
	(5) If field goal, press E		
	(6) If punt, press *D′	P_s	Yards gained or lost, then new line of scrimmage

Note: A flashing display of 9.99 indicates a fumble or interception

C. Repeat steps 8A and 8B until one of the
   following occurs: (?? is 36 for Player A
   and 37 for Player B)
   (1) Touchdown
       (a) Add 6 points (Remember,
           ?? will be entered as 36 or 37)   6 SUM ??   6.
       (b) Place ball 2 yards from goal   2 (or 98) *B'   2. or 98.
       (c) Conduct one play as in steps
           8A and 8B. If 2 or more yards
           are gained, add 1 point to
           score.   1 SUM ??   1.
       (d) Return to step 4.
   (2) Field Goal
       (a) If successful, add 3 points and
           return to step 4   3 SUM ??   3.
       (b) If not successful, place ball on
           last line of scrimmage, L_s, and
           return to step 7 (If last L_s was L_s *B' L_s
           less than 20 yards from goal,
           place ball on line 20 yards from
           goal, 20 or 80.)
   (3) Safety
       (a) Add 2 points to *defense*   2 SUM ??   2.
       (b) Return to step 4 and defense
           will receive
   (4) Fumble or Interception
       (a) Place ball on last line of
           scrimmage, L_s L_s *B' L_s
           Return to step 7
   (5) Loss of ball on downs
       (a) Defense becomes offense with
           line of scrimmage at location
           of ball, L_b, when the last play
           ended L_b *B' L_b
   (6) Punt
       (a) After punt, note location of
           ball, L_b, and enter L_b *8' L_b
       (b) Return to step 7

9. Note: At any time during the game when
    the program is not in operation, you can
    use the RCL key to see any of the
    following:
    A. Current down   RCL 35   Down 1 – 4
    B. Offensive player number (Player A is 1
       and Player B is 2.)   RCL 33   Player number
    C. Line of scrimmage   RCL 32   Yard line
    D. Last gain (or loss)   RCL 30   Number of yards

E. Original line of scrimmage for this
series   RCL 34   Yard number

Data Registers

00–05	Spinner probability	20–25	Digits 0 – 5 (N_s)
10	Seed	30	Yards gained (lost)
11	Generator number	31	Defense probability factor
13	Indirect counter	32	Current line of scrimmage
14	Counter	33	Player identification
15	N_s	34	Original line of scrimmage
16	Sum of probabilities	35	Down number
17	Indirect counter	36	Score for Player A
18	Indirect counter	37	Score for Player B

Football

LOC	CODE	KEY	COMMENTS	LOC	CODE	KEY	COMMENTS
000	91	R/S		034	78	Σ+	
001	76	LBL		035	00	0	
002	36	PGM		036	42	STO	
003	01	1		037	17	17	
004	42	STO		038	42	STO	
005	17	17		039	16	16	
006	02	2		040	02	2	
007	00	0		041	00	0	
008	42	STO		042	42	STO	
009	13	13		043	18	18	
010	00	0		044	43	RCL	
011	42	STO		045	10	10	
012	14	14	Generate	046	65	×	
013	43	RCL	random	047	43	RCL	
014	15	15	numbers	048	11	11	
015	32	X⟷T	using the	049	95	=	
016	76	LBL	spinner	050	22	INV	
017	18	C'	program	051	59	INT	
018	43	RCL		052	42	STO	
019	14	14	(locations	053	10	10	
020	72	ST*	000–075)	054	32	X⟷T	
021	13	13		055	76	LBL	
022	01	1		056	89	π	
023	44	SUM		057	73	RC*	
024	13	13		058	17	17	
025	44	SUM		059	44	SUM	
026	14	14		060	16	16	
027	43	RCL		061	43	RCL	
028	14	14		062	16	16	
029	67	EQ		063	77	GE	
030	78	Σ+		064	79	X̄	
031	61	GTO		065	01	1	
032	18	C'		066	44	SUM	
033	76	LBL		067	17	17	

114

LOC	CODE	KEY	COMMENTS		LOC	CODE	KEY	COMMENTS
068	44	SUM			123	30	TAN	Flag 3
069	18	18			124	87	IFF	transfer
070	61	GTO			125	03	03	
071	89	π			126	34	ΓX	
072	76	LBL			127	02	2	
073	79	x̄			128	42	STO	
074	73	RC*			129	15	15	
075	18	18			130	93	.	Fumble
076	92	RTN			131	00	0	probabilities
077	76	LBL	Kicking		132	05	5	
078	19	D'	subroutine		133	42	STO	
079	01	1			134	00	00	
080	42	STO			135	93	.	
081	30	30			136	09	9	
082	04	4			137	05	5	
083	42	STO			138	42	STO	
084	15	15			139	01	01	
085	93	.			140	71	SBR	Transfer to
086	01	1			141	36	PGM	spinner
087	42	STO			142	22	INV	Fumble
088	00	00	Set		143	49	PRD	"flasher"
089	93	.	probabilities		144	30	30	
090	02	2	for spinner		145	43	RCL	Recall yards
091	05	5	segments		146	30	30	and transfer
092	42	STO			147	61	GTO	
093	01	01			148	91	R/S	
094	93	.			149	76	LBL	
095	05	5			150	37	P/R	
096	42	STO			151	07	7	
097	02	02			152	49	PRD	
098	93	.			153	30	30	
099	01	1			154	76	LBL	
100	05	5			155	47	CMS	
101	42	STO			156	87	IFF	
102	03	03			157	01	01	Determine
103	76	LBL			158	30	TAN	number of
104	28	LOG			159	86	STF	yards ball
105	71	SBR			160	01	01	is kicked
106	36	PGM			161	61	GTO	
107	32	X!T			162	28	LOG	
108	02	2			163	76	LBL	
109	67	EQ	Logic		164	38	SIN	
110	37	P/R	transfers		165	06	6	
111	01	1			166	49	PRD	
112	67	EQ			167	30	30	
113	38	SIN			168	61	GTO	
114	00	0			169	47	CMS	
115	67	EQ			170	76	LBL	
116	39	COS			171	39	COS	
117	08	8			172	05	5	
118	49	PRD			173	49	PRD	
119	30	30			174	30	30	
120	61	GTO	Transfer		175	61	GTO	Transfer
121	47	CMS			176	47	CMS	
122	76	LBL			177	76	LBL	

LOC	CODE	KEY	COMMENTS	LOC	CODE	KEY	COMMENTS
178	11	A		234	04	4	
179	05	5		235	95	=	
180	42	STO		236	61	GTO	Transfer
181	15	15		237	91	R/S	
182	93	.		238	76	LBL	Subtract
183	02	2	Initialize	239	95	=	three yards
184	42	STO	and set	240	03	3	from gain
185	00	00	probabilities	241	94	+/-	
186	93	.		242	61	GTO	Transfer
187	01	1		243	91	R/S	
188	42	STO		244	76	LBL	
189	01	01		245	12	B	
190	93	.		246	01	1	
191	03	3		247	42	STO	
192	42	STO		248	30	30	
193	02	02		249	93	.	
194	93	.		250	05	5	
195	02	2		251	42	STO	
196	42	STO		252	00	00	
197	03	03		253	93	.	
198	93	.		254	03	3	
199	02	2		255	42	STO	Set
200	42	STO		256	01	01	probabilities
201	04	04		257	93	.	for a run and
202	71	SBR	Transfer	258	01	1	initialize
203	36	PGM		259	05	5	
204	42	STO		260	42	STO	
205	30	30		261	02	02	
206	01	1	Check for	262	93	.	
207	75	-	perfect	263	00	0	
208	43	RCL	defense	264	05	5	
209	31	31	against	265	42	STO	
210	95	=	run	266	03	03	
211	32	X⇄T		267	71	SBR	Transfer
212	01	1		268	36	PGM	
213	67	EQ		269	32	X⇄T	
214	95	=		270	00	0	
215	93	.	Check for	271	67	EQ	
216	03	3	poor defense	272	75	-	Identify the
217	77	GE		273	01	1	random number
218	94	+/-		274	67	EQ	
219	01	1		275	85	+	
220	75	-	Average	276	02	2	
221	32	X⇄T	defense,	277	67	EQ	
222	95	=	determine	278	55	÷	
223	49	PRD	yards gained	279	08	8	
224	30	30		280	00	0	
225	43	RCL		281	42	STO	Determine base
226	30	30		282	30	30	yards gained
227	61	GTO	Transfer	283	61	GTO	for running
228	91	R/S		284	81	RST	plays
229	76	LBL		285	76	LBL	
230	94	+/-	Add four yards	286	75	-	
231	43	RCL	to gain	287	09	9	
232	30	30	because of	288	42	STO	
233	85	+	poor defense	289	30	30	

116

LOC	CODE	KEY	COMMENTS
290	76	LBL	
291	81	RST	
292	87	IFF	Check for weak
293	02	02	defense
294	52	EE	
295	01	1	
296	75	-	
297	43	RCL	
298	31	31	
299	95	=	
300	32	X⇄T	
301	93	.	
302	00	0	
303	09	9	
304	09	9	
305	77	GE	
306	93	.	
307	93	.	
308	09	9	Check for
309	22	INV	strong
310	77	GE	defense
311	61	GTO	
312	43	RCL	
313	31	31	Average
314	49	PRD	defense
315	30	30	
316	43	RCL	
317	30	30	
318	61	GTO	Transfer
319	91	R/S	
320	76	LBL	
321	85	+	Select
322	06	6	appropriate
323	42	STO	"base"
324	30	30	
325	61	GTO	Transfer
326	81	RST	
327	76	LBL	
328	55	÷	
329	02	2	Select
330	01	1	appropriate
331	42	STO	"base"
332	30	30	
333	61	GTO	
334	81	RST	
335	76	LBL	
336	93	.	
337	43	RCL	Add yards
338	31	31	gained
339	65	×	because of
340	01	1	weak defense
341	00	0	
342	95	=	
343	44	SUM	
344	30	30	
345	43	RCL	

LOC	CODE	KEY	COMMENTS
346	30	30	
347	61	GTO	
348	91	R/S	Transfer
349	76	LBL	
350	61	GTO	
351	93	.	Reduce yards
352	05	5	because of
353	94	+/-	strong
354	49	PRD	defense
355	30	30	
356	43	RCL	
357	30	30	
358	61	GTO	Transfer
359	30	TAN	
360	76	LBL	
361	13	C	Utilize run
362	86	STF	segment for
363	02	02	short pass
364	61	GTO	
365	12	B	
366	76	LBL	
367	52	EE	
368	43	RCL	Check for
369	31	31	weak defense
370	32	X⇄T	
371	93	.	
372	03	3	
373	77	GE	
374	54	)	
375	93	.	
376	08	8	Check for
377	22	INV	strong defense
378	77	GE	
379	53	(	
380	43	RCL	
381	30	30	Regular
382	87	IFF	defense,
383	04	04	transfer
384	43	RCL	if pass
385	61	GTO	
386	91	R/S	Transfer
387	76	LBL	
388	54	)	
389	43	RCL	
390	31	31	Weak defense,
391	85	+	add yards
392	93	.	gained
393	00	0	
394	03	3	
395	95	=	
396	35	1/X	
397	44	SUM	
398	30	30	
399	43	RCL	
400	30	30	
401	87	IFF	

117

LOC	CODE	KEY	COMMENTS
402	04	04	Transfer if pass
403	35	1/X	
404	61	GTO	Transfer
405	91	R/S	
406	76	LBL.	
407	53	(	
408	32	X!T	
409	33	X²	
410	75	−	Strong defense, reduce yards gained
411	93	.	
412	03	3	
413	01	1	
414	95	=	
415	94	+/−	
416	42	STO	
417	30	30	
418	87	IFF	
419	04	04	
420	42	STO	
421	61	GTO	Transfer to fumble
422	30	TAN	
423	76	LBL.	
424	14	D	Initialize and transfer
425	86	STF	
426	02	02	
427	86	STF	
428	04	04	
429	61	GTO	
430	12	B	
431	76	LBL.	
432	35	1/X	Long pass multiplier
433	65	×	
434	01	1	
435	93	.	
436	05	5	
437	95	=	
438	61	GTO	Transfer
439	91	R/S	
440	76	LBL.	
441	42	STO	Reduce yards gained
442	01	1	
443	00	0	
444	22	INV	
445	44	SUM	
446	30	30	
447	61	GTO	Transfer to fumble
448	30	TAN	
449	68	NOP	Extra locations for possible program expansion
450	68	NOP	
451	68	NOP	
452	68	NOP	
453	68	NOP	
454	68	NOP	
455	68	NOP	
456	68	NOP	

LOC	CODE	KEY	COMMENTS
457	68	NOP	
458	76	LBL	
459	15	E	
460	86	STF	Field goal try, cut kickoff yardage by 50%
461	03	03	
462	61	GTO	
463	19	D'	
464	76	LBL.	
465	34	√X	
466	93	.	
467	05	5	
468	49	PRD	
469	30	30	
470	43	RCL.	
471	30	30	
472	76	LBL.	Display gain or loss yardage
473	91	R/S	
474	59	INT	
475	99	PRT	
476	66	PAU	
477	66	PAU	
478	66	PAU	
479	42	STO	
480	30	30	
481	43	RCL.	
482	33	33	
483	32	X!T	Transfer when Player A is on the offense
484	01	1	
485	67	EQ	
486	44	SUM	
487	43	RCL.	
488	30	30	
489	22	INV	Keep track of yard line and downs for Player B
490	44	SUM	
491	32	32	
492	43	RCL.	
493	32	32	
494	01	1	
495	00	0	
496	32	X!T	
497	43	RCL.	
498	34	34	
499	75	−	
500	43	RCL.	
501	32	32	
502	95	=	
503	61	GTO	Transfer
504	33	X²	
505	76	LBL.	
506	44	SUM	
507	43	RCL.	
508	30	30	
509	44	SUM	
510	32	32	
511	43	RCL.	
512	32	32	

LOC	CODE	KEY	COMMENTS		LOC	CODE	KEY	COMMENTS
513	01	1	Keep track of		540	34	34	
514	00	0	yard line and		541	91	R/S	
515	32	X:T	downs for		542	76	LBL	————
516	43	RCL	Player A		543	16	A'	Use when the
517	32	32			544	42	STO	ball changes
518	75	-			545	33	33	hands
519	43	RCL			546	01	1	
520	34	34			547	42	STO	
521	95	=			548	35	35	
522	76	LBL			549	43	RCL	
523	33	X²			550	32	32	
524	77	GE			551	42	STO	
525	45	YX			552	34	34	
526	01	1	Increment		553	91	R/S	————
527	44	SUM	down		554	76	LBL	
528	35	35			555	17	B'	Initialize
529	43	RCL	Display		556	42	STO	down counters
530	32	32	yard line		557	32	32	
531	91	R/S	————		558	42	STO	
532	76	LBL			559	34	34	
533	45	YX			560	91	R/S	————
534	01	1	Initialize		561	76	LBL	
535	42	STO	yard line		562	10	E'	Initialize
536	35	35	when a first		563	42	STO	and reset
537	43	RCL	down occurs		564	31	31	flags
538	32	32			565	25	CLR	
539	42	STO			566	81	RST	

Sequence   Materials

Programmable calculator

Scratch paper and pencil

Object of the Game

To deduce, as quickly as possible, the next three digits in a sequence of numbers.

General Description

This game is programmed to allow you to select any one of nine different sequences of numbers. The digits are displayed one at a time, and you have an opportunity to guess the next number in the sequence as soon as you feel that you have deduced the algorithm that determines the sequence. If your guess is incorrect, a flashing display of zeros will result, and you must begin again. If your guess is correct, you have another opportunity to guess the next digit. As before, an incorrect guess will result in a display of flashing zeros, while a correct guess will provide an opportunity for a third consecutive guess. If this guess is correct (three in a row), the display will indicate that you have correctly determined the sequence by flashing the number of clues (digits in the sequence) that were presented to you before

119   your guesses. The object, of course, is to determine the sequence with as few clues as possible; therefore, a low number in the final display is better than a high number.

To avoid inadvertently seeing the algorithm, you should have a nonparticipant enter the program into the calculator.

Solutions

Caution: Do not read this section unless you are seeking the solution to one or more of the sequences.

Sequence A:	Consecutive odd numbers beginning with $n = 5$.
	5, 7, 9, 11, 13, 15, 17, 19, 21, 23

Sequence B:
1. Begin with $n = 4$
2. Add 3
3. Subtract 1
4. Repeat steps 2 and 3
   4, 7, 6, 9, 8, 11, 10, 13, 12, 15

Sequence C:
1. Begin with $n = 0$
2. Add 1
3. Add 1
4. Double
5. Repeat steps 2–4
   0, 1, 2, 4, 5, 6, 12, 13, 14, 28, 29

Sequence D:
1. Begin with $n = 2$ and $k = 3$
2. Add k to n
3. Add 1
4. Add 1
5. Increment k by 1
6. Repeat steps 2–5
   2, 5, 6, 7, 11, 12, 13, 18, 19, 20

Sequence E:
1. Set the initial value of k to 0 and determine n as follows:
   $$n = (k + 2) \times (k - 1)$$
2. Increment k by 1 and determine n
3. Repeat step 2 using the formula in step 1 to calculate n
   −2, 0, 4, 10, 18, 28, 40, 54, 70, 88

Sequence A′:
1. Set $k = 2$ and $j = 2$
2. Determine n as follows:
   $$n = \frac{k^2}{2} + j$$
3. Increment k by 2
4. Set j equal to current n
5. Repeat steps 2–4
   4, 12, 30, 62, 112, 184, 282, 410, 572, 772

Sequence B′:
1. Begin with $n = 1$
2. Next n is 3 times the sum of the last two values of n

3. Repeat step 2
    1, 3, 12, 45, 171, 648, 2457, 9315, 35,316, 133,893

Sequence C':

1. Begin with $n = 0$
2. Add 1
3. Add 2
4. Add 3
5. Repeat steps 2-4
    0, 1, 3, 6, 7, 9, 12, 13, 15, 18

Sequence D':

1. Set $k = 1$ and begin with $n = 7$
2. Subtract k from n
3. Add $(k - 1)$ to n
4. Increment k by 1
5. Repeat steps 2-4
    7, 6, 6, 4, 5, 2, 4, 0, 3, -2

Program Notes

Although there are only nine different sequences, each can easily be modified. For example, assume that sequence B was to be modified to match the following algorithm:

1. Begin with $n = 8$
2. Subtract 2
3. Add 7
4. Repeat steps 2 and 3

At program location 083, change the 4 to an 8. At location 093, change the 3 to a 2. Between locations 093 and 094 insert the INV command. At location 101 (before the above insertion) change the 1 to 7. Delete the INV command at location 102.

The output for this sequence will now be: 8, 6, 13, 11, 18, 16, 23, 21, 28, 26.

User Instructions

Step	Procedure	Press	Display
1.	Enter program		
2.	Initialize	*E'	-3.
3.	Select sequence: (This can be any of the ten user-defined keys *except* *E'.)	A-D'	First digit of sequence
4.	Continue displaying sequence	R/S	Next digit of sequence
5.	If you want to make a guess, G:		
	A. Enter first guess (If guess was incorrect, display will flash zeros. Press CLR. Go to step 2 and begin again.)	G_1 *St flg 1 R/S	G_1
	B. Enter second guess	G_2 R/S	G_2

C. Enter third guess G_3 R/S   Number of clues
  (If you make three correct guesses
  in a row, the calculator assumes
  that you know the algorithm and
  the display will flash the number
  of clues (digits of sequence)
  shown to you before your
  guesses.)

6.   For a new sequence, or to try the
  same sequence again, go to step 2

Data Registers
00   Guess

01   *n*

02   Number of clues

03   Number of guesses

04   Counter

Sequence

LOC	CODE	KEY	COMMENTS	LOC	CODE	KEY	COMMENTS
000	91	R/S		030	67	EQ	
001	76	LBL		031	22	INV	
002	10	E'		032	01	1	
003	47	CMS		033	44	SUM	Keep track of
004	03	3		034	03	03	guess and
005	94	+/-	Initialize	035	43	RCL	check for
006	42	STO		036	03	03	win
007	02	02		037	32	X:T	
008	58	FIX		038	03	3	
009	00	00		039	67	EQ	
010	81	RST		040	23	LNX	
011	76	LBL		041	43	RCL	
012	44	SUM		042	00	00	
013	01	1	Check to	043	92	RTN	
014	44	SUM	determine	044	76	LBL	
015	02	02	if a guess	045	22	INV	Display
016	43	RCL	has been	046	00	0	flashing
017	01	01	made	047	55	÷	zeros
018	87	IFF		048	55	÷	
019	01	01		049	58	FIX	
020	87	IFF		050	08	08	
021	92	RTN		051	91	R/S	
022	76	LBL		052	76	LBL	
023	87	IFF		053	23	LNX	Flash number of
024	43	RCL	Check	054	43	RCL	clues before
025	01	01	accuracy	055	02	02	solution
026	32	X:T	of guess	056	55	÷	
027	43	RCL		057	55	÷	
028	00	00		058	91	R/S	
029	22	INV		059	76	LBL	

122

LOC	CODE	KEY	COMMENTS
060	11	A	
061	05	5	
062	42	STO	
063	01	01	
064	71	SBR	
065	44	SUM	
066	91	R/S	
067	42	STO	Sequence A
068	00	00	
069	76	LBL	
070	32	X‡T	
071	02	2	
072	44	SUM	
073	01	01	
074	71	SBR	
075	44	SUM	
076	91	R/S	
077	42	STO	
078	00	00	
079	61	GTO	
080	32	X‡T	
081	76	LBL	
082	12	B	
083	04	4	
084	42	STO	
085	01	01	
086	71	SBR	Sequence B
087	44	SUM	
088	91	R/S	
089	42	STO	
090	00	00	
091	76	LBL	
092	33	X²	
093	03	3	
094	44	SUM	
095	01	01	
096	71	SBR	
097	44	SUM	
098	91	R/S	
099	42	STO	
100	00	00	
101	01	1	
102	22	INV	
103	44	SUM	
104	01	01	
105	71	SBR	
106	44	SUM	
107	91	R/S	
108	42	STO	
109	00	00	
110	61	GTO	
111	33	X²	
112	76	LBL	
113	13	C	
114	71	SBR	
115	44	SUM	

LOC	CODE	KEY	COMMENTS
116	91	R/S	
117	42	STO	
118	00	00	
119	76	LBL	
120	94	+/-	
121	01	1	
122	44	SUM	
123	01	01	
124	71	SBR	Sequence C
125	44	SUM	
126	91	R/S	
127	42	STO	
128	00	00	
129	01	1	
130	44	SUM	
131	01	01	
132	71	SBR	
133	44	SUM	
134	91	R/S	
135	42	STO	
136	00	00	
137	43	RCL	
138	01	01	
139	65	×	
140	02	2	
141	95	=	
142	42	STO	
143	01	01	
144	71	SBR	
145	44	SUM	
146	91	R/S	
147	42	STO	
148	00	00	
149	61	GTO	
150	94	+/-	
151	76	LBL	
152	14	D	
153	02	2	
154	42	STO	
155	01	01	
156	03	3	
157	42	STO	
158	04	04	
159	71	SBR	
160	44	SUM	
161	91	R/S	
162	42	STO	
163	00	00	
164	76	LBL	
165	34	√X	
166	43	RCL	
167	04	04	
168	44	SUM	Sequence D
169	01	01	
170	01	1	
171	44	SUM	

LOC	CODE	KEY	COMMENTS	LOC	CODE	KEY	COMMENTS
172	04	04		228	01	1	
173	71	SBR		229	44	SUM	
174	44	SUM		230	04	04	
175	91	R/S		231	71	SBR	
176	42	STD		232	44	SUM	
177	00	00		233	91	R/S	
178	01	1		234	42	STD	
179	44	SUM		235	00	00	
180	01	01		236	61	GTD	
181	71	SBR		237	35	1/X	
182	44	SUM		238	76	LBL	
183	91	R/S		239	16	A'	
184	42	STD		240	02	2	
185	00	00		241	42	STD	
186	01	1		242	01	01	
187	44	SUM		243	02	2	
188	01	01		244	42	STD	
189	71	SBR		245	04	04	
190	44	SUM		246	76	LBL	
191	91	R/S		247	45	YX	
192	42	STD		248	43	RCL	
193	00	00		249	04	04	
194	61	GTD		250	33	X²	
195	34	ГX		251	55	÷	
196	76	LBL		252	02	2	
197	19	D'		253	95	=	
198	07	7		254	44	SUM	
199	42	STD		255	01	01	Sequence A'
200	01	01		256	71	SBR	
201	01	1		257	44	SUM	
202	42	STD		258	91	R/S	
203	04	04		259	42	STD	
204	71	SBR		260	00	00	
205	44	SUM		261	02	2	
206	91	R/S		262	44	SUM	
207	42	STD		263	04	04	
208	00	00		264	61	GTD	
209	76	LBL		265	45	YX	
210	35	1/X		266	76	LBL	
211	43	RCL		267	17	B'	
212	04	04		268	01	1	
213	22	INV		269	42	STD	
214	44	SUM	Sequence D'	270	01	01	
215	01	01		271	71	SBR	
216	71	SBR		272	44	SUM	
217	44	SUM		273	91	R/S	
218	91	R/S		274	42	STD	
219	42	STD		275	00	00	
220	00	00		276	76	LBL	
221	43	RCL		277	43	RCL	
222	04	04		278	53	(	
223	75	-		279	43	RCL	Sequence B'
224	01	1		280	04	04	
225	95	=		281	85	+	
226	44	SUM		282	43	RCL	
227	01	01		283	01	01	

LOC	CODE	KEY	COMMENTS	LOC	CODE	KEY	COMMENTS
284	54	)		327	44	SUM	
285	65	×		328	91	R/S	
286	03	3		329	42	STO	
287	95	=		330	00	00	
288	32	X:T		331	03	3	
289	43	RCL		332	44	SUM	
290	01	01		333	01	01	
291	42	STO		334	71	SBR	
292	04	04		335	44	SUM	
293	32	X:T		336	91	R/S	
294	42	STO		337	42	STO	
295	01	01		338	00	00	
296	71	SBR		339	61	GTO	
297	44	SUM		340	42	STO	
298	91	R/S		341	76	LBL	————
299	42	STO		342	15	E	
300	00	00		343	53	(	
301	61	GTO		344	43	RCL	
302	43	RCL		345	04	04	
303	76	LBL ————		346	85	+	
304	18	C'		347	02	2	
305	00	0		348	54	)	
306	42	STO		349	65	×	
307	01	01		350	53	(	
308	71	SBR		351	43	RCL	
309	44	SUM		352	04	04	
310	91	R/S		353	75	-	
311	42	STO		354	01	1	
312	00	00		355	54	)	Sequence E
313	76	LBL		356	95	=	
314	42	STO		357	42	STO	
315	01	1	Sequence C'	358	01	01	
316	44	SUM		359	71	SBR	
317	01	01		360	44	SUM	
318	71	SBR		361	91	R/S	
319	44	SUM		362	42	STO	
320	91	R/S		363	00	00	
321	42	STO		364	01	1	
322	00	00		365	44	SUM	
323	02	2		366	04	04	
324	44	SUM		367	61	GTO	
325	01	01		368	15	E	
326	71	SBR					

125

Materials

TI–59 calculator

Paper and pencil

Object of the Game

To guess a secret number generated by the calculator.

The Play

This program will generate a secret number (code), and, utilizing clues provided by the calculator, you must deduce the code with as few guesses as possible. The game is similar to Master Mind and Codebreaker; however, "Mystery Number" provides you with an opportunity to specify the length of the secret number ($2 \leqslant n \leqslant 8$) as well as the *range* of numbers utilized in the selection of each digit of the code ($2 \leqslant$ range $\leqslant 9$). This unique option allows you to select the degree of difficulty for each game as indicated in Table 2-1. As you can see from this table, the number of permutations, and hence the degree of difficulty, increases as you select longer codes and a greater range of digits. Note that the digit 0 is *never* part of the secret number. Further, duplication of digits may occur within the code.

TABLE 2-1   Permutations for the 56 Levels of Difficulty

| Length of code | Range of numbers composing each digit of the code | | | | | | | |
	1 to 2	1 to 3	1 to 4	1 to 5	1 to 6	1 to 7	1 to 8	1 to 9
2	4	9	16	25	36	49	64	81
3	8	27	64	125	216	343	512	729
4	16	81	256	625	1296	2401	4096	6561
5	32	243	1024	3125	7776	16807	32768	59049
6	64	729	4096	15625	46656	117649	262144	531441
7	128	2187	16384	78125	279936	823543	2097152	4782969
8	256	6561	65536	390625	1679616	5764801	16777216	43046721

For example, if you select 4 as the length of the secret number and a digit range of 1–7, the code generated by the calculator will have four digits, and each digit could be a 1, 2, 3, 4, 5, 6, or 7. Duplication of digits could occur, resulting in 7375 as a possible secret number.

Once the secret number has been generated, you make a series of guesses to "break the code." After each guess the calculator will provide you with a clue in the form of *x.y,* where *x* represents the number of digits in your guess that are in the code *and* are in the proper relative position. The number of digits in your guess that are in the code but *not* in the proper relative position is represented by *y.*

The following examples will clarify the meaning of the clues:

Secret Number	Guess	Clue (x.y)	Comments
7375	2716	0.1	The 7 in the guess is *not* counted twice.
7385	2477	0.1	Only one 7 in the guess is counted, as there is only one 7 in the secret number.
73785	27976	0.2	Both 7s in the guess are counted since there are two 7s in the secret number.
13945	26689	0.0	Sorry, no matches
13945	13945	5.0	You win! Each digit in your guess corresponds to a digit in the code.

You continue to make educated guesses until you discover the code. The calculator will display a flashing number that indicates the number of guesses it took you to break the code.

Sample Game

After the program is properly entered into the calculator, the following sample game may be played. (The procedure steps correspond to the user instruction steps.)

Step	Procedure	Enter		Display
2A.	Select seed	.32	A	0.3
2B.	Select length of code	4	B	4.0
2C.	Select range of digits	9	C	1.0
3.	Establish secret number		D	20.0
4.	Enter first guess, 1234	1	E	1.0
		2	E	1.0
		3	E	1.0
		4	E	1.0
5.	Evaluate guess (One digit of the guess is in the code *and* in the correct location, while another digit of the guess is in the code but *not* in the correct position.)	*A′		1.1 (clue)
4.	Enter second guess, 1356	1	E	1.0
		3	E	1.0
		5	E	1.0
		6	E	1.0
5.	Evaluate second guess (All four digits of the guess are in the code; however, none is in the correct position.)	*A′		0.4 (clue)

4.	Enter third guess, 5631	5 E	1.0
		6 E	1.0
		3 E	1.0
		1 E	1.0
5.	Evaluate third guess (All digits of guess are in the code *and* in the correct position.	*A′	4.0 is displayed briefly, then a flashing 3.0 will be displayed
7.	Stop flashing (Code solved in three guesses).	CLR	3.0

Strategy

Although strategy is a matter of personal preference, the following suggestions may help beginning players:

1. Use a pencil and paper to keep track of your guesses and corresponding clues.
2. Attempt to identify the specific digits in the secret number *and then* determine their exact position.
3. Use a *systematic* approach that allows you to deduce information from each clue.
4. It is also useful to determine which digits are *not* in the code.
5. Specific moves will depend on the length of the code as well as the range of possible digits; however, L.H. Ault[1] thoroughly analyzes alternative moves for several similar variations of this game.

Program Notes

1. This program demonstrates the use of a TI-59 library program as a subroutine (locations 203–223 and 251–257). In this case information previously entered by the player is recalled to set the parameters of the random number generator (program 15 of the TI-59 master library).
2. The two single-digit numbers representing the two clues are displayed (location 196) at the same time using an $x.y$ format. This is accomplished by dividing the second digit by 10 and summing the resulting decimal to the first number (locations 178–185).
3. Clues are established as a result of direct, single-digit comparisons between the code and the guess. When "matches" are found, that digit of the code is made negative (locations 48–50 and 81–84), while the corresponding digit of the guess is made to equal zero (locations 40–42 and 85–87). This system prevents erroneous duplication of clues and also provides a mechanism for reestablishing the original code as a positive number (locations 156–177).
4. The flashing display at the end of the game results from an "illegal," but intentional, division by zero (locations 296–298).

[1] L. H. Ault, *The Official Mastermind Handbook* (New York: Signet, 1972), pp. 54–74.

5. As the length of the code is increased arithmetically, the number of comparisons increases exponentially, resulting in increased operating times for the *A′ subroutine. For example:

Length of Code	Approximate Running Time (sec.)
2	17
3	28
4	44
5	62
6	83
7	106
8	133

6. Zero is *never* a code digit, and duplication of digits *is* possible.
7. Data registers 20–24 are used for different purposes during different segments of the program. This is a good technique to use when data registers are at a premium; however, it does add complexity to the program and could make future program modification more difficult.

User Instructions

Step	Procedure	Press	Display
1.	Enter program into calculator		
2.	Enter playing variables		
2A.	Seed for random number generator, S ($0 \leqslant S \leqslant 199017$)	S A	S
2B.	Length of code, L, number of digits ($2 \leqslant L \leqslant 8$)	L B	L
2C.	Range, R, of different digits from which each code digit will be selected ($2 \leqslant R \leqslant 9$)	R C	1.0
3.	Calculator will establish and store secret code as specified in step 2	D	20.0
4.	Enter guess one digit at a time		
4A.	Begin with left digit	digit E	1.0
4B.	Repeat step 4A until guess is entered		
5.	Calculator will evaluate guess and display clue	*A′	$x.y$ where $x.y$ is the clue as described on page 126.
6.	Repeat steps 4 and 5 until you discover code		
7.	Stop flashing	CLR	(Number of tries flashes at end of game)
8.	For a new game, go to step 2		

Data Registers

01–11	Random number generator	24	Counter
12–19	Code digits	20–27	Hold guess
20	Indirect counter	28	*x*
21	Seed	29	*y*
22	Lower limit of random number	30	Number of guesses to win
23	Upper limit of random number	31	Number of digits in code

Mystery Number

LOC	CODE	KEY	COMMENTS	LOC	CODE	KEY	COMMENTS
000	76	LBL		043	01	1	Increment y
001	45	Y×		044	44	SUM	and
002	43	RCL		045	29	29	counter
003	31	31		046	44	SUM	
004	32	X:T		047	08	08	
005	43	RCL	Locations	048	94	+/−	Make matched
006	05	05	000-066	049	64	PD*	code negative
007	67	EQ	compare	050	07	07	
008	34	⌐X	guess to	051	61	GTO	
009	01	1	code	052	45	Y×	
010	44	SUM	looking	053	76	LBL	
011	09	09	for y	054	34	⌐X	
012	44	SUM	portion	055	01	1	Initialize and
013	05	05	of the	056	44	SUM	increment
014	43	RCL	clue	057	07	07	counters
015	31	31		058	02	2	
016	33	X²		059	00	0	
017	32	X:T		060	42	STO	
018	43	RCL		061	08	08	
019	09	09		062	00	0	
020	22	INV		063	42	STO	
021	67	EQ		064	05	05	
022	35	1/X		065	61	GTO	
023	92	RTN		066	45	Y×	Transfer
024	76	LBL		067	76	LBL	
025	35	1/X		068	65	×	
026	73	RC*	Compare	069	73	RC*	Compare code
027	07	07	code to	070	07	07	digit to
028	32	X:T	guess	071	32	X:T	guess digit
029	73	RC*		072	73	RC*	
030	08	08		073	08	08	
031	67	EQ		074	67	EQ	
032	32	X:T		075	55	÷	
033	01	1		076	01	1	
034	44	SUM	Increment	077	61	GTO	Transfer
035	08	08	and	078	75	−	
036	61	GTO	transfer	079	76	LBL	Make matched
037	45	Y×		080	55	÷	digit of code
038	76	LBL		081	01	1	negative and
039	32	X:T	Substitute	082	94	+/−	matched digit
040	00	0	zero for a	083	64	PD*	of guess
041	72	ST*	matched	084	07	07	zero
042	08	08	guess	085	00	0	

130

LOC	CODE	KEY	COMMENTS
086	72	ST*	
087	08	08	
088	01	1	Increment x
089	44	SUM	
090	28	28	
091	76	LBL	Locations 067-
092	75	-	107 compare
093	44	SUM	guess to code
094	07	07	looking for x
095	44	SUM	
096	08	08	
097	44	SUM	
098	09	09	
099	43	RCL	
100	31	31	
101	32	X:T	
102	43	RCL	
103	09	09	
104	22	INV	
105	67	EQ	Count
106	65	×	number of
107	92	RTN	guesses
108	76	LBL	
109	16	A'	
110	01	1	
111	44	SUM	
112	30	30	
113	00	0	
114	42	STO	
115	28	28	
116	42	STO	
117	29	29	
118	01	1	
119	02	2	Initialize
120	42	STO	
121	07	07	
122	02	2	
123	00	0	
124	42	STO	
125	08	08	
126	00	0	
127	42	STO	
128	09	09	
129	71	SBR	x
130	65	×	
131	01	1	
132	94	+/-	
133	42	STO	
134	09	09	
135	00	0	
136	42	STO	
137	05	05	Initialize
138	01	1	
139	02	2	
140	42	STO	
141	07	07	

LOC	CODE	KEY	COMMENTS
142	02	2	
143	00	0	
144	42	STO	
145	08	08	
146	71	SBR	y
147	45	Y×	
148	02	2	
149	00	0	
150	42	STO	
151	00	00	Initialize
152	01	1	
153	02	2	
154	42	STO	
155	07	07	
156	76	LBL	
157	50	.I×I	
158	73	RC*	
159	07	07	
160	50	I×I	
161	72	ST*	Restore code
162	07	07	to its
163	01	1	original,
164	44	SUM	positive
165	07	07	condition
166	43	RCL	
167	07	07	
168	32	X:T	
169	43	RCL	
170	31	31	
171	85	+	
172	01	1	
173	02	2	
174	95	=	
175	22	INV	
176	67	EQ	
177	50	I×I	
178	43	RCL	
179	29	29	Convert y to
180	55	÷	a decimal
181	01	1	
182	00	0	
183	95	=	
184	44	SUM	Establish x.y
185	28	28	
186	43	RCL	
187	28	28	
188	59	INT	Check for a
189	32	X:T	win
190	43	RCL	
191	31	31	
192	67	EQ	
193	66	PAU	
194	43	RCL	Display x.y
195	28	28	if not a win
196	91	R/S	
197	76	LBL	

LOC	CODE	KEY	COMMENTS	LOC	CODE	KEY	COMMENTS
198	14	D		250	91	R/S	
199	01	1		251	76	LBL	
200	02	2		252	18	C'	Generate
201	42	STO	Initialize	253	36	PGM	additional
202	20	20		254	15	15	random numbers
203	36	PGM		255	13	C'	
204	15	15	Call	256	61	GTO	
205	10	E'	program 15	257	80	GRD	
206	43	RCL	Seed for	258	76	LBL	
207	21	21	random	259	11	A	
208	36	PGM	number	260	47	CMS	Fix decimal
209	15	15	generator	261	58	FIX	and store
210	15	E		262	01	01	seed for
211	43	RCL		263	42	STO	random number
212	22	22	Lower limit	264	21	21	
213	36	PGM	for random	265	91	R/S	
214	15	15	number	266	76	LBL	
215	11	A		267	12	B	Store code
216	43	RCL		268	42	STO	length
217	23	23	Upper limit	269	31	31	
218	36	PGM	for random	270	91	R/S	
219	15	15	number	271	76	LBL	
220	12	B		272	13	C	
221	36	PGM	Calculate	273	42	STO	Store upper
222	15	15	random number	274	23	23	and lower
223	13	C		275	01	1	limits for
224	76	LBL		276	42	STO	code
225	80	GRD		277	22	22	generation
226	59	INT		278	91	R/S	
227	72	ST*		279	76	LBL	
228	20	20		280	15	E	Store guess
229	01	1		281	72	ST*	in R20-R27
230	44	SUM		282	00	00	and
231	20	20	Place	283	01	1	increment
232	44	SUM	random numbers	284	44	SUM	counter
233	24	24	in R12-R19	285	00	00	
234	43	RCL		286	91	R/S	
235	31	31		287	76	LBL	
236	32	X!T		288	66	PAU	
237	43	RCL		289	43	RCL	The code has
238	24	24		290	28	28	been broken!
239	22	INV		291	66	PAU	
240	67	EQ		292	66	PAU	Display x.y
241	18	C'		293	66	PAU	
242	68	NOP		294	66	PAU	
243	68	NOP		295	66	PAU	
244	68	NOP		296	55	÷	Flash number of
245	68	NOP		297	00	0	guesses needed
246	02	2		298	95	=	to break code
247	00	0	Initialize	299	43	RCL	
248	42	STO		300	30	30	
249	00	00		301	91	R/S	

Calculaser   Materials

Programmable calculator

Paper and pencil (optional)

Object of the Game
To locate and destroy your opponent's spaceships before he or she locates and destroys yours.

General Description
Calculaser is played by two players, A and B. The game board may be envisioned as the face of a compass with 36 rays, beginning at 10° and continuing to 360°. Each ray is 999 units in length. Although it is not essential, many people prefer to sketch and use a working model of the game board (see Figure 2-2).

The Play
Each player secretly places five spaceships somewhere in the playing grid; however, no player can place more than one ship on a specific ray. Each ship can be represented by a point on one of the rays and must be located between 1 and 999 units from the center of the grid. The object of the game is to use a laser, located at the center of the grid, to locate and destroy all

FIGURE 2-2   Calculaser Circle

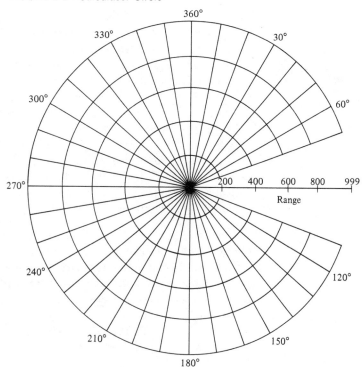

five of the opponent's ships. The laser, with a range capability between 1 and 999 units, may be fired along any of the rays. The greater the assigned range of the laser, the greater its fuel consumption will be. Each unit of energy will send the laser beam outward for a distance of 1 unit. (Since each player begins the game with only 8000 units of energy for his or her laser, fuel consumption will frequently be a factor in planning strategy.) When a laser beam is properly directed with sufficient energy, it will pass through an opponent's spaceship and destroy it; however, if the beam possesses any excess energy, that energy will be captured by the destroyed ship and immediately transferred to the central energy supply of its team.

After the location of each spaceship has been entered into the calculator, players alternate firing a laser beam in search of an opponent's hidden ship. A laser beam is fired by entering into the calculator the range and degree of the beam as follows: RRR.DDD, where RRR represents the *range* of the ray (determined by the amount of fuel you wish to use) and DDD represents the *degree* of the ray along which the beam is to be fired. When entering data, leading zeros are required for DDD. For example, 10° should be entered as 010, not 10.

After a laser beam has been fired, the calculator will provide *one* of the following clues as feedback:

1. DISPLAY 0.7 (Upside down this reads, "LO" for low fuel). You did not have enough fuel energy remaining to fire the laser.
2. DISPLAY 0.401. The zero integer indicates that the laser beam was *not* on a correct ray, and the 401 decimal indicates that the beam ended at a range *greater* than 400 units from the nearest enemy ship.
3. DISPLAY 0.RRR. The zero indicates that the laser beam was *not* on a correct ray, and the RRR indicates the distance from the end of the beam to the nearest enemy ship. Note: RRR will always be equal to or less than 400.
4. DISPLAY 1.07. The 1 indicates that the laser beam *is* on a correct ray; however, the 07 indicates that the beam did *not* have enough fuel to reach the target.
5. DISPLAY 1.00. Direct hit! The 1 indicates a correct ray and the zero indicates the amount of fuel captured by the enemy.
6. DISPLAY 1.FFF. Hit! The 1 indicates a correct ray, and the FFF indicates how much excess fuel was captured by the enemy.
7. 111111111111 continues to flash. *You win!* All enemy spaceships have been destroyed.

If you are attempting to fire a laser without sufficient fuel, the 0.7 clue indicates that you have lost your turn and it is now your opponent's turn. If you have no energy remaining, you must wait to capture some before your laser beam will again become operational. If both you and your opponent run out of fuel, the player with the greatest number of spaceships remaining is the winner. You can get a fuel reading by recalling register 08 for Player A and register 09 for Player B.

Strategy

It is risky to use a pattern when placing your five spaceships into the grid because your opponent may detect your pattern and more easily find your remaining ships. Placing spaceships on the periphery of the grid will force your opponent to use significant amounts of energy to locate and destroy them; however, spaceships placed very close to the center of the grid have greater opportunities to capture excess fuel from an "overshot" by the opponent. Two or more spacecraft located near each other (about 100 units apart) will sometimes confuse your opponent when he or she receives feedback from lasers ending in that general part of the grid.

Sample Game

After the program has been *carefully* entered into the calculator, use this sample game in conjunction with the user instructions. The procedure numbers in the sample game correspond to the step numbers in the user instructions.

Step	Procedure	Press	Display
4.	Player A hides five spaceships	530.200 * A′	1.00
		210.090 * A′	1.00
		5.180 * A′	1.00
		999.360 * A′	1.00
		872.020 * A′	1.00
5.	Player B hides five spaceships	351.260 * B′	1.00
		901.120 * B′	1.00
		10.040 * B′	1.00
		451.180 * B′	1.00
		850.220 * B′	1.00
6.	Player A fires a laser beam (A hit, but with 140 units of fuel captured by Player B)	150.040 A	1.140
7.	Player B fires a laser beam (Miss! Beam not on correct vector and all enemy ships farther than 400 units away.)	400.350 B	0.401
6.	Player A (Laser on correct ray, but low fuel)	900.120 A	1.07
7.	Player B (A direct hit!)	999.360 B	1.00
6.	Player A (A hit, but with 98 units of fuel captured by Player B)	999.120 A	1.098
10B.	Player B checks fuel (6839 units of fuel remaining for B)	RCL 09	6839
7.	Player B fires laser (Incorrect ray, but enemy ship 37 units away)	210.100 B	0.037
6.	Player A fires (Incorrect ray, but enemy ship is 352 units away)	1.090 A	0.352
10A.	Player A checks fuel (5950 units left)	RCL 08	5950.000

6. and 7.	Players A and B continue to take turns searching for enemy targets. Let us *assume* that after several turns (not indicated), Player A has destroyed four of his or her opponent's ships, and Player B has destroyed three enemy ships. Further, Player A is almost out of fuel. The game *could* end as follows. (Since the assumed turns did not actually occur, the display from this point forward is only illustrative.)		
6.	Player A fires (Not enough fuel to make the shot)	600.280 A	0.7
10A.	Player A checks fuel	RCL 08	280
7.	Player B shoots (Hit, but 100 units of fuel captured by Player A)	972.020 B	1.100
6.	Player A shoots (Player A wins!)	351.260 A	1111111 (flashing)

Program Notes

This program utilizes the $P \rightarrow R$ conversion key to determine the x and y coordinates of the targets as well as the x and y coordinates of the point at which the laser beam ends. The distance between these two points (closest target to the end of the beam) is then computed and provides the players with useful feedback. (A sort routine is used to determine the closest target to the laser beam.)

Flags, which are set each time a player makes a guess, allow the program to utilize a specific subroutine for both players. In addition, they allow one player to move two or more times in succession—as may occur when one player is temporarily out of fuel.

At user instruction steps 6 and 7, it takes approximately 30 seconds for the calculator to respond.

The difficulty of the game may be increased in several different ways:

1. Reduce the initial fuel allocation at locations 486–493.
2. Modify the rules to allow ships to be placed on every degree ray instead of just the rays evenly divisible by ten. (No program modifications are required for this change.)
3. *Reduce* the distance requirement, which provides feedback when the end of the laser is near an opponent's ship. To accomplish this change the 400 at locations 275–277 to whatever value you desire. A value of zero will eliminate that feedback completely.
4. Expand the diameter of the playing grid. Place the value of the new diameter in locations 25–28, 42–45, and 498–501. If the diameter you select is not a four-digit figure, you will need to insert or delete program locations through editing techniques described in your owner's manual.

User Instructions

Step	Procedure	Press	Display
1.	Repartition calculator	3 *op 17 CLR	0
2.	Enter program		
3.	Initialize	*E' *Fix 2	1000.00
4.	Enter Player A's spaceships	RRR.DDD *A'	1.00
	where RRR = *Range* of laser	RRR.DDD *A'	1.00
	DDD = *Degree* of ray	RRR.DDD *A'	1.00
	(Be sure to include leading zeros when	RRR.DDD *A'	1.00
	entering DDD.)	RRR.DDD *A'	1.00
5.	Enter Player B's spaceships	RRR.DDD *B'	1.00
		RRR.DDD *B'	1.00
		RRR.DDD *B'	1.00
		RRR.DDD *B'	1.00
		RRR.DDD *B'	1.00
6.	Player A fires a laser	RRR.DDD A	Varies
7.	Player B fires a laser	RRR.DDD B	Varies
8.	Continue play by repeating steps 6 and 7 until someone wins or all of the fuel is gone		
9.	To check fuel:		
	A. Player A	RCL 08	Fuel remaining
	B. Player B	RCL 09	Fuel remaining
10.	For another game, or to start over, go to step 3		

Data Registers

00	1000	10	Indirect counter
01	0	11–15	Data for A
02	1111111	16–20	Data for B
03	Change in fuel	21	A's guess
04	Holder for hit data	22	B's guess
05	Counter for win	23	x coordinate of guess
06	Maximum distance	24	y coordinate of guess
07	Counter	25	x coordinate of ship
08	A's fuel supply	26	y coordinate of ship
09	B's fuel supply		

137

LOC	CODE	KEY	COMMENTS	LOC	CODE	KEY	COMMENTS
000	76	LBL		050	76	LBL	
001	16	A'	Player A	051	48	EXC	
002	72	ST*	data entry	052	87	IFF	
003	10	10	in R11-R15	053	02	02	
004	01	1		054	43	RCL	
005	44	SUM		055	43	RCL	
006	10	10		056	08	08	
007	91	R/S		057	61	GTD	
008	76	LBL		058	44	SUM	
009	17	B'	Player B	059	76	LBL	
010	72	ST*	data entry	060	43	RCL	
011	10	10	in R16-R20	061	43	RCL	
012	01	1		062	09	09	
013	44	SUM		063	76	LBL	Check for
014	10	10		064	44	SUM	adequate
015	91	R/S		065	32	X!T	fuel
016	76	LBL	Store Player A's	066	87	IFF	
017	11	A	guess and set	067	01	01	
018	42	STD	flag 1	068	22	INV	
019	21	21		069	43	RCL	
020	86	STF		070	22	22	
021	01	01		071	61	GTD	
022	22	INV		072	24	CE	
023	86	STF		073	76	LBL	
024	02	02		074	22	INV	
025	02	2		075	43	RCL	
026	00	0		076	21	21	
027	00	0	Initialize	077	76	LBL	
028	00	0		078	24	CE	
029	42	STD		079	59	INT	
030	06	06		080	77	GE	
031	61	GTD		081	23	LNX	
032	48	EXC		082	87	IFF	
033	76	LBL		083	01	01	Reduce
034	12	B	Store Player B's	084	50	IxI	Player B's
035	42	STD	guess and	085	22	INV	fuel
036	22	22	set flag 2	086	44	SUM	
037	86	STF		087	09	09	
038	02	02		088	61	GTD	Transfer
039	22	INV		089	25	CLR	(fuel OK)
040	86	STF		090	76	LBL	
041	01	01		091	50	IxI	Reduce
042	02	2		092	22	INV	Player A's
043	00	0	Initialize	093	44	SUM	fuel
044	00	0		094	08	08	
045	00	0		095	61	GTD	Transfer
046	42	STD		096	25	CLR	(fuel OK)
047	06	06		097	76	LBL	
048	61	GTD		098	23	LNX	
049	48	EXC		099	00	0	

LOC	CODE	KEY	COMMENTS
100	93	.	
101	07	7	Not enough
102	95	=	fuel,
103	58	FIX	display 0.7
104	01	01	
105	91	R/S	
106	76	LBL	
107	25	CLR	
108	05	5	
109	94	+/-	
110	42	STD	Begin to
111	07	07	determine
112	87	IFF	if the
113	01	01	guess is on
114	32	X:T	the correct
115	43	RCL	vector
116	22	22	
117	61	GTD	
118	33	X²	
119	76	LBL	
120	32	X:T	
121	43	RCL	
122	21	21	Place angle
123	76	LBL	in test
124	33	X²	register
125	22	INV	
126	59	INT	
127	65	X	
128	43	RCL	
129	00	00	
130	95	=	
131	32	X:T	
132	87	IFF	Check Player
133	01	01	B's data
134	34	⌐X	locations
135	01	1	
136	01	1	Initialize
137	42	STD	
138	10	10	
139	61	GTD	Player A's
140	35	1/X	data locations
141	76	LBL	
142	34	⌐X	
143	01	1	
144	06	6	
145	42	STD	
146	10	10	
147	76	LBL	
148	35	1/X	
149	73	RC*	

LOC	CODE	KEY	COMMENTS
150	10	10	
151	22	INV	
152	59	INT	
153	65	X,	
154	43	RCL	Ray on correct
155	00	00	vector, search
156	95	=	for hit
157	67	EQ	
158	42	STD	
159	01	1	
160	44	SUM	
161	10	10	
162	97	DSZ	
163	07	07	
164	35	1/X	
165	76	LBL	
166	37	P/R	Angle of data
167	05	5	and guess do not
168	42	STD	match; begin to
169	07	07	calculate
170	87	IFF	distance between
171	01	01	guess and
172	45	Y^X	closest target
173	01	1	
174	01	1	
175	42	STD	
176	10	10	
177	43	RCL	Player B's
178	22	22	distance into
179	59	INT	t-register
180	32	X:T	
181	43	RCL	
182	22	22	Player B's
183	61	GTD	angle
184	52	EE	
185	76	LBL	
186	45	Y^X	
187	01	1	Initialize
188	06	6	
189	42	STD	
190	10	10	
191	43	RCL	Player A's
192	21	21	distance into
193	59	INT	t-register
194	32	X:T	
195	43	RCL	
196	21	21	Calculate
197	76	LBL	Player A's
198	52	EE	angle
199	22	INV	

LOC	CODE	KEY	COMMENTS
200	59	INT	
201	65	×	
202	43	RCL	
203	00	00	
204	95	=	
205	37	P/R	Place value of
206	42	STO	x in R23
207	23	23	
208	32	X⇄T	Place value of
209	42	STO	y in R24
210	24	24	
211	76	LBL	
212	65	×	
213	00	0	
214	32	X⇄T	
215	73	RC*	
216	10	10	
217	67	EQ	
218	60	DEG	
219	59	INT	Calculate x
220	32	X⇄T	and y values
221	73	RC*	of original
222	10	10	data
223	22	INV	
224	59	INT	
225	65	×	
226	43	RCL	
227	00	00	
228	95	=	
229	37	P/R	
230	42	STO	
231	25	25	
232	32	X⇄T	
233	42	STO	
234	26	26	
235	53	(	
236	53	(	
237	43	RCL	
238	23	23	
239	75	-	
240	43	RCL	
241	25	25	
242	54	)	
243	33	X²	
244	85	+	
245	53	(	
246	53	(	
247	43	RCL	
248	24	24	
249	75	-	

LOC	CODE	KEY	COMMENTS
250	43	RCL	
251	26	26	Calculate
252	54	)	distance
253	33	X²	between
254	54	)	target and
255	54	)	guess
256	34	√X	
257	71	SBR	
258	55	÷	
259	76	LBL	
260	60	DEG	
261	01	1	Increment
262	44	SUM	and test for
263	10	10	distances
264	22	INV	within 400
265	97	DSZ	units of
266	07	07	guess
267	61	GTO	
268	61	GTO	
269	65	×	
270	76	LBL	
271	61	GTO	
272	43	RCL	
273	06	06	
274	32	X⇄T	
275	04	4	
276	00	0	
277	00	0	
278	22	INV	
279	77	GE	
280	71	SBR	
281	58	FIX	
282	03	03	Display 0.RRR
283	43	RCL	(a miss, but
284	06	06	within 400 units
285	55	÷	of enemy ship)
286	43	RCL	
287	00	00	
288	95	=	
289	91	R/S	
290	76	LBL	
291	55	÷	
292	32	X⇄T	
293	43	RCL	Sort distances
294	06	06	from guess to
295	22	INV	closest target
296	77	GE	and keep track
297	18	C'	of closest
298	32	X⇄T	distance
299	42	STO	

140

LOC	CODE	KEY	COMMENTS
300	06	06	
301	76	LBL	
302	18	C'	
303	92	RTN	_____
304	76	LBL	
305	71	SBR	
306	93	.	
307	04	4	Display 0.401
308	00	0	to indicate
309	01	1	a miss
310	95	=	
311	91	R/S	_____
312	76	LBL	
313	42	STO	
314	73	RC*	
315	10	10	
316	59	INT	Guess is on
317	32	X!T	a correct
318	87	IFF	vector
319	01	01	
320	75	-	Search to
321	43	RCL	determine
322	22	22	if a hit
323	61	GTO	occurred
324	81	RST	
325	76	LBL	
326	75	-	
327	43	RCL	
328	21	21	
329	76	LBL	
330	81	RST	
331	59	INT	
332	22	INV	
333	77	GE	
334	85	+	Store location
335	73	RC*	of hit ship for
336	10	10	future use
337	42	STO	
338	04	04	_____
339	00	0	Eliminate
340	72	ST*	hit ship
341	10	10	
342	61	GTO	_____
343	91	R/S	Laser is on a
344	76	LBL	correct vector,
345	85	+	but without
346	01	1	enough fuel
347	93	.	
348	00	0	Display 1.07
349	07	7	

LOC	CODE	KEY	COMMENTS
350	95	=	
351	58	FIX	
352	02	02	
353	91	R/S	_____
354	76	LBL	
355	91	R/S	
356	87	IFF	
357	01	01	
358	93	.	
359	01	1	
360	01	1	
361	42	STO	
362	10	10	
363	61	GTO	
364	94	+/-	
365	76	LBL	
366	93	.	
367	01	1	
368	06	6	Search for
369	42	STO	a win
370	10	10	
371	76	LBL	
372	94	+/-	
373	00	0	
374	42	STO	
375	05	05	
376	32	X!T	
377	05	5	
378	42	STO	
379	07	07	
380	76	LBL	
381	59	INT	
382	73	RC*	
383	10	10	
384	71	SBR	
385	95	=	
386	01	1	
387	44	SUM	
388	10	10	
389	97	DSZ	
390	07	07	
391	59	INT	
392	43	RCL	
393	05	05	
394	32	X!T	
395	05	5	
396	67	EQ	
397	28	LOG	
398	61	GTO	
399	29	CP	_____

LOC	CODE	KEY	COMMENTS	LOC	CODE	KEY	COMMENTS
400	76	LBL		450	44	SUM	Add Player B's
401	28	LOG		451	08	08	fuel excess to
402	55	÷	Create a	452	76	LBL	Player A's amount
403	00	0	flashing	453	49	PRD	
404	95	=	display of	454	58	FIX	
405	43	RCL	ones to	455	03	03	
406	02	02	indicate win	456	43	RCL	
407	91	R/S		457	03	03	Adjust fuel
408	76	LBL		458	55	÷	
409	95	=		459	43	RCL	
410	67	EQ		460	00	00	
411	20	CLR	Search	461	95	=	
412	92	RTN	for a	462	85	+	
413	76	LBL	win	463	01	1	
414	20	CLR		464	95	=	
415	01	1		465	91	R/S	
416	44	SUM		466	76	LBL	
417	05	05		467	36	PGM	
418	92	RTN		468	01	1	Display 1.0 to
419	76	LBL		469	93	.	indicate a
420	29	CP		470	00	0	direct hit
421	43	RCL		471	95	=	
422	04	04		472	91	R/S	
423	59	INT		473	76	LBL	
424	32	X:T		474	39	COS	Add Player A's fuel
425	87	IFF		475	44	SUM	excess to Player B's
426	01	01		476	09	09	amount
427	30	TAN		477	61	GTO	
428	43	RCL		478	49	PRD	
429	22	22	Search for a	479	76	LBL	
430	61	GTO	direct hit	480	10	E'	Clear registers
431	38	SIN		481	47	CMS	and initialize
432	76	LBL		482	01	1	R10 for data
433	30	TAN		483	01	1	storage
434	43	RCL		484	42	STO	
435	21	21		485	10	10	
436	76	LBL		486	08	8	
437	38	SIN		487	00	0	Place 8000 units
438	59	INT		488	00	0	of fuel in R08
439	67	EQ		489	00	0	and R09
440	36	PGM		490	42	STO	
441	75	-		491	09	09	
442	32	X:T		492	42	STO	
443	95	=		493	08	08	
444	50	I×I		494	05	5	Initialize R07
445	42	STO		495	94	+/-	with -5 for Dsz
446	03	03		496	42	STO	
447	87	IFF		497	07	07	
448	01	01		498	02	2	
449	39	COS		499	00	0	

LOC	CODE	KEY	COMMENTS	LOC	CODE	KEY	COMMENTS
500	00	0	Initialize	511	02	02	
501	00	0	maximum	512	00	0	
502	42	STO	distance	513	42	STO	Initialize
503	06	06	from target	514	01	01	
504	01	1		515	01	1	
505	01	1		516	00	0	Divide by
506	01	1		517	00	0	1000
507	01	1	Initialize R02	518	00	0	
508	01	1		519	42	STO	
509	01	1		520	00	00	
510	42	STO		521	91	R/S	Halt

Race Car Driver

Materials

Programmable calculator for each player

Paper and pencil

Graph paper (8–10 squares per inch)

Object of the Game

The object of this game is to be the first person to "drive" your car across the finish line without hitting another car or going off the track. If you are playing solitaire, attempt to complete the racecourse in the fewest possible moves.

General Description

"Race Car Driver" is a "racing" game played on a racecourse drawn to your specifications on a sheet of graph paper as in Figure 2-3. The course can be any size and shape; however, until you get a feeling for the game, we recommend that you use a track similar to the one in Figure 2-3.

The rules for this rectangular coordinate game are very simple.

1. If your car hits the rail or another car, you are out of the race.
2. At the end of each turn, indicate the position of each car by placing a small dot at the appropriate location on the track. Connect each dot to the previous dot with a straight line to represent the path of the car.
3. The lines (paths of cars) may touch and even cross, since they represent *previous* positions of the cars; however, it is important to remember that no two cars can be in the same location *at the same time*.
4. At the beginning of the game each player places a dot on the starting line (0,0 on the rectangular coordinates) to represent the position of his or her car. It is helpful to use different colors of ink so the "cars" may be more easily distinguished from one another.
5. Flip a coin or roll a die to determine who moves first.
6. Each car has two components to its movement, horizontal (x-axis) and vertical (y-axis). On this course the horizontal component represents the car's speed in an east-west direction, while the vertical component represents the car's speed in a north-south direction. At

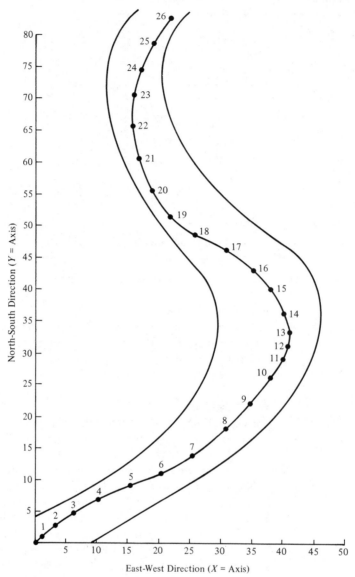

FIGURE 2-3   Sample Track for Race Car Driver

the beginning of the game the cars have not yet begun to move, hence they each have a 0 horizontal and a 0 vertical component. When it is your turn to move, you can modify each component independently by either adding or subtracting *one* unit of speed from *either or both* of the components. You also have the option of *not* modifying either component. Increasing the absolute value of a component simulates acceleration, while deceleration results from decreasing the absolute value of a component. If you choose not to modify either component, your car maintains its current speed. After you modify (or do not modify, as the case may be) the horizontal and/or the vertical component(s), move your car across the *x*-axis a distance equal to the value of the horizontal component. Then move the car up or down the *y*-axis a distance equal to the value of the vertical component. In other words, the new position of your car is determined by adding the previous location of the car to the result of the two movement components.

7. Either component may have a negative or positive value. Positive values represent movement east or north, while negative values signify movement west or south.

8. Players take turns moving their cars, and the first player to drive his or her car across the finish line without hitting another car or the rail wins the race.

Sample Game (Solitaire Mode)

A dot at location 0,0 (see Figure 2-3) indicates the initial position of the car. The first move involved the addition of 1 to *both* the horizontal and vertical components. This resulted in a new position of 1,1. The second move was again the addition of 1 to both components. The horizontal speed of the car became 2, as did the vertical speed. The location at the end of the second move was 3,3. The third move involved another acceleration for the horizontal component; however, the vertical component remained at a speed of 2. A complete summary of the moves for this game appears in Table 2-2.

Two-player games are played in a similar manner, with each player having his or her own calculator to assist in the "bookkeeping," reducing the chance of error in the routine data.

Enthusiastic players could modify the racecourse to create a stock car race, road rally, or other variation. Advanced players may wish to play on a "figure 8" track with several players participating.

User Instructions

Step	Procedure	Press	Display
1.	Enter program		
2.	Initialize	RST *CMs	
3.	Enter a horizontal modification value, *H,* where *H* may be −1, 0, or +1	*H* R/S	*H*
4.	Enter a vertical modification value, *V,* where *V* may be −1, 0, or +1	*V* R/S	Horizontal and vertical speed Horizontal and vertical position
5.	Continue play by repeating steps 3 and 4		

TABLE 2-2 Summary of Moves for a Sample Game of Race Car Driver

| | Input | | Output | | |
Move	Horizontal Modification Value	Vertical Modification Value	Horizontal Speed	Vertical Speed	Location
1	1	1	1	1	1,1
2	1	1	2	2	3,3
3	1	0	3	2	6,5
4	1	0	4	2	10,7
5	1	0	5	2	15,9
6	0	0	5	2	20,11
7	0	1	5	3	25,14
8	0	1	5	4	30,18
9	−1	0	4	4	34,22
10	−1	0	3	4	37,26
11	−1	−1	2	3	39,29
12	−1	−1	1	2	40,31
13	−1	0	0	2	40,33
14	−1	1	−1	3	39,36
15	−1	1	−2	4	37,40
16	−1	−1	−3	3	34,43
17	−1	0	−4	3	30,46
18	−1	−1	−5	2	25,48
19	1	1	−4	3	21,51
20	1	1	−3	4	18,55
21	1	1	−2	5	16,60
22	1	0	−1	5	15,65
23	1	0	0	5	15,70
24	1	−1	1	4	16,74
25	1	0	2	4	18,78
26	1	0	3	4	21,82

6.　　To observe the:
A. Horizontal speed　　　RCL 01
B. Vertical speed　　　　RCL 02
C. Horizontal location　　RCL 03
D. Vertical location　　　RCL 04

7.　　For a new game, go to step 2

Data Registers
01　Horizontal speed
02　Vertical speed
03　Horizontal location
04　Vertical location

146

Race Car Driver

LOC	CODE	KEY	COMMENTS
000	44	SUM	Enter and
001	01	01	modify H
002	91	R/S	
003	44	SUM	Enter and
004	02	02	modify V
005	43	RCL	
006	01	01	Display
007	66	PAU	current H
008	66	PAU	
009	66	PAU	
010	44	SUM	Modify H
011	03	03	location
012	43	RCL	
013	02	02	

LOC	CODE	KEY	COMMENTS
014	66	PAU	Display
015	66	PAU	current V
016	66	PAU	
017	44	SUM	Modify V
018	04	04	location
019	43	RCL	
020	03	03	Display
021	66	PAU	horizontal
022	66	PAU	location
023	66	PAU	
024	43	RCL	Display
025	04	04	vertical
026	91	R/S	location
027	81	RST	Halt

147

Simulations

PROBABILITY

Random Numbers Random numbers are frequently employed in applying probability concepts. For example, you may wish to sample 5% of a given product to check on specific tolerances; however, you must decide which 5% to examine. One solution would be to select every nth item. But if periodicities exist in the manufacturing process, this method would not be appropriate. Another method would be to examine the first items off the assembly line. This is also inappropriate, as it makes no allowance for the items produced later in the production run.

One acceptable method of sampling relies on random numbers. This technique requires a supply of random numbers to indicate which of the items should be examined. Frequently, the random numbers are taken from tables designed for this purpose. In constructing a random number table you must ensure that all of the numbers were selected from a set of digits, each of which had an equal chance of being chosen. Although random number tables are useful in identifying a sample, some large problems quickly exhaust an average sized table. Hence, methods have been developed to generate random numbers as they are needed.

149

One such method utilizes the programmable calculator. Strictly speaking, programs for programmable calculators do not generate true random numbers. This is because the numbers are generated in a deterministic manner, and they may eventually recur in the same order. These numbers are therefore termed pseudorandom numbers. With a good program the period of recurrence is so long that this limitation is generally not a concern.

Several algorithms exist for generating pseudorandom numbers; however, we will focus on a method described by Lennart Rade.[1] His scheme requires that you begin with a 5 to 10 digit, decimal number, x_0, between 0 and 1.

The first step is to multiply x_0 by 147 and take only the decimal portion of the product. The first four digits of this product, x_1, are the first four pseudorandom numbers. To generate four additional random numbers multiply x_1 by 147 and again take only the decimal portion of the product. The first four digits of this new product, x_2, are the second set of pseudorandom numbers. Continue in this manner until you have generated a sufficient list of random numbers.

The above scheme is known as the 147 generator. It is possible to substitute other numbers for 147 to create a similar, but different, pseudorandom number generator. When this is done, the new generator should be tested. A simple test, assuming that the output is haphazard, would be to generate a few hundred random numbers and then examine the frequency of occurrence for each digit. The frequencies should be approximately equal.

Testing New Generators

If you wanted to test a specific generator, the following program can assist you. It allows you to select the seed, generator number, and the number of digits to be generated. As the digits are generated, a frequency distribution is developed for examination at the conclusion of the generating process.

Assume that you want to test a 101 random number generator with a seed of 0.987654321. Further, you are willing to accept 100 generated digits as a significantly large sample from which to decide the suitability of 101 as a generator.

After entering and initializing the program, you would enter 0.987654321 from the keyboard and store the seed in register 10. The number of digits to be generated, 100, would be entered and stored in register 16. Finally, 101 would be entered and stored in register 11. Push R/S and wait for the program to stop and display the number of digits generated. In this case the program will run approximately 11 minutes.

A recall of each register, 00–09, should provide the following output data:

[1] Lennart Rade, *Take a Chance with Your Calculator* (Forest Grove, Oregon: Dilithium Press, 1977), pp. 3–4.

Digit	0	1	2	3	4	5	6	7	8	9	Total
Frequency	8	12	5	4	11	10	19	8	11	12	100

Although other seeds could be tried with the 101 generator, it appears that this generator is not adequate, since the frequency of the digits is too varied.

Program Notes

To see each pseudorandom number as it is generated, insert a Pause command at location 074. (If you have a printer, the command *Prt could be inserted at location 074 in place of the Pause.)

An interesting aspect of this program is the way a four-digit decimal number is "broken down" into four, single-digit numbers (locations 015–036). The *Int and INV *Int keys are used to isolate the integer and decimal portions of a number.

Once a random digit is isolated, subroutine A is used to "identify" this digit so that a frequency distribution can be constructed in registers 00–09.

User Instructions

Step	Procedure	Press	Display
1.	Enter program and return to run mode		
2.	Initialize program	RST *CMs	
3.	Enter seed (0 < seed < 1)	Seed STO 10	Seed
4.	Enter number, n, of random digits to be generated	n STO 16	n
5.	Enter 147 or the generator number, g, which you want to test	g STO 11	g
6.	Run program	R/S	n
7.	Examine frequency of occurrence for each digit, 0–9, by recalling R00–R09	RCL 00	Frequency of 0
		RCL 01	Frequency of 1
		RCL 02	Frequency of 2
		.	.
		.	.
		.	.
		RCL 09	Frequency of 9
8.	For a new case, go to step 2		

Data Registers

00–09	Frequency of digits 0 to 9
10	Seed
11	g
12	Counter
13	Random digit
14	Modified random string
15	Number of digits generator
16	Number of digits desired
17	Counter

Random Numbers

LOC	CODE	KEY	COMMENTS	LOC	CODE	KEY	COMMENTS
000	01	1		038	13	13	
001	42	STO	Initialize	039	71	SBR	Transfer
002	17	17		040	11	A	
003	58	FIX		041	43	RCL	
004	04	04		042	17	17	Test to be sure
005	43	RCL		043	32	X:T	that four, and
006	10	10		044	04	4	only four, digits
007	65	×		045	67	EQ	from string are
008	43	RCL	Calculate	046	97	DSZ	isolated
009	11	11	random number	047	01	1	
010	95	=	string	048	44	SUM	
011	22	INV		049	17	17	
012	59	INT		050	43	RCL	
013	42	STO		051	14	14	
014	10	10		052	61	GTO	Transfer
015	65	×		053	98	ADV	
016	01	1		054	76	LBL	
017	00	0		055	97	DSZ	
018	00	0		056	04	4	
019	00	0		057	44	SUM	
020	00	0		058	15	15	Test to
021	95	=	Isolate a	059	43	RCL	determine
022	76	LBL	single	060	16	16	when to
023	98	ADV	random number	061	32	X:T	halt the
024	59	INT	from string	062	43	RCL	program
025	55	÷		063	15	15	
026	01	1		064	77	GE	
027	00	0		065	16	A'	
028	95	=		066	61	GTO	
029	42	STO		067	00	00	Transfer
030	14	14		068	00	00	
031	22	INV		069	76	LBL	
032	59	INT		070	16	A'	
033	65	×		071	91	R/S	
034	01	1		072	76	LBL	
035	00	0		073	11	A	
036	95	=		074	68	NOP	
037	42	STO		075	00	0	

LOC	CODE	KEY	COMMENTS	LOC	CODE	KEY	COMMENTS
076	42	STO	Identify	089	12	12	
077	12	12	a single	090	61	GTO	
078	76	LBL	random	091	90	LST	Transfer
079	90	LST	digit	092	76	LBL	commands
080	43	RCL		093	99	PRT	
081	12	12		094	92	RTN	
082	32	XIT		095	76	LBL	
083	43	RCL		096	12	B	Sum one to
084	13	13		097	01	1	appropriate
085	67	EQ		098	74	SM*	register,
086	12	B		099	12	12	00-09
087	01	1		100	61	GTO	Transfer
088	44	SUM		101	99	PRT	

Pseudorandom Numbers

Once you have tested and are satisfied with a specific pseudorandom number generator, it is no longer necessary to use the relatively slow program in the previous section. By eliminating unwanted sections, such as the frequency counter, the program can be made both shorter and faster in the generation of random numbers. The following program is one such modification. The user instructions for this modification are identical to the instructions for the previous program and have not been repeated. Note that this program will *not* provide an opportunity to view the frequency distribution of the random digits.

Pseudorandom Numbers

LOC	CODE	KEY	COMMENTS	LOC	CODE	KEY	COMMENTS
000	01	1		023	98	ADV	Isolate a
001	42	STO		024	59	INT	single
002	17	17	Initialize	025	55	÷	random
003	58	FIX		026	01	1	number
004	04	04		027	00	0	from string
005	43	RCL		028	95	=	
006	10	10		029	42	STO	
007	65	×		030	14	14	
008	43	RCL	Calculate	031	22	INV	
009	11	11	random	032	59	INT	
010	95	=	number	033	65	×	
011	22	INV	string	034	01	1	
012	59	INT		035	00	0	
013	42	STO		036	95	=	
014	10	10		037	66	PAU	Display
015	65	×		038	66	PAU	random
016	01	1		039	66	PAU	digit
017	00	0		040	43	RCL	
018	00	0		041	17	17	Test to be
019	00	0		042	32	XIT	sure that
020	00	0		043	04	4	four digits
021	95	=		044	67	EQ	from string
022	76	LBL		045	97	DSZ	are isolated

LOC	CODE	KEY	COMMENTS	LOC	CODE	KEY	COMMENTS
046	01	1		060	32	X:T	
047	44	SUM		061	43	RCL	
048	17	17		062	15	15	
049	43	RCL		063	77	GE	
050	14	14		064	16	A'	
051	61	GTO	Transfer	065	61	GTO	
052	98	ADV		066	00	00	Transfer
053	76	LBL		067	00	00	
054	97	DSZ		068	76	LBL	
055	04	4	Test to halt	069	16	A'	Halt
056	44	SUM	the program	070	91	R/S	
057	15	15	when all random				
058	43	RCL	digits have been				
059	16	16	generated				

Dice Simulation Many different types of games require the tossing of standard, six-sided dice. Some games, such as Dungeons and Dragons, use dice with 4, 8, 12, and 20 sides. Modification of the previously described random number generator will allow you to roll one or more dice. The following modification allows you to define the number of sides, n, on the die, and generate and display pseudorandom digits from 1 through n.

Sample Simulation
The following program and user instructions will allow you to simulate as many die tosses as you desire. Assume that you are rolling a single, eight-sided die.

For example, using the 147 generator with a seed of 0.583924, the first 20 outcomes will be: 7, 5, 3, 7, 6, 3, 1, 1, 2, 5, 1, 1, 1, 8, 7, 3, 4, 8, 7, and 1. Additional rolls might smooth out this rather uneven distribution, but maybe the 147 generator is not a suitable generator. If you wish, you can use the random number program to check this generator.

Program Notes
This program is a modification of the previous one. To make the modification replace the instructions at locations 034–040 in the previous program with the following: RCL 18 + 1 = Int R/S. These commands multiply the random decimal by a value equal to the number of sides on the die. The number 1 is added to this product to allow the final outcome to range from 1 to n, where n is the number of sides on the die.

If two dice need to be rolled, simply roll one die two times and treat the two rolls as a pair.

User Instructions

Step	Procedure	Press	Display
1.	Enter program and return to run mode		

154

2.	Initialize	RST *CMs	
3.	Enter seed, s $(0 < s < 1)$	s STO 10	Seed (s)
4.	Estimate and enter the maximum number, n_d, of random digits you will need	n_d STO 16	n
5.	Enter the number of the generator, g, you want to use. If in doubt, use 147.	g STO 11	g
6.	Enter the number of sides, n_s, on the die	n_s STO 18	s
7.	Run program	R/S	Outcome of roll
8.	Repeat step 7 for additional rolls of the die. If n is exceeded, it will be displayed. Additional random digits can be generated by going to step 2 and beginning again.		

Note: You can change the number of sides on the die at any time by entering the new s and storing it in R18 as in step 6.

Data Registers
10 s
11 g
14 Modified random string
15 Number of digits generated
16 n
17 Counter
18 n_s

LOC	CODE	KEY	COMMENTS		LOC	CODE	KEY	COMMENTS
000	01	1			039	59	INT	
001	42	STO			040	91	R/S	Display die
002	17	17	Initialize		041	43	RCL	
003	58	FIX			042	17	17	
004	04	04			043	32	X:T	Test to be
005	43	RCL			044	04	4	sure that
006	10	10			045	67	EQ	four digits
007	65	×			046	97	DSZ	from the
008	43	RCL	Calculate		047	01	1	string are
009	11	11	random		048	44	SUM	isolated
010	95	=	decimal		049	17	17	
011	22	INV	string		050	43	RCL	
012	59	INT			051	14	14	
013	42	STO			052	61	GTO	Transfer
014	10	10			053	98	ADV	
015	65	×			054	76	LBL	
016	01	1			055	97	DSZ	
017	00	0			056	04	4	
018	00	0			057	44	SUM	
019	00	0			058	15	15	Test to halt
020	00	0			059	43	RCL	program when
021	95	=	Isolate		060	16	16	all random
022	76	LBL	a single		061	32	X:T	digits have
023	98	ADV	random		062	43	RCL	been generated
024	59	INT	number		063	15	15	
025	55	÷	from string		064	77	GE	
026	01	1			065	16	A'	
027	00	0			066	61	GTO	
028	95	=			067	00	00	
029	42	STO			068	00	00	
030	14	14			069	76	LBL	
031	22	INV			070	16	A'	Halt
032	59	INT			071	91	R/S	
033	65	×	Modify digit					
034	43	RCL	based on					
035	18	18	number of					
036	85	+	sides on die					
037	01	1						
038	95	=						

Spinner Simulation   Some games use spinners in place of dice. These spinners are generally circular with a free-moving arrow attached to the center of the circle. The surface of the circle is subdivided into two or more segments, and the segments may be of equal size, resulting in an equal chance of selecting each segment.

An advantage of spinners over dice is that the spinners can easily be "loaded" so that unequal selection of each segment will intentionally occur. Assuming that the arrow of the spinner moves freely, the size of each segment determines the probability of selection. Of course, the sum of the probabilities must equal one.

156

Programs for calculators can easily be written to simulate these two types of spinners. If the spinner is equally divided, the dice simulation program can be used by substituting the number of segments on the spinner for the number of sides on the die. For spinners with unequal segments, the following program will simulate the spin.

Sample Simulation

Simulate several spins of a spinner that has three segments. Assume that one segment encompasses 50% of the circle, while the remaining two segments each comprise 25% of the circle. Through experimentation with the random numbers program, you have decided to use the 135 generator with a seed of 0.8392417.

After entering and initializing the program, you enter and store the seed, 0.8392417, as indicated in step 3 of the user instructions. In a similar manner you enter and store the number of the generator, 135. Since the spinner has three segments, enter a 3 for n_s and store it in register 15.

In this example the first segment of the spinner is the 50% segment, hence, you enter and store 0.5 in register 00. (In this program the first segment is always labeled as segment 0.) Enter and store 0.25 in registers 01 and 02 for each of the remaining two segments.

To simulate a spin start the program by pushing R/S. The display will indicate the segment of the spinner that was selected. In this case the first result is 0. Additional spins can be achieved by pushing the R/S key. For this example, the following output results from nine additional spins: 0, 0, 0, 0, 2, 1, 1, 2, and 0. As expected, approximately 50% (actually 60%) of the spins resulted in the selection of segment 0, while approximately 25% of the spins selected segments 1 and 2. If the 135 generator that you are using to generate the random decimal is suitable, the percentages would continue to approach the expected value as the number of spins increases. In fact, 30 additional spins result in a total of 52.5% selection for segment 0, 25% selection for segment 1, and 22.5% selection for segment 2.

Program Notes

The maximum number of segments, n_s, for this program is ten, and as the number of segments increases from two to ten, the running time of the program also increases. For example, it takes approximately three seconds to simulate a spinner with two segments; however, it may take four to ten seconds to simulate a ten-segment spinner.

The time for individual spins may also vary depending on which segment is being selected and the order and magnitude of the probabilities for each segment. For example, it takes longer for a spin that selects the tenth segment than for one that selects the first segment. (More loops are processed in the former.) Hence, designating *lower* number segments as the higher probability segments will result in a slightly faster spin.

Step	Procedure	Press	Display
1.	Enter program and return to run mode		
2.	Initialize	RST *CMs	
3.	Enter seed, s	s STO 10	Seed (s)
4.	Enter generator number, g	g STO 11	g
5.	Enter number of segments, n_s, of spinner ($0 < n_s < 10$)	n_s STO 15	n_s
6.	Enter, as a *decimal,* the desired probability for *each* segment of the spinner.		
	Probability of segment 0	p_0 STO 00	p_0
	Probability of segment 1	p_1 STO 01	p_1
	Probability of segment 2	p_2 STO 02	p_2
	.	.	.
	.	.	.
	.	.	.
	Probability of segment 9	p_9 STO 09	p_9

Note: The number of probabilities entered *must* equal the number of segments in the spinner. The sum of the probabilities must equal 1.00

7.	Simulate the spin	R/S	Result of spin

Note: The first segment of the spinner is always labeled as zero; therefore the output will range from zero to $n_s - 1$

8.	Repeat step 7 to continue the simulation		
9.	To change only the probabilities go to step 6. To change any of the other parameters go to step 2.		

Data Registers

00–09	Probability for spinner segments 0–9	15	n_s
10	Seed, s	16	Sum of probabilities
11	Generator number, g	17	Indirect counter
13	Indirect counter	18	Indirect counter
14	Counter	20–29	Digits 0–9 (n_s)

Spinner Simulation

LOC	CODE	KEY	COMMENTS
000	01	1	
001	42	STO	
002	17	17	
003	58	FIX	
004	04	04	Initialize
005	02	2	counters
006	00	0	
007	42	STO	
008	13	13	
009	00	0	
010	42	STO	
011	14	14	
012	43	RCL	
013	15	15	
014	32	X;T	
015	76	LBL	
016	13	C	Load R20-Rn$_S$
017	43	RCL	with digits
018	14	14	1 to n$_S$ where
019	72	ST*	n$_S$ is the
020	13	13	number of
021	01	1	spinner
022	44	SUM	segments
023	13	13	
024	44	SUM	
025	14	14	
026	43	RCL	
027	14	14	
028	67	EQ	
029	78	Σ+	
030	13	C	
031	76	LBL	
032	78	Σ+	
033	00	0	
034	42	STO	
035	17	17	
036	42	STO	
037	16	16	Generate
038	02	2	random
039	00	0	decimal
040	42	STO	
041	18	18	
042	43	RCL	
043	10	10	
044	65	×	
045	43	RCL	
046	11	11	
047	95	=	
048	22	INV	
049	59	INT	

LOC	CODE	KEY	COMMENTS
050	42	STO	
051	10	10	
052	32	X;T	
053	76	LBL	
054	89	π	
055	73	RC*	
056	17	17	
057	44	SUM	Seqment
058	16	16	probabilities
059	43	RCL	used to
060	16	16	determine
061	77	GE	output
062	79	X̄	
063	01	1	
064	44	SUM	
065	17	17	
066	44	SUM	
067	18	18	
068	61	GTO	
069	89	π	
070	76	LBL	Select random
071	79	X̄	output and
072	73	RC*	display
073	18	18	
074	91	R/S	
075	61	GTO	Repeat
076	78	Σ+	

BIOLOGICAL SCIENCE

Dieting: Calories or Pounds

All living systems must have a sufficient supply of energy to maintain essential body functions, and humans are no exception. Our supply of energy comes from the food we eat; however, we sometimes oversupply our bodies with excess food energy. We generally consider the resulting adipose tissue a liability, and we promise to go on a diet.

Going on a diet, for most people, means counting calories. The calories being counted are generally *large calories;* a large calorie is defined as the amount of energy needed to raise the temperature of one pound of water 4° Fahrenheit. The number of calories needed to maintain your weight depends on several factors, including your body weight, general metabolic rate, and level of physical activity.

If we oversimplify a little and assume that the level of physical activity is near zero, then the number of calories needed per day to maintain a given body weight for a typical adult human could be determined as follows: $C = W \times k$, where W is the weight in pounds and k is a species-specific constant. For humans $k = 15$, but for elephants k would equal approximately 6. The value of k for a rabbit would be about 26. As the general size of the animal increases, the value of k decreases. This is another way of saying that larger animals eat a smaller percent of their weight to maintain essential body functions. This is not surprising, since larger animals have a smaller ratio of surface area to body volume, reducing the rate of body heat loss and the need for additional energy.

As an alternative to "calorie counting," you could count pounds of food. To maintain basic functions and body weight an adult human must eat approximately 2 pounds of food per day per 100 pounds of body weight. This, of course, assumes that the food is of "average" energy content. Obviously, 2 pounds of animal fat will yield more usable energy than 2 pounds of celery.

Regardless of whether you choose to count calories or pounds, this program will simulate weight loss and provide, as output, the associated number of calories or pounds of food needed to maintain basic body functions.

Sample Simulation

An inactive 385 pound human does not want to gain additional weight. In fact weight loss is this person's goal. He or she wants to know the maximum number of calories that can be eaten per day without causing additional weight gain. In other words, how many calories are needed to maintain basic body functions? Further, the output data should be provided for each 15 pounds of weight loss until the person's weight is less than 185 pounds.

The initial weight in this simulation is 385, the final weight is 185, and the increment is 15. Enter this information into the calculator as indicated in the user instructions, and the output in Table 3-1 will result.

TABLE 3-1 Weights
and Calories for the
Sample Simulation
Dieting Person

Weight	Calories
385	5775
370	5550
355	5325
340	5100
325	4875
310	4650
295	4425
280	4200
265	3975
250	3750
235	3525
220	3300
205	3075
190	2850
175	2625

Program Notes

To run the program for nonhumans, the value of k at program locations
018–019 must be changed. Further, nonhuman simulations *must* receive
the output in calories. The program can also simulate weight gain by
deleting the INV command at location 028 and making the value of the
increment negative.

Remember that this program provides output based on the energy
needed to maintain basic body functions. In reality an individual could
increase his or her energy intake by some value that would depend on the
actual level of physical activity. However, it takes a considerable amount
of exercising to "work off" even a few additional calories of food energy.

User Instructions

Step	Procedure	Press	Display
1.	Enter program		
2.	Initialize:		
	A. Reset pointer	RST *CMs	0
	B. If output is to be in pounds of food, then	*St flg 1	0.
3.	Enter initial weight, W_I, in pounds	W_I R/S	W_I
4.	Enter final weight, W_F, in pounds	W_F R/S	t-register

161

5.   Enter increment of weight loss, i i R/S   Current weight, then calories *or* pounds depending on the status of flag 1 (step 2B)

        Note: The program halts with the last weight in display

6.   For a new case, go to step 2

Data Registers
00   W_I
01   i

Dieting: Calories or Pounds

LOC	CODE	KEY	COMMENTS	LOC	CODE	KEY	COMMENTS
000	42	STO	Enter and store W_I	024	66	PAU	
001	00	00		025	66	PAU	
002	91	R/S		026	43	RCL	
003	32	X:T	Enter and store W_F	027	00	00	Compare W_I to W_F
004	91	R/S		028	22	INV	
005	42	STO	Enter and store I	029	77	GE	
006	01	01		030	11	A	
007	76	LBL		031	43	RCL	
008	22	INV		032	01	01	
009	43	RCL	Display W_I	033	22	INV	Modify weight
010	00	00		034	44	SUM	
011	66	PAU		035	00	00	
012	66	PAU		036	61	GTO	
013	66	PAU		037	22	INV	
014	65	×		038	76	LBL	
015	87	IFF	Transfer for pounds	039	11	A	Halt
016	01	01		040	91	R/S	
017	23	LNX		041	76	LBL	
018	01	1		042	23	LNX	Calculate pounds
019	05	5		043	93	.	
020	76	LBL	Calculate and display calories or pounds	044	00	0	
021	24	CE		045	02	2	
022	95	=		046	61	GTO	Transfer
023	66	PAU		047	24	CE	

Cell Growth   Imagine a science fiction thriller that depicts a small, single-celled creature with a horrendous appetite busily eating its way to bigger and better things. The spherical-shaped creature assimilates food through "pores" in its surface membrane in a manner not too different from that of an amoeba. As the creature eats, it grows. Before long the amoebalike creature has grown to gigantic proportions and now "eats" trees and people—it even threatens to engulf entire villages! Could a single-celled organism grow this large?

162   To answer this question we must first consider a few facts of biological growth. As cells grow in size their rate of growth generally decreases until growth stops entirely. One of the factors that contributes to this decreasing rate of growth is the relationship between a cell's surface area and its volume. As a cell grows in size, the need for materials essential for cellular activity increases; however, the available surface area through which the materials must pass tends to increase at a slower rate than the volume of the cell.

This situation can be demonstrated through a program that simulates cell growth. Assume that a spherical cell has a radius of 0.5 microns (μ). Its surface area would be 3.14 μ^2, and its volume would be 0.52 μ^3. Thus, the ratio of area to volume (reduced to its simplest terms) would be approximately 6:1. Since the volume of the cell increases with the cube of the radius ($V = 4/3\pi r^3$), and the area of the cell only increases with the square of the radius ($A = 4\pi r^2$), it is clear that the ratio of area to volume will decrease as the radius of the cell increases.

Using the following cell growth program, you can watch this ratio change for each 20% of growth in cell radius.

User Instructions (Single Cell Growth)

Step	Procedure	Press	Display
1.	Enter program		
2.	Initialize	RST	
3.	Enter initial size of cell radius, r	r STO 01	r
4.	Run program	R/S	Ratio of area to one unit of volume
	Program will continue to calculate the units of area per one unit of volume until the R/S key is pressed again		
5.	Stop program by holding R/S key down for about one second while the display is visible	R/S	
6.	View length of radius	RCL 01	r
7.	For a new case, go to step 2		

Data Registers

01   r

05   Area; area/volume

06   Volume

LOC	CODE	KEY	COMMENTS	LOC	CODE	KEY	COMMENTS
000	58	FIX	Set decimal	024	95	=	
001	02	02		025	42	STO	Store volume
002	76	LBL		026	06	06	
003	11	A		027	43	RCL	
004	04	4		028	06	06	Calculate
005	65	×		029	22	INV	area/volume
006	89	π	Calculate	030	49	PRD	ratio
007	65	×	area	031	05	05	
008	43	RCL		032	43	RCL	
009	01	01		033	05	05	
010	33	X²		034	66	PAU	Display
011	95	=		035	66	PAU	area/unit volume
012	42	STO	Store area	036	66	PAU	
013	05	05		037	66	PAU	
014	04	4		038	66	PAU	
015	55	÷		039	43	RCL	
016	03	3		040	01	01	
017	65	×		041	65	×	Calculate
018	89	π	Calculate	042	93	.	20% "growth"
019	65	×	volume	043	02	2	of radius
020	43	RCL		044	95	=	
021	01	01		045	44	SUM	
022	45	Yˣ		046	01	01	
023	03	3		047	11	A	Transfer

Discussion of Output

After six "growth spurts" the radius of the cell is 1.49 μ (recall register 01) and the ratio of surface area to cell volume has been reduced to approximately 2:1.

Since this reduction in relative surface area will continue to impede a cell's ability to grow, it is reasonable to assume that our village-eating "blob" could never occur outside the realm of science fiction. Indeed, specific cells have upper limits to their growth. Hence, if an organism is to achieve an exceptionally large physical size, it must do so through an increase in the *number* of cells composing its body, not through an increase in the size of its cells.

A related question now arises. Could a multicellular organism, such as a human, grow to a gigantic size? Gulliver, as you may remember, encountered a civilization of giants approximately 70 feet tall. Hollywood horror movies provide us with numerous examples of "oversized" but normally proportioned organisms. Can these large creatures, whose anatomy is in proportion to that of their regular-sized counterparts, be expected to have the same functions?

To answer this question we must realize that, in part, the strength of a bone depends on the area of its cross section. This area, like the surface area of a single cell, increases with the *square* of its linear measurements; however, the volume (which can be used as an approximation of weight) that a bone must support increases with the *cube* of its linear measurements.

This principle was discussed as early as 1638 by Galileo in his *Discorsi.* He argued that the bones of a large animal must thicken disproportionately to provide the same relative strength as the thin bones of a smaller animal. So to retain the same functions, animals must change their form as they grow. The study of these types of changes in form is called *scaling theory,* and the following program will simulate a simplified investigation in this area.

Program Description

Using the area of a bone's cross section as an indication of its strength, and the volume of a limb as an approximation of the weight the bone must support, this program will simulate a 20% growth in all the linear measurements of the bone and limb. As the growth occurs, the program will display the total percent of growth followed by the total percent increase in bone strength and the total percent of weight increase. In this manner you may easily plot percentage increases in bone strength and limb weight as linear growth of the organism occurs. Since the weight gain increases much more rapidly than the ability of the bone to support that weight, it is clear that exceptional giants of a species cannot exist without a corresponding change in form or function.

User Instructions (Multicellular Growth)

Step	*Procedure*	*Press*	*Display*
1.	Enter program		
2.	Initialize	RST *CMs	
3.	Enter data (in inches):		
	A. Enter size of initial radius of bone's cross section, R_b	R_b R/S	R_b
	B. Enter initial radius of limb's cross section, R_L	R_L R/S	R_L
	C. Enter length of limb, L	L R/S	L
	D. Enter percent growth, G, at which you want all linear measurements to increase (Since $0 < G < 1$, 50% growth would be entered as 0.5)	G R/S	Initial area Initial volume

Note: Program simulates growth and displays total percent growth, the number of times strength has increased, and the number of times weight has increased

4.   To stop program press
R/S   R/S

5.   For a new case, go to step 2

Data Registers

01 Bone radius

02 Limb radius

03 Limb length

04 Percent growth

05 Initial area

06 Initial volume

07 Total percent growth

Multicellular Growth

LOC	CODE	KEY	COMMENTS	LOC	CODE	KEY	COMMENTS
000	42	STO		030	03	03	
001	00	00	Store	031	95	=	
002	42	STO	bone	032	42	STO	Store volume
003	01	01	radius	033	06	06	
004	91	R/S		034	66	PAU	Display volume
005	42	STO	Store	035	66	PAU	
006	02	02	limb	036	76	LBL	
007	91	R/S	radius	037	11	A	
008	42	STO	Store	038	43	RCL	
009	03	03	limb	039	04	04	Increase all
010	91	R/S	length	040	65	×	linear
011	42	STO	Store	041	43	RCL	dimensions
012	04	04	growth rate	042	01	01	by the
013	43	RCL		043	95	=	growth rate
014	01	01		044	44	SUM	
015	33	X²	Calculate	045	01	01	
016	65	×	original	046	43	RCL	
017	89	π	area of	047	04	04	
018	95	=	bone cross	048	65	×	
019	42	STO	section,	049	43	RCL	
020	05	05	store, and	050	02	02	
021	66	PAU	display	051	95	=	
022	66	PAU		052	44	SUM	
023	43	RCL		053	02	02	
024	02	02		054	43	RCL	
025	33	X²	Calculate	055	04	04	
026	65	×	original	056	65	×	
027	89	π	volume of	057	43	RCL	
028	65	×	limb	058	03	03	
029	43	RCL		059	95	=	

LOC	CODE	KEY	COMMENTS	LOC	CODE	KEY	COMMENTS
060	44	SUM		082	05	05	
061	03	03		083	95	=	
062	43	RCL		084	66	PAU	
063	01	01		085	66	PAU	Display
064	55	÷	Calculate	086	66	PAU	
065	43	RCL	total percent	087	43	RCL	Calculate new
066	00	00	growth and	088	02	02	volume and
067	65	×	display	089	33	x²	divide by
068	01	1		090	65	×	original volume
069	00	0		091	89	π	of limb to
070	00	0		092	65	×	determine the
071	95	=		093	43	RCL	number of times
072	66	PAU		094	03	03	larger the new
073	66	PAU		095	95	=	volume is than
074	43	RCL	Calculate new	096	55	÷	the original
075	01	01	area and	097	43	RCL	
076	33	x²	divide by	098	06	06	
077	65	×	original area	099	95	=	
078	89	π	to determine	100	66	PAU	
079	95	=	the number	101	66	PAU	Display
080	55	÷	of times it	102	66	PAU	
081	43	RCL	has grown	103	11	A	Transfer

Mammalian Life Spans

As indicated in the cell growth programs, biological growth is not without limitations. Further, biological form and function are partially defined by scaling theory. If we consider growth through time, a related concept emerges—*life span*. Mammalian life span is related to body size. Robert Kohn indicates that 60% of life span variance can be accounted for by the regression of log life span in years (x) on log body weight in grams (y) as follows: $x = 0.198y + 0.471$.[2] Humans are an important exception to the general rule. Based on our size, we live almost three times longer than "expected."

The following program was developed to predict quickly the life span of any species of mammal (except humans) from its average adult body weight.

Sample Simulation

A given species of dog has an average adult weight of 15 pounds. Approximately, what is its expected life span?

After the program has been entered and initialized, the weight of the dog is entered and key A is pushed rather than R/S because the weight was entered in pounds rather than grams. The display indicates that the expected life span for this species of dog is approximately 16.98 years.

Although this program will provide a "ball park" estimate of a mammal's life span, remember that life span is affected by other factors as well—diet, physical environment, and general health, among others.

[2] Robert Kohn, *Principles of Mammalian Aging,* 2nd ed. (Englewood Cliffs, New Jersey: Prentice-Hall, Inc., 1978), p. 192.

Step	Procedure	Press	Display
1.	Key in program		
2.	Initialize	RST	
3.	Enter mammal's weight:		
	A. If in grams, *G*	*G* R/S	Life span
	or		
	B. If in pounds, *P*	*P* A	Life span
4.	For another case, go to step 2		

Mammalian Life Spans

LOC	CODE	KEY	COMMENTS	LOC	CODE	KEY	COMMENTS
000	76	LBL		018	91	R/S	Display year
001	12	B	Initialize	019	76	LBL	
002	58	FIX		020	11	A	
003	02	02		021	65	×	
004	28	LOG		022	01	1	
005	65	×		023	06	6	
006	93	.		024	65	×	Convert
007	01	1		025	02	2	pounds
008	09	9	Calculate	026	08	8	to grams
009	08	8	log life	027	93	.	
010	85	+	span	028	03	3	
011	93	.		029	04	4	
012	04	4	Convert	030	09	9	
013	07	7	to years	031	05	5	
014	01	1		032	02	2	
015	95	=		033	95	=	
016	22	INV		034	12	B	Transfer
017	28	LOG					

Metabolic Rates   A mammal's metabolic rate is related to that animal's body size. Robert Kohn states that this relationship is almost perfect.[3] If this were not true the heat loss of smaller animals, which have a larger ratio of body surface to volume, would eventually surpass their heat production. The regression of log metabolic rate (*m*) on log body weight (*y*) is: $m = -.266y + 1.047$. Hence, if the animal's body weight is known, its metabolic rate can easily be determined. The following program can be used to simulate mammalian "growth" with the resulting decrease in metabolic rate.

Sample Simulation
A mammal's weight is 3175 grams. After each 10% increase of body weight, what will be the associated metabolic rate?

[3] Kohn, *Principles of Mammalian Aging*, p. 193.

After the program has been entered and initialized, enter 3175 and push R/S. Enter 0.1 to represent the 10% growth spurts. The output will show the following weights and associated metabolic rates: 3175, 1.3; 3492.5, 1.27; 3841.75, 1.24; 4225.93, 1.21; and 4648.52, 1.18.

User Instructions

Step	Procedure	Press	Display
1.	Key in program		
2.	Initialize	RST	
3.	Enter weight of mammal:		
	A. If in grams, *Gr*	*Gr* R/S	*Gr*
	B. If in pounds, *P*	*P* A	*P*
4.	Enter percent growth, *g%*, which you wish to simulate (enter as decimal)	*g%* R/S	Weight in grams, then metabolic rate

Note: The weight, followed by the metabolic rate, continues until R/S is pushed

5.	For a new case, go to step 2	

Data Registers
01 Body weight
02 Growth rate
03 Metabolic rate

Metabolic Rates

LOC	CODE	KEY	COMMENTS	LOC	CODE	KEY	COMMENTS
000	76	LBL		017	06	6	
001	13	C	Store and	018	06	6	
002	42	STO	display	019	94	+/-	
003	01	01	body	020	85	+	
004	91	R/S	weight	021	01	1	
005	42	STO	Enter	022	93	.	
006	02	02	growth rate	023	00	0	
007	58	FIX		024	04	4	
008	02	02		025	07	7	
009	76	LBL		026	95	=	
010	12	B		027	22	INV	
011	43	RCL		028	28	LOG	
012	01	01		029	42	STO	Store
013	28	LOG		030	03	03	metabolic rate
014	65	×	Calculate	031	43	RCL	
015	93	.	metabolic	032	01	01	Display body
016	02	2	rate	033	66	PAU	weight

LOC	CODE	KEY	COMMENTS		LOC	CODE	KEY	COMMENTS
034	66	PAU			050	76	LBL	
035	66	PAU	_____		051	11	A	
036	43	RCL			052	65	×	
037	03	03	Display		053	01	1	
038	66	PAU	metabolic rate		054	06	6	Convert
039	66	PAU			055	65	×	pounds
040	66	PAU	_____		056	02	2	to grams
041	43	RCL			057	08	8	
042	01	01			058	93	.	
043	65	×			059	03	3	
044	43	RCL	Increase		060	04	4	
045	02	02	body weight		061	09	9	
046	95	=	by 20%		062	05	5	
047	44	SUM			063	02	2	
048	01	01			064	95	=	
049	12	B	_____		065	13	C	

Habit Formation   Within the discipline of animal behavior many concepts lend themselves to simulation. Habit formation is one.

Clark Hull, a psychologist, defined habit formation as:

$$_sH_R = 1 - 10^{-.0305\dot{N}}$$

where $_sH_R$ is habit strength, and $\dot{N}$ is the number of reinforcements from the beginning of learning.[4]

Hence, to simulate habit formation and determine habit strength through a series of reinforced trials, we need only input the number of reinforcements since the beginning of learning. As the value of $_sH_R$ increases from 0 to 1, the habit strength increases.

Sample Simulation

An individual is asked to push a series of buttons each time a specific light is flashed. If the subject makes the correct response, praise and a reward are given.

To what extent will the habit strength, $_sH_R$, increase as the number of reinforcements ranges from 4 to 8?

As indicated in step 3 of the user instructions, the value of the initial $\dot{N}$, 4, is entered and stored in register 00. The final $\dot{N}$ is then entered and automatically stored by pressing R/S.

The output will display each $\dot{N}$ and the associated habit strength, $_sH_R$. The program will halt with the final $_sH_R$ in display. In this case the output will be 4.00, 0.24; 5.00, 0.30; 6.00, 0.34; 7.00, 0.39; 8.00, 0.43.

[4]Clark L. Hull, *A Behavior System: An Introduction to Behavior Theory concerning the Individual Organism* (New Haven: Yale University Press, 1952), pp. 357–60.

Program Notes

Hull's equation for habit formation has been criticized by others as premature and not generalizable. For example, the −0.0305 value in the equation does not allow for the realistic possibility that some individuals may form habits (learn) more rapidly than others. Therefore, it is clear that this simulation, as all classroom simulations, is for illustrative purposes only.

   To vary the simulation store values other than −0.0305 in register 01 by changing the program at locations 003–006.

User Instructions

Step	Procedure	Press	Display
1.	Enter program and return to run mode		
2.	Initialize	RST	
3.	Enter initial $\dot{N}$	$\dot{N}$ STO 00	$\dot{N}$
4.	Enter final $\dot{N}$	$\dot{N}$ R/S	$\dot{N}$
			Then the associated $_sH_R$

Note: The display continues to pause for each $\dot{N}$ and the associated $_sH_R$ until the final $_sH_R$ is displayed at which time the program halts.

5.	For another simulation, go to step 2

Data Registers
00   Current $\dot{N}$
01   −0.0305
02   Exponent
03   Final $\dot{N}$
04   $_sH_R$

LOC	CODE	KEY	COMMENTS		LOC	CODE	KEY	COMMENTS
000	42	STO			031	32	X⁞T	
001	03	03			032	95	=	
002	93	.			033	42	STO	
003	00	0			034	04	04	
004	03	3			035	43	RCL	
005	00	0			036	00	00	Display .
006	05	5	Initialize		037	66	PAU	current N
007	94	+/-			038	66	PAU	
008	42	STO			039	66	PAU	
009	01	01			040	43	RCL	
010	58	FIX			041	04	04	Display $_SH_R$
011	02	02			042	66	PAU	
012	76	LBL			043	66	PAU	
013	24	CE			044	66	PAU	
014	43	RCL			045	43	RCL	
015	01	01			046	03	03	Compare final
016	65	×			047	32	X⁞T	$\dot{N}$ to current
017	43	RCL			048	43	RCL	$\dot{N}$
018	00	00			049	00	00	
019	95	=			050	67	EQ	
020	42	STO			051	91	R/S	
021	02	02	Calculate		052	01	1	
022	01	1	and store		053	44	SUM	Increment current
023	00	0	$_SH_R$		054	00	00	$\dot{N}$ and transfer
024	45	Yˣ			055	61	GTO	
025	43	RCL			056	24	CE	
026	02	02			057	76	LBL	
027	95	=			058	91	R/S	Display $_SH_R$
028	32	X⁞T			059	43	RCL	and halt
029	01	1			060	04	04	
030	75	-			061	91	R/S	

PHYSICAL SCIENCE

Aging through Space

The distance between objects in the universe is so great that we use the term *light-years* in place of miles. A light-year is the distance you would travel in one year if you moved at the speed of light. Since the speed of light is approximately 186,000 miles per second, a light-year would be about 5.9×10^{12} miles.

Even when using the light-year as a unit of measure, distances in space are very large numbers. For example, the galaxy M31 in the constellation Andromeda is 2.2 million light-years away! The width of our galaxy, the Milky Way, is over 80,000 light-years, and we are more than 4 light-years from Alpha Centauri, the *nearest* star to our solar system.

These tremendous distances make manned space travel to locations beyond our solar system impractical. Even if we quadrupled the speed of

172

our fastest spacecraft, it would take more than 26,000 years to reach Alpha Centauri! To reach Andromeda at this speed it would take over 1.4×10^{10} years.

The only way we know to make trips like this at all plausible is to think in terms of very fast spaceships. If we could travel at velocities that approach the speed of light, an interesting phenomenon would occur: The aging process of those in space would slow down relative to that of the people remaining on earth. This process is described by the following formula:

$$A = \sqrt{1 - (\frac{v}{c})^2}$$

Where: v = speed of travel

c = speed of light

A = astronaut's aging, expressed as a decimal part of a year, per each earth-year

This formula forms the basis for our program, which simulates space travel for any distance and for speeds between 1 and 186,000 miles per second. The output will indicate the number of earth-years elapsed during the journey as well as the number of years the astronauts will have aged.

Sample Simulation

Assume that you want to travel to Barnard's Star, which is approximately 6.1 light-years from earth. If your speed were to be 80% of the speed of light, how many earth-years would have elapsed and how many earth-years would you have aged by the time you reached your destination?

After entering the program into the calculator, initialize as indicated in the user instructions. Then enter the distance to be traveled, 6.1, and press B, since the distance is in light-years. The speed is entered as 80, and after pressing R/S the display will indicate 4.60 as the number of earth-years you will age while making the journey. People on earth would have aged 7.66 years, as indicated in the display after pressing RCL 05.

If the distance had been in miles (36,000,000,000,000) instead of light-years, you would have needed to use scientific notation in step 4B. (See the program notes for more information on using scientific notation.)

Program Notes

Since this program allows very large distances to be entered, it will sometimes be necessary to use scientific notation in step 4B. To use this mode for data entry, first enter the mantissa (up to 8 digits) and then press the EE key. Finally, enter the power of 10 (exponent) and, in this program, press A. The command to take the calculator out of scientific notation is INV EE. This command is built into the program at locations 058–059, hence the display will be in standard notation when the program halts.

For example, to enter 36,000,000,000,000 miles as the distance in step 4 the following sequence of keystrokes should be followed: 3.6 EE 13 A

User Instructions

Step	Procedure	Press	Display
1.	Key in program		
2.	Set decimal point	*Fix 2	
3.	Initialize	RST	
4.	Enter distance to be traveled: A. If in light-years, enter distance, D_L, and press B	D_L B	D_M
	B. If in miles, enter distance, D_M, and press A (Use scientific notation for large numbers.)	D_M A	D_M
5.	Enter speed of travel, S, as a percent of the speed of light. (For example, a speed of 93,000 miles per second would be entered as 50.) $(0 < S < 100)$	S R/S	Years of astronaut's aging
6.	To see: A. Length of trip in earth-years	RCL 05	
	B. Aging of astronaut in earth-years	RCL 06	
7.	For a new simulation, go to step 3		

Data Registers

01 Distance in miles

02 Speed of light

03 Velocity of travel in miles per second

04 Aging in space per earth-year

05 Length of journey in earth-years

06 Aging of astronaut in earth-years

LOC	CODE	KEY	COMMENTS
000	76	LBL	
001	11	A	Store D_M
002	42	STO	
003	01	01	
004	91	R/S	Enter S
005	55	÷	
006	01	1	
007	00	0	
008	00	0	
009	65	×	
010	01	1	Calculate
011	08	8	speed of
012	06	6	travel in
013	00	0	miles per
014	00	0	second
015	00	0	
016	42	STO	
017	02	02	
018	95	=	
019	42	STO	
020	03	03	
021	55	÷	
022	43	RCL	
023	02	02	
024	95	=	
025	33	X²	
026	32	X:T	Calculate
027	01	1	aging, A
028	75	-	
029	32	X:T	
030	95	=	
031	34	√X	
032	42	STO	
033	04	04	
034	43	RCL	
035	03	03	
036	65	×	
037	03	3	

LOC	CODE	KEY	COMMENTS
038	01	1	Convert
039	05	5	miles per
040	05	5	second to
041	07	7	miles per
042	06	6	year
043	00	0	
044	00	0	
045	95	=	
046	32	X:T	
047	43	RCL	
048	01	01	
049	55	÷	
050	32	X:T	Calculate years
051	95	=	for journey
052	42	STO	
053	05	05	
054	65	×	Calculate aging
055	43	RCL	in years
056	04	04	
057	95	=	
058	22	INV	Remove
059	52	EE	scientific
060	42	STO	notation
061	06	06	
062	91	R/S	Display years
063	76	LBL	
064	12	B	
065	65	×	
066	05	5	Convert
067	93	.	D_L to D_M
068	09	9	
069	52	EE	
070	01	1	
071	02	2	
072	95	=	
073	61	GTO	Transfer
074	11	A	

How Far Is the Storm? Very few people enjoy being caught outdoors in an electrical storm. Possibly for this reason several methods for predicting the arrival of a storm have been passed from generation to generation. Some people look at the behavior of certain tree leaves; leaves that are bottom-side up indicate bad weather. Others judge the arrival of a storm by observing the position of the clouds and the decrease in natural light. Still others depend on their senses to warn of an impending storm. For example, many people claim to be able to "smell" a storm; others "feel" a storm through a change in their leg or arm joints.

These methods for predicting a storm may or may not have a basis in fact; however, one relatively simple method is based on fact and can be used to determine the distance from an electrical storm. This method is based on the difference between the speed of sound and the speed of light.

It is easy to demonstrate that sound travels much slower than light. Spectators at a track meet observe the smoke from the starting pistol long (a second or so) before they can hear the shot. Baseball fans in the outfield bleachers can see a ball flying through the air before they hear the crack of the bat. Many similar examples could be listed, but the one that relates to this situation is observing a flash of lightning before hearing the clap of thunder.

The reason the lightning always arrives ahead of the thunder is that the lightning travels at the speed of light (approximately 186,000 miles per second) while the thunder only travels at the speed of sound (approximately 1100 feet per second). For our purposes, the speed of light is so fast that we can consider that light travels instantaneously, so we can use the flash of lightning to indicate when the electrical discharge took place. By combining this information with the knowledge that sound travels approximately 1100 feet per second, we can easily determine the distance to the storm once we know how long it took for the thunder to travel from its source to our ears.

The calculation for determining the distance to the storm is simply to multiply the speed of sound by the time it takes the thunder to travel from the discharge to our ears. For example, if you measured a ten second delay between the flash of lightning and the clap of thunder, the storm would be approximately 11,000 feet from you. Keep in mind that since the electrical discharge can be between two high clouds, this calculation does not necessarily measure *ground* distance between you and the storm, but rather *straight-line* distance. If the discharge were close to the ground, then ground distance and straight-line distance would be approximately equal.

One additional consideration will increase the accuracy of your calculation. That is, the speed of sound varies with the temperature of the air. The warmer the air, the faster the sound travels. At 32° Fahrenheit the speed of sound in air is 1090 feet per second. For each Fahrenheit degree increase, sound travels approximately 1.11 feet per second faster. Hence, at 70° F, the speed of sound will be approximately 1132 feet per second. (If you are measuring the temperature on the Centigrade scale, the increase in the speed of sound is approximately 2 feet per second for each Centigrade degree increase.) Since the speed of sound in air is not significantly affected by changes in air pressure, we can ignore this variable in our calculations.

Sample Simulation

Assume that you are playing golf and you see a flash of lightning followed by a clap of thunder. This sequence repeats itself several times with increasing intensity, and you begin to wonder if you are safe with a nine iron in your hand.

To determine whether or not the storm is moving closer, you need to measure its distance from you on at least two separate occasions— preferably a few minutes apart. To use your programmable calculator you only need to input the estimated temperature in degrees Fahrenheit. The program uses a counting loop as a clock to help you determine the number of seconds between the lightning and the thunder.

Assume that the temperature is 80° F. The first step is to key in the program and return the calculator to the run mode. Next, initialize the program by pressing the RST and *CMs keys. Enter the temperature and store it in register 03. When you see a flash of lightning *immediately* push the R /S key, and a counter will begin to measure elapsed time. When you hear the clap of thunder again push the R /S key to stop the counter. To begin the calculations press the A key. The display will indicate the distance (in miles) to the storm.

If the elapsed time had been 6.30 seconds, the counter in register 01 would have a value approximately equal to 44, and the display would indicate that the storm was approximately 1.36 miles away.

A few minutes later the above process is repeated, and the display indicates that the storm is now only 0.45 miles away. From these two calculations, it is easy to see that the storm is moving closer, and a wise golfer would immediately seek shelter.

Program Notes

A short loop that continues to sum the value of one into register 01 builds a timer into your program easily. Although the number of loops per second may vary somewhat depending on the charge in the battery pack as well as from calculator to calculator, it is a simple matter to program this short loop into your calculator and determine the number of loops per second. If you find that your calculator completes significantly more or fewer than 7.142 loops per second, simply enter your data into the program at locations 026–030.

Note that this program assumes that the temperature of the air is constant between the individual on the ground and the location of the electrical discharge. If the clouds providing the discharge are very high, the air temperature at that point could be slightly lower. However, for the purpose of this simulation this variable can be ignored.

If this program is to be used at temperatures lower than 0° F, the base value for the speed of sound should be appropriately reduced at program locations 014–019.

User Instructions

Step	Procedure	Press	Display
1.	Key in program		
2.	Initialize	RST *CMs	
3.	Enter temperature of air in degrees Fahrenheit	Temperature STO 02	Temperature
4.	Determine time between lightning and thunder: A. When lightning is seen, *immediately* begin		

	operation	R/S	
	B. When thunder is heard, *immediately* stop operation	R/S	
5.	Calculate distance (in miles) to the storm	A	Miles
6.	To see the speed of sound in feet	RCL 03	Speed of sound, in feet, corrected for temperature
7.	For another case, go to step 2		

Data Registers

01 Time counter

02 Temperature

03 Speed of sound

How Far Is the Storm?

LOC	CODE	KEY	COMMENTS	LOC	CODE	KEY	COMMENTS
000	01	1		021	42	STO	
001	44	SUM	Loop for	022	03	03	
002	01	01	timer	023	43	RCL	
003	81	RST	_____	024	01	01	Convert
004	76	LBL		025	55	÷	counter to
005	11	A		026	07	7	seconds
006	43	RCL		027	93	.	
007	02	02		028	01	1	(7.142 is a
008	65	×		029	04	4	constant)
009	01	1		030	02	2	
010	93	.	Correct speed	031	95	=	
011	01	1	of sound for	032	65	×	_____
012	01	1	temperature	033	43	RCL	
013	85	+		034	03	03	Calculate
014	01	1		035	55	÷	distance:
015	00	0		036	05	5	
016	05	5		037	02	2	Seconds times
017	04	4		038	08	8	speed divided
018	93	.		039	00	0	by 5280
019	05	5		040	95	=	_____
020	95	=		041	91	R/S	Display distance

Compute Your Radiation Dose   We live in a radioactive world. Much of this radiation is from our natural environment; however, some additional radiation is manmade. One unit frequently used to measure both types of radiation is called the millirem (mrem), and a "typical" natural environment (background) may give you an annual dose of approximately 100 mrem, depending upon where you live.

In addition to where you live, other factors, such as how you live and **178** what you eat, drink, and breathe affect your annual radiation dosage.

Although scientists and doctors do not know the full health-related effects of different dosages of radiation, the National Council on Radiation Protection and Measurement (NCRP) has established 500 mrems per year as the dose limit for the public.

Various federal agencies such as the EPA and the NRC have established limits for the addition into the environment of "human-created" radiation. The EPA standard allows for an increase in the annual background dosage of 25 mrem—far below the NCRP's 500 mrem limit for "safety." The NRC's standard permits an increase into the environment of 10–15 mrems per year. The design objectives for a nuclear power plant are stated as 5 mrem per year.

Although it is difficult to accurately determine the number of mrems of radioactivity that you receive each year, the following worksheet and program will assist you in making a rough estimate.

Worksheet

(To be completed *before* using the program)

1. Approximately how many feet above sea level do you live? (See Table 3-2) _____

2A. From what material is your home made?
Wood = 1 Concrete = 2 Brick = 3 Stone = 4 _____

2B. On average, how many hours per day do you spend in your house? (Remember to include nights) _____

3. On average, how many hours per day are you outside? _____

4. If the sum of your answers to 2B and 3 does not equal 24, in what type of building do you spend the rest of your day?
Wood = 1 Concrete = 2 Brick = 3 Stone = 4 _____
(If the sum of 2B and 3 is equal to 24, enter 0.)

5. Water, food, and air account for about 25 mrems per year. Estimate your dosage (22 to 29). _____

6. Fallout from weapons tests (worldwide) may add about 4 mrems per year to your dosage. Estimate a value for your case. _____

7. How many miles of high-altitude (20,000 feet[+]) flying do you do in a year? _____

8. Do you wear a radium dial wristwatch?
Yes = 1 No = 0 _____

9. On average, how many hours per day are you in a room with a television set that is turned on? _____

10. X-rays:

Type	mrem		Number per year		
Chest	150	×	_____	=	_____
Colon	450	×	_____	=	_____
Dental	20	×	_____	=	_____
G.I. tract	2000	×	_____	=	_____
Head	50	×	_____	=	_____
Limb	420	×	_____	=	_____
Spinal	250	×	_____	=	_____
Stomach	350	×	_____	=	_____
Other	???	×	_____	=	_____
			Total	=	_____

What is your total of mrems from X-rays?   _____

11. How close to a nuclear power plant do you live?
Site boundary = 1
One mile away = 2
Five miles away = 3
Over fives miles away = 4   _____

12. On average, how many hours per day do you spend
in or around your home?   _____

Now, use the above information with the user instructions of the following
program to calculate your estimated mrem dosage. An "average" annual
dose is in the 150–200 mrem range.

TABLE 3-2 Elevations for Selected Cities

City	Elevation	City	Elevation
Abilene, Texas	1710	Kansas City, Kansas	750
Akron, Ohio	874	Knoxville, Tennessee	890
Albuquerque, New Mexico	4945	Lincoln, Nebraska	1150
Ann Arbor, Michigan	880	Little Rock, Arkansas	286
Atlanta, Georgia	1050	Los Angeles, California	340
Atlantic City, New Jersey	10	Madison, Wisconsin	860
Billings, Montana	3120	New York, New York	55
Boise, Idaho	2704	Peoria, Illinois	470
Boston, Massachusetts	21	Pittsburgh, Pennsylvania	745
Buffalo, New York	585	Portland, Oregon	77
Cheyenne, Wyoming	6100	Richmond, Virginia	160
Chicago, Illinois	595	Raleigh, North Carolina	365
Cincinnati, Ohio	550	St. Louis, Missouri	455
Dallas, Texas	435	Santa Fe, New Mexico	6950
El Paso, Texas	3695	Terre Haute, Indiana	496
Fairbanks, Alaska	448	Waterbury, Connecticut	260
Johnstown, Pennsylvania	1185	Tulsa, Oklahoma	804

Step	Procedure	Press	Display
1.	Enter program		
2.	Initialize	*E'	0
3.	Enter		
	A. Elevation (feet above sea level)	Elevation R/S	Elevation
	B. Home construction, H_C Wood = 1		
	Concrete = 2 Brick = 3 Stone = 4	H_C R/S	H_C
	C. Hours per day in home	Hours R/S	Hours
	D. Hours per day outside	Hours R/S	Hours
	E. Construction of other building, O_C	O_C R/S	O_C
	F. Mrem from water, food, and air	Mrem R/S	Mrem
	G. Mrem from fallout	Mrem R/S	Mrem
	H. Miles of jet flight per year	Miles R/S	Miles
	I. Radium dial watch? Yes = 1 No = 0	1 or 0 R/S	1 or 0
	J. Hours per day with television	Hours R/S	Hours
	K. Mrem from X-rays (see worksheet)	Mrem R/S	Mrem
	L. Distance from nuclear plant; site		
	boundary = 1 1 mile away = 2;		
	5 miles away = 3 over 5 = 4	1-4 R/S	1-4
	M. Hours in house plus hours near house	Hours R/S	Total mrem
4.	To check any given variable in relation to:		
	A. Elevation	A	Elevation dose
	B. Home construction	B	Dose at home
	C. Outside background	C	Outside dose
	D. Other buildings	D	Building dose
	E. Jet travel	E	Air dose
	F. Radium watch	*A'	Radium dose
	G. Television	*B'	Television dose
	H. Power plant	*C'	Power plant dose
	I. Total mrem	*D'	Total dose
5.	For a new case, reinitialize and go to step 2	*E'	0

Data Registers

01	Elevation	08	Jet miles
02	Home material	09	Watch
03	Hours in home	10	Television
04	Hours outside	11	X-rays
05	Other place	12	Power plant
06	Water, food, air	13	Hours near home
07	Fallout	15	mrem total

181

Compute Your Radiation Dose

LOC	CODE	KEY	COMMENTS
000	43	RCL	
001	01	01	
002	55	÷	
003	01	1	
004	00	0	
005	00	0	
006	95	=	Elevation
007	85	+	dosage
008	04	4	
009	02	2	
010	95	=	
011	42	STO	
012	01	01	
013	44	SUM	
014	15	15	
015	43	RCL	
016	02	02	
017	32	X⁀T	
018	01	1	
019	67	EQ	
020	22	INV	
021	04	4	
022	67	EQ	
023	22	INV	Home
024	02	2	building
025	93	.	materials
026	05	5	dosage
027	65	×	
028	43	RCL	
029	03	03	
030	95	=	
031	42	STO	
032	02	02	
033	44	SUM	
034	15	15	
035	76	LBL	
036	24	CE	
037	43	RCL	
038	04	04	
039	65	×	
040	02	2	Outside
041	93	.	background
042	05	5	dosage
043	95	=	
044	42	STO	
045	04	04	
046	44	SUM	
047	15	15	
048	43	RCL	
049	05	05	

LOC	CODE	KEY	COMMENTS
050	32	X⁀T	
051	00	0	Check for
052	22	INV	24 hours
053	67	EQ	
054	25	CLR	
055	76	LBL	
056	34	⌐X	Water, food,
057	43	RCL	and air
058	06	06	dosage
059	44	SUM	
060	15	15	
061	43	RCL	
062	07	07	Fallout
063	44	SUM	dosage
064	15	15	
065	43	RCL	
066	08	08	
067	65	×	
068	93	.	
069	00	0	
070	00	0	Jet travel
071	00	0	dosage
072	07	7	
073	95	=	
074	42	STO	
075	08	08	
076	44	SUM	
077	15	15	
078	43	RCL	
079	09	09	
080	32	X⁀T	Check for
081	01	1	radium watch
082	67	EQ	
083	35	1/X	
084	76	LBL	
085	42	STO	
086	43	RCL	
087	10	10	
088	65	×	
089	93	.	Television
090	01	1	dosage
091	05	5	
092	95	=	
093	42	STO	
094	10	10	
095	44	SUM	
096	15	15	
097	43	RCL	
098	11	11	X-ray
099	44	SUM	dosage

182

LOC	CODE	KEY	COMMENTS
100	15	15	
101	43	RCL	
102	12	12	
103	32	X:T	
104	01	1	Determine
105	67	EQ	distance
106	43	RCL	to the
107	68	NOP	nuclear
108	02	2	plant
109	67	EQ	
110	44	SUM	
111	03	3	
112	67	EQ	
113	45	YX	
114	00	0	If over five
115	42	STO	miles, no
116	12	12	dosage
117	76	LBL	
118	52	EE	Display mrem
119	43	RCL	per year
120	15	15	
121	91	R/S	
122	76	LBL	
123	22	INV	
124	01	1	
125	93	.	
126	09	9	
127	04	4	Wooden house
128	65	×	dosage
129	43	RCL	
130	03	03	
131	95	=	
132	42	STO	
133	02	02	
134	44	SUM	
135	15	15	
136	61	GTO	Transfer
137	24	CE	
138	76	LBL	
139	23	LNX	
140	02	2	
141	93	.	Stone house
142	07	7	dosage
143	08	8	
144	65	×	
145	43	RCL	
146	03	03	
147	95	=	
148	42	STO	
149	02	02	

LOC	CODE	KEY	COMMENTS
150	44	SUM	
151	15	15	
152	61	GTO	Transfer
153	24	CE	
154	76	LBL	
155	25	CLR	Dosage from
156	01	1	other than
157	67	EQ	home and
158	32	X:T	outside
159	04	4	
160	67	EQ	
161	33	X²	
162	02	2	
163	93	.	
164	05	5	
165	65	×	
166	53	(	Brick or
167	02	2	concrete
168	04	4	building
169	75	−	dosage
170	43	RCL	
171	03	03	
172	75	−	
173	43	RCL	
174	04	04	
175	54	)	
176	95	=	
177	42	STO	
178	05	05	
179	44	SUM	
180	15	15	
181	61	GTO	Transfer
182	34	ГX	
183	76	LBL	
184	32	X:T	
185	01	1	
186	93	.	
187	09	9	
188	04	4	
189	65	×	
190	53	(	Wooden
191	02	2	building
192	04	4	dosage
193	75	−	
194	43	RCL	
195	03	03	
196	75	−	
197	43	RCL	
198	04	04	
199	54	)	

LOC	CODE	KEY	COMMENTS
200	95	=	
201	42	STO	
202	05	05	
203	44	SUM	
204	15	15	
205	61	GTO	
206	34	√X	
207	76	LBL	
208	33	X²	
209	02	2	
210	93	.	
211	07	7	
212	08	8	
213	65	×	
214	53	(	
215	02	2	Stone
216	04	4	building
217	75	-	dosage
218	43	RCL	
219	03	03	
220	75	-	
221	43	RCL	
222	04	04	
223	54	)	
224	95	=	
225	42	STO	
226	05	05	
227	44	SUM	
228	15	15	
229	61	GTO	Transfer
230	34	√X	
231	76	LBL	
232	35	1/X	Dosage
233	02	2	from
234	42	STO	radium
235	09	09	watch
236	44	SUM	
237	15	15	
238	61	GTO	Transfer
239	42	STO	
240	76	LBL	
241	43	RCL	
242	93	.	
243	02	2	Dosage at
244	65	×	site
245	43	RCL	boundary
246	13	13	
247	95	=	
248	42	STO	
249	12	12	

LOC	CODE	KEY	COMMENTS
250	44	SUM	
251	15	15	
252	61	GTO	Transfer
253	52	EE	
254	76	LBL	
255	45	Y×	
256	93	.	
257	00	0	
258	00	0	
259	02	2	Dosage five
260	65	×	miles from
261	43	RCL	site
262	13	13	
263	95	=	
264	42	STO	
265	12	12	
266	44	SUM	
267	15	15	
268	61	GTO	Transfer
269	52	EE	
270	76	LBL	
271	44	SUM	
272	93	.	
273	00	0	Dosage one
274	02	2	mile from
275	65	×	site
276	43	RCL	
277	13	13	
278	95	=	
279	42	STO	
280	12	12	
281	44	SUM	
282	15	15	
283	61	GTO	Transfer
284	52	EE	
285	76	LBL	
286	90	LST	Enter
287	91	R/S	elevation
288	42	STO	
289	01	01	
290	91	R/S	Enter home
291	42	STO	construction
292	02	02	
293	91	R/S	Enter hours
294	42	STO	in home
295	03	03	
296	91	R/S	Enter hours
297	42	STO	outside
298	04	04	
299	91	R/S	

LOC	CODE	KEY	COMMENTS
300	42	STO	Enter other
301	05	05	construction
302	91	R/S	Enter mrem
303	42	STO	from food
304	06	06	
305	91	R/S	Enter mrem
306	42	STO	from fallout
307	07	07	
308	91	R/S	Enter jet
309	42	STO	miles
310	08	08	
311	91	R/S	Enter radium
312	42	STO	watch
313	09	09	
314	91	R/S	Enter hours
315	42	STO	of television
316	10	10	
317	91	R/S	Enter mrem
318	42	STO	from X-rays
319	11	11	
320	91	R/S	Enter
321	42	STO	distance to
322	12	12	nuclear site
323	91	R/S	Enter hours
324	42	STO	at home
325	13	13	
326	81	RST	
327	76	LBL	Display mrem
328	11	A	from
329	43	RCL	elevation
330	01	01	
331	91	R/S	
332	76	LBL	
333	12	B	Display mrem
334	43	RCL	from home
335	02	02	
336	91	R/S	
337	76	LBL	
338	13	C	Display mrem
339	43	RCL	from outside
340	04	04	
341	91	R/S	
342	76	LBL	
343	14	D	Display mrem
344	43	RCL	from other
345	05	05	buildings
346	91	R/S	
347	76	LBL	
348	15	E	Display mrem
349	43	RCL	from jet
350	08	08	travel
351	91	R/S	
352	76	LBL	
353	16	A'	Display mrem
354	43	RCL	from radium
355	09	09	watch
356	91	R/S	
357	76	LBL	
358	17	B'	Display mrem
359	43	RCL	from
360	10	10	television
361	91	R/S	
362	76	LBL	
363	18	C'	Display mrem
364	43	RCL	from power
365	12	12	plant
366	91	R/S	
367	76	LBL	
368	19	D'	Display total
369	43	RCL	mrem
370	15	15	
371	91	R/S	
372	76	LBL	
373	10	E'	Reinitialize
374	47	CMS	
375	25	CLR	
376	61	GTO	Transfer
377	90	LST	

Where Is Your Horizon? Assume that you and your friend are standing on the shore of a large lake. As you look straight across the water you will see the horizon—the point at which the sky and the water appear to come together. Is the horizon you see located at the same distance from you as the horizon your friend sees? It may or may not be. As indicated in Figure 3-1, it will depend on the height of your eyes above ground level.

A person whose eyes are at point h_2 could see a horizon, B_2, at a greater distance than a person whose eyes are at point h_1. But can we be more specific?

Yes, since the Pythagorean theorem indicates that the hypotenuse of a right triangle is equal to the square root of the sum of the squares of the other two sides ($c^2 = a^2 + b^2$), we can say that:

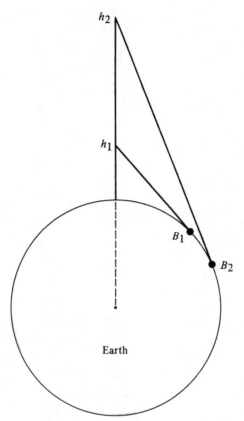

FIGURE 3-1   Position of the Horizon from Two
Different Elevations

$$r^2 + d^2 = (r + h)^2$$
$$d^2 = (r + h)^2 - r^2$$
$$d = \sqrt{(r + h)^2 - r^2}$$

where h is the height of a person's eyes above ground level, r is the radius of the earth, and d is the distance from the person to the horizon (see Figure 3–2).

Then, assuming a radius of 3959 miles, the distance to the horizon for a person whose eyes are 5 feet above the ground would be 2.74 miles.

$$d = \sqrt{(3959 + \frac{5}{5280})^2 - (3959)^2}$$
$$d = \sqrt{15673688.50 - 15673681.00}$$
$$d = \sqrt{7.50}$$
$$d = 2.74 \text{ miles}$$

For a person whose eyes are 6 feet from the ground, the calculations would be:

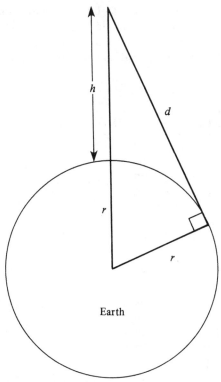

FIGURE 3-2   Distance to the Horizon from a
Specific Elevation

$$d = \sqrt{(3959 + \frac{6}{5280})^2 - (3959)^2}$$
$$d = \sqrt{16000009.09 - 15673681.00}$$
$$d = \sqrt{9.00}$$
$$d = 3.00 \text{ miles}$$

In this example, an increase of one foot in h resulted in an increase of 1372.8 feet (0.26 mile) in the distance to the horizon. This is why the line-of-sight antennas on small boats are placed several feet above the deck. This is also the principle that helps determine the necessary height for a communications satellite that will receive an electronic signal from one point on the earth and redirect it to another.

The following program will calculate d for any value of h. Further, you may select a value by which to increase h, and the program will repeatedly display the new h with its associated value d.

Variations
Since the distance to the horizon is, in part, determined by the radius of the planet on which you are standing, it will be necessary to make a slight modification in the program if you want to simulate these activities on another planet. To make this modification simply change the planet's

radius at program locations 002–005. (For radii with less than four digits, one or more program steps should be deleted, and for radii with more than four digits, program steps must be inserted.) Table 3-3 will provide approximate radii for several planets and some of their natural satellites.

TABLE 3-3   Radii of Selected Planets and Satellites

Planet/Satellite	Radii in Miles
Mercury	1,500
Venus	3,800
Earth	3,959
Moon	1,080
Mars	2,100
Phobos	9
Uranus	14,789
Titania	294
Miranda	97
Asteroids	
Ceres	239
Icarus	0.5
Vesta	118

User Instructions

Step	Procedure	Press	Display
1.	Key in program		0
2.	Initialize	RST *Fix 2	0.00
3.	Enter increment, I, in feet (this is the amount by which the previous height will be increased)	I R/S	5280
4.	Enter height, h, in feet where h is the distance of your eyes above ground level	h R/S	Height in feet Distance in miles
	The display continues to show a new height with the associated distance to the horizon		
5.	To stop program, press R/S for a second while a number is in display	R/S	
6.	For a new case, go to step 2		

Data Registers

01	Increment in feet
02	Height in feet
03	Radius of planet or satellite
04	5280 feet
05	Distance to horizon

Where Is Your Horizon?

LOC	CODE	KEY	COMMENTS	LOC	CODE	KEY	COMMENTS
000	42	STO	Store I	027	75	−	
001	01	01		028	43	RCL	
002	03	3		029	03	03	
003	09	9		030	33	X²	
004	05	5		031	95	=	
005	09	9		032	34	√X	
006	42	STO		033	42	STO	Store distance
007	03	03	Initialize	034	05	05	
008	05	5		035	43	RCL	
009	02	2		036	02	02	
010	08	8		037	66	PAU	Display
011	00	0		038	66	PAU	height
012	42	STO		039	66	PAU	
013	04	04		040	66	PAU	
014	91	R/S	Enter h	041	43	RCL	
015	42	STO	Store h	042	05	05	
016	02	02		043	66	PAU	Display
017	76	LBL		044	66	PAU	distance
018	11	A		045	66	PAU	
019	55	÷		046	66	PAU	
020	43	RCL		047	43	RCL	
021	04	04		048	01	01	
022	85	+		049	44	SUM	
023	43	RCL	Calculate	050	02	02	Increment
024	03	03	distance	051	43	RCL	current
025	95	=	in miles	052	02	02	height
026	33	X²		053	11	A	Transfer

CHEMISTRY

Acid/Base Determination

Acids and bases are common substances in chemistry, and they must frequently be identified and quantified. Acids taste sour and turn blue litmus paper red, while bases turn red litmus paper blue. However, it is the quantity of the hydronium ion that identifies the solution as an acid or a base. Water contains 1×10^{-7} mole of H_3O^+ per liter and is neutral. If the H_3O^+ ion concentration is greater than that of pure water, the solution is acidic. Conversely, solutions containing less than 1×10^{-7} mole of H_3O^+ per liter are basic. This system of quantifying acids and bases is accurate but cumbersome, and chemists frequently use an alternative method known as the pH scale.

The pH scale was developed as a relatively simple way to express quantitatively the acidity or alkalinity of a solution. The scale is logarithmic and ranges from 0 to 14. Acidic solutions have a pH less than 7, while basic solutions have a pH greater than 7. A pH of 7 indicates that the solution is neutral. The pH is defined as follows:

$$pH = \log \frac{1}{H_3O^+}$$

If the pH is known, the H_3O^+ can be calculated as follows: H_3O^+ = antilog $(-pH)$.

Within the parameters you select this program will continuously increase or decrease the concentration of H_3O^+ and display the resulting pH. Single pH determinations from a given concentration of H_3O^+ are also possible.

Sample Simulation

The H_3O^+ concentration of a given solution is 1×10^{-7} mole per liter. If this concentration increased in increments of 0.4×10^{-5} mole per liter until a final concentration of 1×10^{-5} mole per liter H_3O^+ was exceeded, what would be the associated pH values for each new solution that had a H_3O^+ concentration of less than 1×10^{-5}?

After entering and initializing the program, store the initial concentration, 1×10^{-7}, in register 00 as follows: 1 EE 7 +/− STO 00. In a similar manner store the final concentration, 1×10^{-5}, in register 02 and the increment, 0.4×10^{-5}, in register 01. Push R/S, and the initial concentration will be briefly displayed followed by the associated pH value. In this case:

H_3O^+	pH
1.00×10^{-7}	7.00
4.10×10^{-6}	5.39
8.10×10^{-6}	5.09

Program Notes

Scientific notation (EE instruction at locations 002, 034, and 044) is necessary so that answers less than 1×10^{-8} can be displayed. The INV EE instructions at locations 012–013 provide for a display of the pH in standard notation.

If the solutions have a decreasing H_3O^+ concentration, it is necessary to enter a negative increment in step 3C2. Setting flag 1 when the increment is negative provides a mechanism for the program to halt at the appropriate time. Single pH values for any H_3O^+ concentration can be determined by setting C_F equal to C_I. The increment can be a nonzero, positive number.

When entering the program be careful to enter 1, not 01, at locations 021 and 022. The keystroke sequence would be: *If flg 1, not *If flg 01.

User Instructions

Step	Procedure	Press	Display
1.	Enter program		
2.	Initialize	RST	
3.	Enter data (use scientific notation)		
	A. Enter initial concentration, C_I, of H_3O^+	C_I STO 00	C_I
	B. Enter final concentration, C_F of H_3O^+	C_F STO 02	C_F
	C. Enter size of increment, S		
	1. If $C_I \leqslant C_F$	S STO 01	S
	2. If $C_I > C_F$	$S +/-$ *Stflg 1	S
4.	Run program	R/S	
	The program will halt and display the final concentration when this concentration has been exceeded.		Concentration of H_3O^+ then associated pH value
5.	For another simulation, return to step 2		

Data Registers
00   Initial and current concentration

01   Increment

02   Final concentration

Acid/Base Determination

LOC	CODE	KEY	COMMENTS	LOC	CODE	KEY	COMMENTS
000	58	FIX		021	87	IFF	Check for
001	02	02	Initialize	022	01	01	negative
002	52	EE		023	12	B	increment
003	43	RCL		024	43	RCL	
004	00	00		025	00	00	
005	66	PAU	Display C_I	026	32	X:T	Compare
006	66	PAU		027	43	RCL	current
007	66	PAU		028	02	02	concentration
008	76	LBL		029	76	LBL	and C_F when
009	11	A		030	70	RAD	C_F is greater
010	35	1/X	Calculate	031	22	INV	than or equal
011	28	LOG	and display	032	77	GE	to C_I
012	22	INV	pH	033	16	A'	
013	52	EE		034	52	EE	
014	66	PAU		035	43	RCL	Display
015	66	PAU		036	00	00	current
016	66	PAU		037	66	PAU	concentration
017	43	RCL		038	66	PAU	
018	01	01	Increment	039	66	PAU	
019	44	SUM	concentration	040	61	GTO	Transfer
020	00	00		041	11	A	

191

LOC	CODE	KEY	COMMENTS		LOC	CODE	KEY	COMMENTS
042	76	LBL			050	43	RCL	
043	16	A'			051	02	02	Compare
044	52	EE	Display C_F		052	32	X:T	current
045	43	RCL			053	43	RCL	concentration
046	02	02			054	00	00	and C_F when C_F
047	91	R/S			055	61	GTO	is less than C_I
048	76	LBL			056	70	RAD	
049	12	B						

General Gas Law   Compressibility is a characteristic property of gases that is summarized quantitatively in Boyle's law, which states that at constant temperature a fixed weight of gas occupies a volume inversely proportional to the pressure exerted on it. Thus, for a given mass of an ideal gas, $P_1 V_1 = P_2 V_2$ at a constant temperature.

Thermal expansion is another characteristic property of gases, summarized by Charles's law, which states that at constant pressure the volume occupied by a fixed weight of an ideal gas is directly proportional to the absolute temperature. Thus,

$$\frac{V_1}{T_1} = \frac{V_2}{T_2}$$

at constant pressure where T_1 and T_2 denote the absolute temperature of the gas.

When gases are mixed they sometimes react with each other as summarized by Gay-Lussac's law of combining volumes, which states that at a given pressure and temperature gases combine in simple proportion by volume, and the volume of any gaseous product bears a whole-number ratio to that of any gaseous reactant. Thus, at constant volume

$$\frac{P_1}{T_1} = \frac{P_2}{T_2}$$

The above laws may be combined:

$$\frac{P_1 \times V_1}{T_1} = \frac{P_2 \times V_2}{T_2}$$

Since the majority of gas calculations are concerned with determining a new volume from an old volume, this program uses the following formula:

$$V_2 = V_1 \times \frac{T_2}{T_1} \times \frac{P_1}{P_2}$$

(Note that these formulas assume "ideal gas behavior.") For example, if 2 grams of an ideal gas occupy 8.4 liters at a temperature of $0°$ C ($273°$ K) and a pressure of 760mm/Hg, what would be its volume at $91°$C and

840mm/Hg? (Answer = 10.13 liters.) This program will allow you to visualize the results of manipulating the variables in various ways.

User Instructions

Step	Procedure	Press	Display
1.	Enter program		
2.	Initialize	RST R/S	5
3.	Enter data:		
	A. Initial temperature in Centigrade degrees	T_1 R/S	T_1
	B. Initial pressure in mm/Hg	P_1 R/S	P_1
	C. Initial volume in liters	V_1 R/S	V_1
	D. Final temperature in Centigrade degrees	T_2 R/S	T_2
	E. Final pressure in mm/Hg	P_2 R/S	Final volume
4.	For a new case, go to step 2		

Data Registers

01	P_2
02	T_2
03	V_1
04	P_1
05	T_1

General Gas Laws

LOC	CODE	KEY	COMMENTS	LOC	CODE	KEY	COMMENTS
000	05	5		021	65	×	Multiply
001	42	STO		022	53	(	
002	00	00		023	43	RCL	
003	76	LBL		024	02	02	P_1
004	11	A		025	55	÷	
005	91	R/S	Store data in	026	43	RCL	P_2
006	72	ST*	R01-R05	027	05	05	
007	00	00		028	54	)	
008	97	DSZ		029	65	×	Multiply
009	00	00		030	53	(	
010	11	A		031	43	RCL	
011	02	2		032	04	04	
012	07	7		033	55	÷	T_2
013	03	3		034	43	RCL	T_1
014	44	SUM		035	01	01	
015	05	05		036	54	)	
016	44	SUM		037	95	=	
017	02	02		038	58	FIX	Set decimal
018	53	(		039	02	02	
019	43	RCL	V_1	040	91	R/S	Halt
020	03	03					

Heat is a concept that surrounds us in our everyday life, although too frequently it is not clearly understood. A common misconception relates to the direction of heat flow. For example, when an ice cube is placed in a glass of warm water, the ice cube does not give off cold; rather, it extracts heat from the water. In other words, heat flows from areas of high temperature to areas of low temperature.

The use of temperature as a measure of heat is another familiar concept. Temperature can be determined by three scales; however, the Fahrenheit (F) scale is the one with which most people in the United States are familiar. On this scale water boils at 212° and freezes at 32°. During the winter season it is not uncommon to experience temperatures below 0° on this scale. The fact that substances have a finite amount of heat to lose suggests that there must be a lower limit to all three scales. This limit on the Fahrenheit scale occurs at −459.7°, absolute zero.

A second scale measures temperature in degrees Centigrade (C). This scale is generally used by scientists and most of the non-English-speaking countries of the world. On this scale water boils at 100° and freezes at 0°. Zero degrees Centigrade does not indicate the absence of heat, as absolute zero on this scale occurs at −273.16°. The size of the Centigrade degree is nine-fifths the size of the Fahrenheit degree.

The third scale is called the Kelvin (K), or absolute, scale. This scale was developed by Sir William Thomson, a physicist better known by his title, Lord Kelvin. The size of the Kelvin degree is the same as the size of the Centigrade degree; however, the Kelvin scale begins at absolute zero. Hence, on this scale water freezes at 273.16° and boils at 373.16°.

It is sometimes necessary to convert temperature from one scale to another, and although any given thermometer could be labeled with all three scales, this is generally not done. Mathematical formulas are used to make the conversions.

This program uses mathematical formulas to simulate a rising or falling temperature in increments of your choice on any of the three scales, with output given in either of the other two scales. Conversion of single temperatures is also possible.

Sample Simulation

A thermometer that is calibrated in degrees Centigrade is placed in a solar collector as part of a data-gathering experiment. A time graph in degrees Fahrenheit is to be constructed, and this program is to be used to convert the temperature from degrees Centigrade to degrees Fahrenheit. Further, the conversions are to be made for every 0.5 degree of Centigrade temperature beginning at 15° C and ending at 78° C.

After the program has been entered in the calculator, enter the data as indicated in the user instructions. In this case the initial temperature is 15, the size of the increment is 0.5, and the final temperature is 78. Since our original temperature is in degrees Centigrade and we want this converted to degrees Fahrenheit, we will select part B of step 6 and press *St flg 1. Next press the R/S key to begin program operation. The output will pause with 15.0° C on display and then pause again showing the converted temperature of 59.0° F. This process continues until the final temperature listed in step 5 of the user instructions is achieved.

Program Notes

How long the output is displayed is determined by the number of consecutive pause statements in the program. Hence, inserting additional pause statements may make the program easier to use. If you want to stop the program to hold the output in display, press the R/S key for approximately half a second while the output is on display. To begin the program press R/S again.

If you want to use this program to convert a single temperature to another scale, set the final temperature (step 5 of user instructions) equal to the initial temperature (step 3 of user instructions). The size of the increment is not relevant and can be ignored. (No entry is necessary in step 4.)

The program utilizes the following formulas to make the temperature conversions:

$$°F = (°K - 273.16 + 40) \times 9/5 - 40$$
$$°F = (°C + 40) \times 9/5 - 40$$
$$°C = (°F + 40) \times 5/9 - 40$$
$$°C = °K - 273.16$$
$$°K = (°F - 32) \times 5/9 + 273.16$$
$$°K = °C + 273.16$$

User Instructions

Step	Procedure	Press	Display
1.	Enter the program and return to run mode		
2.	Initialize	RST	
3.	Enter initial temperature, T_I	T_I STO 00	T_I
4.	Enter size of temperature increment, i. (The temperature scale used here and in step 5 must match the scale used in step 3. Further, this increment must be negative if T_F is lower than T_I).	i STO 01	i
5.	Enter the final temperature, T_F	T_F STO 00	T_F
6.	Select *one* of the following input/output options		

Input	Output	Press	
A. °K to °F		*St flg 1	
B. °C to °F		*St flg 2	
C. °F to °C		*St flg 3	
D. °K to °C		*St flg 4	
E. °F to °K		*St flg 5	
F. °C to °K		*St flg 6	

7.   Run program   R/S   Temperature in input
                                                            degrees (briefly)
                                                            Temperature in output
                                                            degrees (briefly)

Note: The program will pause to display the original input temperature and then pause again to display that temperature in the scale selected as output. The increment is added to the original temperature and the process repeats until the input temperature reaches or exceeds the final temperature as selected in step 5.

8.   For a new case, go to step 2

Data Registers
00   Initial temperature, T_I
01   Temperature increment, i
02   Final temperature, T_F

Temperature Scales

LOC	CODE	KEY	COMMENTS	LOC	CODE	KEY	COMMENTS
000	58	FIX		033	16	A'	
001	01	01		034	76	LBL	
002	93	.	Initialize	035	30	TAN	Increment
003	00	0		036	43	RCL	current
004	00	0		037	01	01	temperature
005	00	0		038	44	SUM	
006	01	1		039	00	00	
007	44	SUM		040	43	RCL	
008	02	02		041	02	02	Compare T_F
009	43	RCL		042	32	X:T	with current
010	00	00	Display T_I	043	43	RCL	temperature
011	66	PAU		044	00	00	when T_F is
012	66	PAU		045	87	IFF	greater than
013	66	PAU		046	07	07	T_I
014	76	LBL		047	18	C'	
015	89	'		048	76	LBL	
016	87	IFF		049	60	DEG	
017	01	01		050	77	GE	
018	11	A		051	17	B'	Display
019	87	IFF		052	66	PAU	current
020	02	02		053	66	PAU	temperature
021	12	B	Select proper	054	66	PAU	
022	87	IFF	conversion	055	61	GTO	
023	03	03		056	89	'	Transfer
024	13	C		057	76	LBL	
025	87	IFF		058	11	A	
026	04	04		059	75	-	
027	14	D		060	02	2	
028	87	IFF		061	07	7	
029	05	05		062	03	3	
030	15	E		063	93	.	
031	87	IFF		064	01	1	
196 032	06	06		065	06	6	

LOC	CODE	KEY	COMMENTS
066	85	+	Convert degrees
067	04	4	Kelvin to
068	00	0	degrees
069	95	=	Fahrenheit, and
070	65	×	display
071	09	9	Fahrenheit
072	55	÷	
073	05	5	
074	75	-	
075	04	4	
076	00	0	
077	95	=	
078	66	PAU	
079	66	PAU	
080	66	PAU	
081	61	GTO	Transfer
082	30	TAN	
083	76	LBL	
084	12	B	
085	85	+	
086	04	4	Convert degrees
087	00	0	Centigrade to
088	95	=	degrees
089	65	×	Fahrenheit, and
090	09	9	display
091	55	÷	Fahrenheit
092	05	5	
093	75	-	
094	04	4	
095	00	0	
096	95	=	
097	66	PAU	
098	66	PAU	
099	66	PAU	
100	61	GTO	Transfer
101	30	TAN	
102	76	LBL	
103	13	C	
104	85	+	
105	04	4	Convert degrees
106	00	0	Fahrenheit to
107	95	=	degrees
108	65	×	Centigrade, and
109	05	5	display
110	55	÷	Centigrade
111	09	9	
112	75	-	
113	04	4	
114	00	0	
115	95	=	
116	66	PAU	
117	66	PAU	
118	66	PAU	
119	61	GTO	Transfer
120	30	TAN	
121	76	LBL	

LOC	CODE	KEY	COMMENTS
122	14	D	
123	75	-	
124	02	2	Convert degrees
125	07	7	Kelvin to
126	03	3	degrees
127	93	.	Centigrade, and
128	01	1	display
129	06	6	Centigrade
130	95	=	
131	66	PAU	
132	66	PAU	
133	66	PAU	
134	61	GTO	Transfer
135	30	TAN	
136	76	LBL	
137	15	E	
138	75	-	Convert degrees
139	03	3	Fahrenheit to
140	02	2	degrees Kelvin,
141	95	=	and display
142	65	×	Kelvin
143	05	5	
144	55	÷	
145	09	9	
146	85	+	
147	02	2	
148	07	7	
149	03	3	
150	93	.	
151	01	1	
152	06	6	
153	95	=	
154	66	PAU	
155	66	PAU	
156	66	PAU	
157	61	GTO	Transfer
158	30	TAN	
159	76	LBL	
160	16	A'	
161	85	+	
162	02	2	Convert degrees
163	07	7	Centigrade to
164	03	3	degrees Kelvin,
165	93	.	and display
166	01	1	Kelvin
167	06	6	
168	95	=	
169	66	PAU	
170	66	PAU	
171	66	PAU	
172	61	GTO	Transfer
173	30	TAN	
174	76	LBL	
175	17	B'	
176	75	-	Display T_F
177	43	RCL	

LOC	CODE	KEY	COMMENTS	LOC	CODE	KEY	COMMENTS
178	01	01		190	02	02	
179	95	=		191	43	RCL	
180	91	R/S		192	00	00	
181	76	LBL		193	22	INV	
182	18	C'		194	77	GE	
183	93	.		195	17	B'	
184	00	0	Compare T_F with	196	66	PAU	
185	00	0	current	197	66	PAU	
186	00	0	temperature	198	66	PAU	
187	02	2	when T_F is less	199	61	GTO	Transfer
188	22	INV	than T_I	200	89	π	
189	44	SUM					

AUTOMOBILE

Automobile Miles per Gallon

In 1974 the personal passenger car accounted for approximately 77% of the total vehicle-miles traveled in America. This represents approximately 7.42×10^{10} gallons of gasoline in a single year! The opportunities for conservation are numerous. In addition to changes in personal driving habits, the automobile itself can be improved to become a much more efficient machine.

Most of the energy in a gallon of gasoline never reaches the drive wheels of your car. A typical gasoline internal combustion engine is, at best, 26% efficient. This means that 74% of the energy in a gallon of gasoline is wasted as engine heat and friction. Additional energy is lost through the transmission, power accessories, idling, braking, rolling resistance, air resistance, and so on.

The effect of each of these variables on the mileage of your car can be simulated with this program, and although there has been some oversimplification and generalization, the program will provide interesting insights into the use of energy by a "typical" car.

The underlying assumptions and formulas for this simulation are given below; however, you may want to skip them and go directly to the operation of the program. Table 3-4 (page 200) will assist you in determining an approximate drag coefficient.

Assumptions and Formulas

1. $$F_d = \frac{C_d \, A_f V^2}{370}$$

   F_d = force of drag in pounds

   C_d = drag coefficient

   A_f = projected frontal area of the car in square feet

   V = speed in miles per hour

   370 compensates for the mixed units

198

2. $F_r = \dfrac{M}{1000} [12 + 0.05 V + 0.004 (V - 40)^2]$ when $V \geqslant 40$ miles per hour

   F_r = rolling force in pounds

   M = mass of car in pounds

   V = speed in miles per hour

3. $F_r = \dfrac{M}{1000} [12 + 0.05 V]$ when $V < 40$ miles per hour

   F_r = rolling force in pounds

   M = mass of car in pounds

   V = speed in miles per hour

4. Engine efficiency is 26% under ideal conditions without accessories; 19% on average.

5. There are 97,155,708 foot-pounds of energy in one gallon of gasoline.

6. An automatic transmission is 75% efficient in urban driving and 90% efficient in highway driving.

7. A manual transmission is 95% efficient overall.

8. Air conditioners account for a loss of approximately 7% of fuel.

9. Open windows at speeds greater than 50 miles per hour account for a loss of approximately 8% of your fuel.

10. Idling accounts for a loss of 7.5% of the fuel.

11. Radial tires at maximum pressure will increase mileage by 7%.

12. The C_d of a "typical car" is 0.5.

13. The projected area of an average car is 22 square feet.

14. Power accessories (not including air conditioning) account for about 4% of the fuel loss.

15. At speeds significantly less than 40 miles per hour, the resulting miles per gallon will be artificially inflated.

16. An "average" small car will weigh approximately 1900–2500 pounds, an "average" medium-sized car will weigh approximately 2700–3300 pounds, while a large car will weigh approximately 3500–4000 pounds.

Note that considerable variation is possible in each of these assumptions. In addition, other factors influence the mileage of a car, such as individual driving habits, gear ratios, tire tread, road conditions, temperature, and time since last engine tune-up. These variables are not considered in this simulation so the input data is not excessively long.

Sample Simulation

Assume that you have a 1980 Citation with the following "options": air conditioning, radial tires with maximum inflation, manual transmission, power steering, power brakes, and a radio. If you took a trip with no

TABLE 3-4   Coefficient of Drag
for Selected Vehicles

Vehicle	C_d
Ordinary truck	0.72
Late 1920s car	0.71
1972 Dodge wagon	0.61
Late 1930s car	0.58
Streamlined truck	0.55
Late 1940s car	0.53
Late 1950s car	0.50
1972 Camaro	0.49
"Typical modern car"	0.48
Jaguar XK-E	0.40
Porsche	0.35
Citroen	0.33
Lower limit for a car	0.30

passengers and drove 90% of the time on interstates at 55 miles per hour with your windows closed and air conditioning turned on, what would your savings be, compared to the identical trip with three additional passengers whose combined weight equaled 550 pounds? (Driver weighs 190 pounds). The procedure numbers correspond to the step numbers in the user instructions.

Step	Procedure	Press	Display
1.	Enter program and initialize	1000 STO 17 A	0
2.	Enter data:		
	A. Gross weight of car and driver	2810 R/S	2810.00
	B. Percent stop/go	.1 R/S	0.10
	C. Average highway speed	55 R/S	55.00
	D. Air conditioning on	1 R/S	1.00
	E. Radial tires	1 R/S	1.00
	F. Power accessories	1 R/S	1.00
	G. Manual transmission	0 R/S	0.00
	H. Coefficient of drag	.5 R/S	0.50
	I. Area	22 R/S	22.00
	J. Windows closed	0 R/S	24.02
	(24 miles per gallon is the estimated answer)		
3.	Reinitialize for the next case with passengers	A	0
2.	Enter new data		
	A. Gross weight of car and people (2620 + 190 + 550)	3360 R/S	3360.00
	B. Percent stop/go	.1 R/S	0.10
200	C. Average highway speed	55 R/S	55.00

D. Air conditioning on	1 R/S	1.00
E. Radial tires	1 R/S	1.00
F. Power accessories (brakes,		
steering, and others)	1 R/S	1.00
G. Manual transmission	0 R/S	0.00
H. Coefficient of drag	.5 R/S	0.50
I. Area	22 R/S	22.00
J. Windows closed	0 R/S	22.62 miles per gallon

In this simulation the three additional people "cost" approximately 1.4 miles per gallon. Thousands of similar comparisons can be made using this program; however, be cautioned that exact prediction of miles per gallon for a specific case (or car) is *not* the intended use of this program. It should be used to study the overall effects of one or more of the variables that influence gasoline mileage.

User Instructions

Step	Procedure	Press	Display
1.	Key in the program and initialize	1000 17 A	0
2.	Enter data as follows:		
	A. Weight of car and passengers (in pounds), W	W R/S	W
	B. Percent stop/go driving (as decimal), D	D R/S	Percent
	C. Average highway speed (in miles per hour), S	S R/S	S
	D. Air conditioning on? Yes = 1, No = 0	1 *or* 0 R/S	1 or 0
	E. Radial tires at maximum pressure? Yes = 0 No = 1	0 *or* 1 R/S	0 or 1
	F. Power accessories other than air? Yes = 1 No = 0	1 *or* 0 R/S	1 or 0
	G. Automatic transmission? Yes = 1 No = 0	1 *or* 0 R/S	1 or 0
	H. Coefficient of drag, C_d. If unknown, use 0.5	C_d R/S	C_d
	I. Frontal area of car (in square feet), A. If unknown, use 22	A R/S	A
	J. Most or all windows open? Yes = 1 No = 0	1 *or* 0 R/S	Miles per gallon
3.	For a new case, reinitialize and go to step 2	A	

Data Registers			
01	W	09	A_f
02	Percent stop/go driving	10	F_d
03	S	11	F_r
04	Air conditioning	12	Available foot-pounds per gallon
05	Radial tires	13	Open windows
06	Power accessories	14	Used
07	Transmission	15	Used
08	C_d	16	Foot-pounds per gallon
		17	1000

Automobile Miles per Gallon

LOC	CODE	KEY	COMMENTS	LOC	CODE	KEY	COMMENTS
000	43	RCL		050	76	LBL	
001	04	04		051	35	1/X	
002	32	X:T	Check for "air"	052	43	RCL	
003	01	1		053	02	02	
004	67	EQ		054	65	×	Reduce energy
005	23	LNX		055	43	RCL	from idle
006	76	LBL		056	16	16	
007	22	INV		057	65	×	
008	43	RCL	Check for	058	93	.	
009	05	05	radial tires	059	00	0	
010	32	X:T		060	07	7	
011	01	1		061	05	5	
012	67	EQ		062	95	=	
013	24	CE		063	22	INV	
014	76	LBL		064	44	SUM	
015	25	CLR		065	12	12	
016	43	RCL	Check for	066	43	RCL	
017	06	06	automatic	067	03	03	
018	32	X:T	transmission	068	32	X:T	
019	01	1		069	05	5	
020	67	EQ		070	00	0	
021	32	X:T		071	22	INV	
022	76	LBL		072	77	GE	
023	33	X²		073	42	STO	
024	43	RCL		074	61	GTO	
025	07	07		075	12	B	Reduce energy
026	32	X:T		076	76	LBL	from open
027	01	1		077	42	STO	windows when
028	67	EQ	Reduce energy	078	43	RCL	speed is
029	34	√X	from manual	079	13	13	greater than
030	43	RCL	transmission	080	32	X:T	or equal to
031	16	16		081	00	0	50 miles per
032	65	×	(urban and	082	67	EQ	hour
033	93	.	highway)	083	12	B	
034	09	9		084	43	RCL	
035	05	5		085	12	12	
036	95	=		086	65	×	
037	42	STO		087	93	.	
038	15	15		088	00	0	
039	43	RCL		089	08	8	
040	16	16		090	95	=	
041	22	INV		091	22	INV	
042	44	SUM		092	44	SUM	
043	15	15		093	12	12	
044	43	RCL		094	61	GTO	
045	15	15		095	12	B	Transfer
046	50	I×I		096	76	LBL	
047	22	INV		097	23	LNX	
048	44	SUM		098	43	RCL	
049	12	12		099	16	16	

202

LOC	CODE	KEY	COMMENTS
100	65	×	
101	93	.	Reduce energy
102	00	0	from air
103	07	7	conditioning
104	95	=	
105	22	INV	
106	44	SUM	
107	12	12	
108	61	GTO	
109	22	INV	Transfer
110	76	LBL	
111	24	CE	
112	43	RCL	Add energy
113	16	16	savings
114	65	×	from radial
115	93	.	tires
116	00	0	
117	07	7	
118	95	=	
119	44	SUM	
120	12	12	
121	61	GTO	Transfer
122	25	CLR	
123	76	LBL	
124	32	X:T	
125	43	RCL	
126	16	16	Reduce energy
127	65	×	from power
128	93	.	accessories
129	00	0	
130	04	4	
131	95	=	
132	22	INV	
133	44	SUM	
134	12	12	
135	61	GTO	Transfer
136	33	X²	
137	76	LBL	
138	34	ГX	
139	43	RCL	Reduce energy
140	12	12	available
141	65	×	from
142	43	RCL	automatic
143	02	02	transmission
144	95	=	in urban
145	22	INV	areas
146	44	SUM	
147	12	12	
148	65	×	
149	93	.	

LOC	CODE	KEY	COMMENTS
150	07	7	
151	05	5	
152	95	=	
153	44	SUM	
154	12	12	
155	43	RCL	
156	12	12	
157	65	×	
158	53	(	
159	01	1	
160	75	−	Reduce energy
161	43	RCL	available from
162	02	02	automatic
163	54	)	transmission
164	95	=	in highway
165	22	INV	driving
166	44	SUM	
167	12	12	
168	65	×	
169	93	.	
170	09	9	
171	95	=	
172	44	SUM	
173	12	12	
174	61	GTO	Transfer
175	35	1/X	
176	76	LBL	
177	52	EE	
178	43	RCL	
179	10	10	
180	44	SUM	
181	11	11	
182	43	RCL	Calculate miles
183	11	11	per gallon and
184	22	INV	display
185	49	PRD	
186	12	12	
187	43	RCL	
188	12	12	
189	55	÷	
190	05	5	
191	02	2	
192	08	8	
193	00	0	
194	58	FIX	
195	02	02	
196	95	=	
197	91	R/S	
198	61	GTO	Transfer
199	65	×	

LOC	CODE	KEY	COMMENTS
200	76	LBL	
201	12	B	
202	43	RCL	
203	08	08	
204	65	×	Calculate
205	43	RCL	force of
206	09	09	drag, F_d
207	65	×	
208	43	RCL	
209	03	03	
210	33	X²	
211	55	÷	
212	03	3	
213	07	7	
214	00	0	
215	95	=	
216	42	STO	
217	10	10	
218	43	RCL	
219	03	03	Check
220	32	X¦T	highway
221	04	4	speed
222	00	0	
223	77	GE	
224	44	SUM	
225	43	RCL	
226	01	01	
227	55	÷	
228	43	RCL	
229	17	17	
230	65	×	Calculate
231	53	(	force of
232	01	1	rolling
233	02	2	resistance
234	85	+	when speed
235	53	(	is less
236	93	.	than 40
237	00	0	miles per
238	05	5	hour
239	65	×	
240	43	RCL	
241	03	03	
242	54	)	
243	54	)	
244	95	=	
245	42	STO	
246	11	11	
247	61	GTO	Transfer
248	52	EE	
249	76	LBL	

LOC	CODE	KEY	COMMENTS
250	44	SUM	
251	43	RCL	
252	01	01	
253	55	÷	
254	43	RCL	
255	17	17	
256	65	×	
257	53	(	
258	01	1	
259	02	2	
260	85	+	
261	53	(	
262	93	.	Calculate
263	00	0	force of
264	05	5	rolling
265	65	×	resistance
266	43	RCL	when speed
267	03	03	is greater
268	54	)	than 40
269	85	+	miles per
270	53	(	hour
271	93	.	
272	00	0	
273	00	0	
274	04	4	
275	65	×	
276	53	(	
277	43	RCL	
278	03	03	
279	75	-	
280	04	4	
281	00	0	
282	54	)	
283	33	X²	
284	54	)	
285	54	)	
286	95	=	
287	42	STO	
288	11	11	
289	61	GTO	
290	52	EE	Transfer
291	76	LBL	
292	11	A	
293	01	1	
294	08	8	
295	04	4	
296	05	5	Initialize
297	09	9	
298	05	5	
299	08	8	

LOC	CODE	KEY	COMMENTS		LOC	CODE	KEY	COMMENTS
300	04	4			319	42	STO	Enter tires
301	42	STO			320	05	05	
302	16	16			321	91	R/S	Enter accessories
303	42	STO			322	42	STO	
304	12	12			323	06	06	
305	25	CLR			324	91	R/S	Enter transmission
306	91	R/S	Enter weight		325	42	STO	
307	42	STO			326	07	07	
308	01	01			327	91	R/S	
309	91	R/S	Enter percent stop/go		328	42	STO	Enter C_d
310	42	STO			329	08	08	
311	02	02			330	91	R/S	Enter area
312	91	R/S	Enter speed		331	42	STO	
313	42	STO			332	09	09	
314	03	03			333	91	R/S	Enter windows
315	91	R/S	Enter "air"		334	42	STO	
316	42	STO			335	13	13	
317	04	04			336	81	RST	Reset
318	91	R/S						

Improved Gas Mileage   If you improve gas mileage from 10 miles per gallon to 15 miles per gallon, would your annual savings in fuel cost be the same as if you improved gas mileage from 15 miles per gallon to 20 miles per gallon?[6]

Solution
Let y be dollars saved with gasoline costing $1.20 per gallon and 10,000 miles being driven per year.

Gas mileage is improved from x miles per gallon to $(x + 5)$ miles per gallon.

$$y_1 = \frac{10,000(1.20)}{x} - \frac{10,000(1.20)}{x + 5}$$

$$= 10,000(1.20)(\frac{1}{x} - \frac{1}{x + 5})$$

$$= 10,000(1.20)(\frac{5}{x(x + 5)})$$

$$= 50,000(1.20)(\frac{1}{x(x + 5)})$$

To solve this problem, write a program to obtain a table of values from $x = 5$ to $x = 50$ in intervals of five units.

[6] Floyd Vest, "Secondary School Mathematics from the EPA Gas Mileage Guide," *Mathematics Teacher,* 72, no. 1 (January 1979), 10–11, by permission of the publisher.

Step	Procedure	Press	Display
1.	Enter program		
2.	Initialize	*CMs *Fix 3 RST	
3.	Run program	R/S	x
			y

Data Registers
01   x

Output

If gasoline costs $1.20 per gallon and you drive 10,000 miles per year, Table 3-5 summarizes the savings when gasoline mileage is improved from 5 miles per gallon to 50 miles per gallon.

Improved Gas Mileage

LOC	CODE	KEY	COMMENTS	LOC	CODE	KEY	COMMENTS
000	05	5		027	00	0	
001	42	STO		028	00	0	
002	01	01	Initialize	029	00	0	
003	05	5		030	00	0	
004	00	0		031	65	×	
005	32	X¦T		032	01	1	
006	76	LBL		033	93	.	
007	11	A		034	02	2	
008	43	RCL	Begin loop	035	95	=	
009	01	01	and	036	66	PAU	
010	66	PAU	display x	037	66	PAU	
011	66	PAU		038	66	PAU	
012	66	PAU		039	66	PAU	
013	53	(		040	43	RCL	Compare x
014	43	RCL		041	01	01	to 50
015	01	01		042	77	GE	
016	65	×		043	12	B	Transfer
017	53	(		044	85	+	
018	43	RCL		045	05	5	Add 5 to x
019	01	01		046	95	=	and loop back
020	85	+		047	42	STO	
021	05	5		048	01	01	
022	54	)		049	61	GTO	
023	54	)	Calculate	050	11	A	
024	35	1/X	and display	051	76	LBL	
025	65	×	savings	052	12	B	Halt
026	05	5		053	91	R/S	

TABLE 3-5   Savings as a
Function of Miles per Gallon

x(mpg)	y(savings)
5	1200
10	400
15	200
20	120
25	80
30	57.143
35	42.857
40	33.333
45	26.667
50	21.818

Impact of Price Increase

What is the effect of an increase in gasoline prices? If the price of gasoline increases 20%, what happens to the savings function?

How does the fuel cost per 10,000 miles increase as the price of gasoline increases (1) 10¢ a gallon, (2) 20¢ a gallon, (3) 50¢ a gallon for gasoline costing x dollars per gallon and a car getting z mpg? Does such an increase create the same increase in annual fuel costs at all ranges of fuel cost per gallon?[7]

Solution
Let: z = the cost per gallon of gasoline in dollars with

a. $z + 0.10 = 10$¢ greater
b. $z + 0.20 = 20$¢ greater
c. $z + 0.50 = 50$¢ greater

x = gasoline mileage in miles per gallon
y_1 = change in fuel cost from an increase of 10¢ for 10,000 miles of driving
y_2 = change in fuel cost from an increase of 20¢ for 10,000 miles of driving
y_3 = change in fuel cost from an increase of 50¢ for 10,000 miles of driving

$$y_1 = \frac{10,000(z + 0.10)}{x} - \frac{10,000z}{x} = \frac{1000}{x}$$

$$y_2 = \frac{10,000(z + 0.20)}{x} - \frac{10,000z}{x} = \frac{2000}{x}$$

$$y_3 = \frac{10,000(z + 0.50)}{x} - \frac{10,000z}{x} = \frac{5000}{x}$$

To solve this problem, write a program to obtain a table of values from $x = 5$ to $x = 50$ in intervals of five units.

[7] Vest, "Secondary School Mathematics from the EPA Gas Mileage Guide," p. 12, by permission of the publisher.

Step	Procedure	Press	Display
1.	Enter program		
2.	Initialize	*CMs *Fix 2 RST	
3.	Enter numerator of y_1, y_2, or y_3.	n	
4.	Run program	R/S	x
			yi

Data Registers
01   numerator
02   x

Output

As you simulate an increase in miles per gallon, the effects of the price increases can be seen in Table 3-6.

TABLE 3-6   Changes in Fuel Costs Resulting from Gasoline Price Increases (at 10,000 miles of Driving)

	Increase of 10¢	Increase of 20¢	Increase of 50¢
x(mpg)	y_1	y_2	y_3
5	$200.00	$400.00	$1000.00
10	100.00	200.00	500.00
15	66.67	133.33	333.33
20	50.00	100.00	250.00
25	40.00	80.00	200.00
30	33.33	66.67	166.67
35	28.57	57.14	142.88
40	25.00	50.00	125.00
45	22.22	44.44	111.11
50	20.00	40.00	100.00

Impact of Price Increase

LOC	CODE	KEY	COMMENTS	LOC	CODE	KEY	COMMENTS
000	42	STO		011	02	02	Display x
001	01	01		012	66	PAU	
002	05	5		013	66	PAU	
003	42	STO	Initialize	014	66	PAU	
004	02	02		015	35	1/X	
005	05	5		016	65	×	
006	00	0		017	43	RCL	Calculate y
007	32	X:T		018	01	01	
008	76	LBL		019	95	=	
009	11	A		020	66	PAU	
010	43	RCL		021	66	PAU	Display y

```
LOC  CODE  KEY      COMMENTS
022   66   PAU
023   66   PAU     _____
024   43   RCL
025   02    02
026   77   GE
027   12    B      Check for end
028   85    +      of program
029   05    5
030   95    =
031   42   STO
032   02    02
033   61   GTO
034   11    A      _____
035   76   LBL
036   12    B      Halt
037   91   R/S
```

GENERAL

Home Heat Simulations

In the northern states it is not uncommon for 50% of the energy used in a typical residence to go for space heating. Nationwide, approximately 38% of all the energy consumed is used for home heating. Within a given region there is considerable variation among the energy use of individual homes. This is caused, in part, by a number of variables related to home heating efficiency, including such things as the amount and type of insulation in the structure, the difference between the inside and outside temperatures, the size and shape of the building, and the type of heating system.

Once a building is constructed and actual fuel consumption has occurred calculating its energy efficiency is a relatively straightforward procedure. It is not so easy, however, to manipulate the variables controlling the efficiency of the building, unless you do so before construction through simulations and models. This program, although it oversimplifies, will provide realistic simulation of many variables relating to home heating efficiency. By using one set of data and changing one variable at a time, it will be easy to compare energy utilization and related costs among the different simulations.

Sample Simulation
(Step numbers correspond to user instruction steps.)

Since there are so many different input variables required for this program, you should make a data sheet similar to the sample below.

2. Degree-days per year = 5800
3. Average thermostat setting = 68° F
4A. Area of single-pane windows = 73 square feet
4B. Area of double-pane windows = 89 square feet

209

4C. Area of thermopane windows = 0 square feet

5A. Area of nonglass doors without storm doors = 0 square feet

5B. Area of nonglass doors with storm doors = 65 square feet

6A. Area of exterior walls, excluding windows, doors, and basement = 2155 square feet

6B. Insulation R value of the walls = Rw = $R11$

7A. Area of the ceiling = 928 square feet

7B. Insulation R value of the ceiling = R_c = $R22$

11A. Exterior wall area of insulated, heated basement not applicable for this sample

11B. Insulation R value of basement walls not applicable for this sample

13A. Perimeter of concrete slab not applicable for this sample

13B. Insulation factor of slab not applicable for this sample

14A. Basement wall area above grade for heated basements that are not insulated not applicable for this sample

14B. Basement wall area below grade for heated basements that are not insulated not applicable for this sample

15B. Area of floor over unheated basements and foundations = 800 square feet = 0.5

16A. Total floor area of heated portion of the building = 1600 square feet

16B. Height of the ceilings = 8.5 feet

17. Air exchange factor = 1.5

18. Type of heating fuel and cost per specified unit = gas at $3.95 per 1000 cubic feet

19. BTU per unit of fuel = 650,000

Once the appropriate data have been collected, they can be entered into the calculator as indicated by the user instructions.

In this case we have a house with an unheated basement. We also rated it as having a tight basement in step 15B. In step 17 we indicated that the house had average caulking. Combining this information with that on the data sheet the program calculated an annual Btu consumption of 86,482,878. The cost of this energy was calculated to be $525.55.

If the house had better caulking and tighter storm windows, the energy consumption would be reduced by 22%. Of course, not all variables will have such a large impact on the total energy budget.

Program Notes

Since the program incorporates the degree-day concept, houses from all climatic zones can be examined. If you do not know the number of degree-days in your average year, your local utility should be able to provide you with this information.

The temperature difference between the inside and the outside will affect the rate at which a building will lose heat. Steps 000–028 of this program account for this change by adjusting the stated number of degree-days to the average indoor thermostat setting. Since this is a simplified approach to the problem, it limits the accuracy of the program. The closer the thermostat setting is to 72°F, the more accurate the calculations will be. The program is designed for inside temperatures between 60° and 84°F. It also requires that the unit of measurement for all areas be square feet.

User Instructions

Step	Procedure	Press	Display
1.	A. Key in program, return to run mode		
	B. Initialize	RST *CMs	
2.	Enter average number of degree-days, DD, for your region	DD STO 11	DD
3.	Enter average thermostat setting, T	T R/S	
4.	Glass doors and windows (in square feet):		
	A. Enter area, A_1, of single-pane windows and doors	A_1 R/S	Btu loss
	B. Enter area, A_2, of double-pane windows and doors	A_2 R/S	Btu loss
	C. Enter area, A_3, of thermopane windows and doors	A_3 R/S	Btu loss
5.	Nonglass doors (in square feet):		
	A. Enter area, A_4, of nonglass doors without storm doors	A_4 R/S	Btu loss
	B. Enter area, A_5, of nonglass doors with storm doors	A_5 R/S	Btu loss
6.	Exterior walls excluding doors, windows, and basement (in square feet):		
	A. Enter area, A_6, of exterior walls	A_6 R/S	A_6
	B. Enter R value of wall insulation, R_w	R_w R/S	Btu loss
7.	Ceiling (in square feet):		
	A. Enter area, A_7, of ceilings under unheated attic and/or roof	A_7 R/S	A_7
	B. Enter R value of ceiling insulation, R_c	R_c R/S	Btu loss
8.	If no basement, press: and skip to step 12. Otherwise, continue to step 9	GTO *D'	
9.	If basement is not heated, press: and skip to step 15B. Otherwise, continue to step 10	GTO *Rad	
10.	If heated basement is not insulated, press: and skip to step 14A	*C'	

11. Basement walls (in square feet):

    A. If heated basement is insulated (or partially insulated), enter exterior wall area, A_8 A_8 R/S A_8

    B. Enter R value for the basement walls, R_b R_b R/S   Btu loss

    C. Skip to step 15

12. If house is *not* on a concrete slab, press: GTO *Rad

    and skip to step 15B. Otherwise, continue to step 13

13. A. If concrete slab, enter perimeter of the slab, P_s, in linear feet P_s R/S P_s

    B. If slab is insulated, enter: 3 R/S   Btu loss

    Or, if slab not insulated, enter: 1.3 R/S   Btu loss

    C. Press: GTO *Rad

    and skip to step 15B

14. A. If basement is *not* fully insulated, enter wall area, A_9, that is above grade (If zero, be *sure* to enter 0) A_9 R/S CLR   Btu loss

    B. Enter area, A_{10}, of the walls that are below grade A_{10} R/S   Btu loss

15. Floor:

    A. If heated basement is under most or all of the heated portion of the house, press: GTO *Deg

    and skip to step 16

    Otherwise:

    B. Enter area, A_{11}, of the floor over unheated basement, crawl space, or foundation. A_{11} R/S A_{11}

    Select *one* of the following:

    (1) If a slab, tight crawl space, or tight basement enter 0.5   0.5 or

    (2) If a skirted crawl space, or rock-wall basement, enter 0.8   0.8 or

    (3) If an open crawl space, enter 1   1 R/S   Btu loss

16. Infiltration:

    A. Enter total floor area, A_{12} (in square feet) of the heated portion of the house A_{12} R/S A_{12}

    B. Enter the height of the ceilings, H H R/S   Adjusted *DD*

17. Air exchanges: (Select one)

    A. If windows and doors are well caulked and the house is generally tight, enter 0.8   0.8 or

    B. If caulking and house are average, enter 1.5   1.5 or

    C. If caulking is poor or absent, enter 2.5   2.5 R/S   Btu loss

18. Cost of fuel:

    Use the following units list and enter the cost of fuel (in dollars) *per unit*   Cost R/S   Cost

212

Units List:
Natural gas/1000 cubic feet
Coal/ton
Oil/gallon
Electricity/kwh

19. Select and enter appropriate net Btu/unit of fuel:
     A. If natural gas heat, enter 650,000 Btu
     B. If coal heat, enter 13,000,000 Btu
     C. If oil heat, enter 100,000 Btu
     D. If electric resistance heat, enter 3414 Btu   Btu R/S   Btu loss, total

20. Output:
     A. To see the estimated annual heating cost   RCL 14 *fix 2   Cost, total
     B. To see the total Btu loss per heating
        season   RCL 00   Btu loss, total

21. For another simulation, press: *CMs RST
     and return to step 2

Data Registers
00   Btu loss
01   Used
02   Degree-days
03   Used
04   Total costs

Home Heat Simulations

LOC	CODE	KEY	COMMENTS	LOC	CODE	KEY	COMMENTS
000	75	–		020	44	SUM	
001	07	7		021	11	11	
002	02	2		022	76	LBL	
003	95	=		023	90	LST	
004	65	×		024	32	X!T	
005	05	5		025	50	I×I	
006	55	÷		026	22	INV	
007	01	1		027	44	SUM	
008	00	0		028	11	11	
009	00	0		029	61	GTO	Transfer
010	65	×		030	80	GRD	
011	43	RCL		031	76	LBL	
012	11	11		032	16	A'	
013	95	=	Correct	033	02	2	
014	32	X!T	degree-day	034	04	4	Subroutine
015	00	0	for	035	65	×	calculates
016	77	GE	thermostat	036	43	RCL	Btu loss
017	90	LST	setting	037	11	11	
018	32	X!T		038	65	×	
019	50	I×I		039	43	RCL	

213

LOC	CODE	KEY	COMMENTS	LOC	CODE	KEY	COMMENTS
040	12	12		096	91	R/S	Exterior
041	55	÷		097	42	STO	wall Btu loss
042	43	RCL		098	10	10	
043	10	10		099	16	A'	
044	95	=		100	91	R/S	
045	44	SUM		101	42	STO	
046	00	00		102	12	12	
047	92	RTN		103	91	R/S	Ceiling
048	76	LBL		104	42	STO	Btu loss
049	80	GRD		105	10	10	
050	91	R/S		106	16	A'	
051	42	STO	Single-window	107	76	LBL	
052	12	12	Btu loss	108	17	B'	
053	93	.		109	91	R/S	
054	08	8		110	42	STO	
055	09	9		111	12	12	Basement wall
056	42	STO		112	91	R/S	Btu loss
057	10	10		113	42	STO	(heated and
058	16	A'		114	10	10	insulated)
059	91	R/S		115	16	A'	
060	42	STO		116	91	R/S	
061	12	12		117	61	GTO	Transfer
062	01	1		118	70	RAD	
063	93	.	Double-window	119	76	LBL	
064	08	8	Btu loss	120	18	C'	
065	42	STO		121	68	NOP	Above grade
066	10	10		122	91	R/S	basement
067	16	A'		123	42	STO	wall Btu
068	91	R/S		124	12	12	loss
069	42	STO		125	02	2	
070	12	12		126	42	STO	(heated
071	02	2		127	10	10	without
072	93	.	Thermopane	128	16	A'	insulation)
073	02	2	window	129	91	R/S	
074	42	STO	Btu loss	130	42	STO	
075	10	10		131	12	12	Below grade
076	16	A'		132	01	1	basement
077	91	R/S		133	07	7	wall Btu loss
078	42	STO		134	42	STO	
079	12	12		135	10	10	(heated
080	01	1	Nonglass	136	16	A'	without
081	93	.	door Btu loss	137	91	R/S	insulation)
082	04	4		138	68	NOP	
083	42	STO	(no storms)	139	76	LBL	
084	10	10		140	19	D'	
085	16	A'		141	42	STO	Slab floor
086	91	R/S		142	12	12	Btu loss
087	42	STO		143	91	R/S	
088	12	12	Nonglass	144	42	STO	
089	03	3	door Btu loss	145	10	10	
090	42	STO		146	16	A'	
091	10	10	(storms)	147	91	R/S	
092	16	A'		148	76	LBL	
093	91	R/S		149	70	RAD	
094	42	STO		150	42	STO	
095	12	12		151	12	12	

LOC	CODE	KEY	COMMENTS	LOC	CODE	KEY	COMMENTS
152	91	R/S	Floor	175	11	11	
153	49	PRD	Btu loss	176	49	PRD	
154	12	12		177	12	12	
155	16	A'		178	91	R/S	
156	91	R/S	_____	179	49	PRD	
157	76	LBL		180	12	12	
158	60	DEG		181	43	RCL	
159	42	STO		182	12	12	
160	12	12		183	44	SUM	
161	91	R/S		184	00	00	
162	49	PRD		185	91	R/S	_____
163	12	12		186	42	STO	
164	93	.		187	14	14	Store fuel
165	00	0		188	91	R/S	cost
166	01	1	Infiltration	189	22	INV	_____
167	08	8	Btu loss	190	49	PRD	
168	49	PRD		191	14	14	Calculate
169	12	12		192	43	RCL	cost of
170	02	2		193	00	00	heating
171	04	4		194	49	PRD	
172	49	PRD		195	14	14	
173	12	12		196	91	R/S	
174	43	RCL					

Personal Energy Budget

Approximately 20% of the nation's energy budget goes for residential use. Of this, space heating is by far the greatest single source of energy consumption. Over half of our residential energy goes to space heating with another 15% going for hot water heating. The remaining 30% of the residential energy budget goes for such things as cooking, air conditioning, and refrigeration. Transportation of materials and people accounts for almost 60% of the transportation budget. Hence, the national energy budget for cars, home heating, and hot water amounts to almost 40% of the total energy consumed in the country.

This program allows you to enter several energy-related variables to simulate a personal energy budget for any number of years. Further, you can simulate the effects of inflation on this budget by entering an annual inflation rate for each of the fuel sources. In times of high inflation this effect will be dramatic.

Sample Simulation

A particular house has an annual home heating expense of $525.55. This can be determined from utility bills or through a simulation with the previous program, "Home Heat." Weekly hot water consumption is estimated to be 410 gallons with a tank temperature of 135° F. The water tank is electric, and the power costs $0.055 per kilowatt hours. This family of four has only one car, which uses regular gas at $1.28 per gallon. They drive the car approximately 12,500 miles per year, and it averages 24 miles per gallon. For this simulation, inflation rates for all fuels will be 10%, and the annual energy budget for each of the next five years will be calculated.

215

Once the program has been keyed into the calculator and initialized, $525.55 is entered as indicated in step 3A of the user instructions, and 135 degrees are entered. Since the hot water tank uses electrical energy, enter the cost of a kilowatt hour (.055) and press R/S *St flg 1. The cost of fuel for vehicle 1 is entered as 1.28, the number of miles per year is entered as 12500, and the miles per gallon is 24. Although this family does not have a second car, entries *must* be made in steps 3H, 3I, and 3J. Note that these entries can be zero in steps 3H and 3I; however, a one must be entered in step 3J. (This prevents a division by zero, which would result in a flashing display.) Since all three inflation rates were selected as 10, enter 10 in steps 3K, 3L, and 3M. We want the program to simulate the situation for five years, so enter 5 in step 3N. The output will be displayed as indicated in the user instructions. For this particular simulation the output is:

Year	Energy Cost
1	$ 998.47
2	1098.32
3	1208.15
4	1328.97
5	1461.87

The program display halts with $6,095.78 in display to indicate the total cost for the five-year period.

User Instructions

Step	Procedure	Press	Display
1.	Enter program and return to run mode		
2.	Initialize	RST *CMs	
3.	Enter data as follows: (All costs are to be in dollars, and *no entry can be omitted.*)		
	A. Annual cost of home heat fuel, C_1	C_1 R/S	1.
	B. Gallons of hot water used per week, G (350 is about average)	G R/S	G
	C. Temperature in hot water tank, T (120° F–140° F is average)	T R/S	T
	D. If electric hot water tank, enter cost of electricity, C_2, per kilowatt hour	C_2 R/S *St flg 1	C_2
	or		

If natural gas hot water, enter
cost of 1000 cubic feet of gas,
C_3 C_3 R/S C_3

E. Cost of fuel for vehicle 1, C_4 C_4 R/S C_4

F. Number of miles per year for
vehicle 1, M_1 (If zero, enter 0) M_1 R/S M_1

G. Miles per gallon, vehicle 1   MPG R/S   Miles per gallon

H. Cost of fuel for vehicle 2, C_5 C_5 R/S C_5

I. Number of miles per year for
vehicle 2, M_2 M_2 R/S M_2

J. Miles per gallon, vehicle 2 (If
zero, enter 1)   MPG R/S   Miles per gallon

K. Average annual inflation rate
for hot water fuel (enter as
percent)   % R/S $\dfrac{\text{percent}}{100}$

L. Average annual inflation rate
for home heating fuel   % R/S $\dfrac{\text{percent}}{100}$

M. Average annual inflation rate
for vehicle fuel   % R/S $\dfrac{\text{percent}}{100}$

N. Length of simulation (in
years), Y Y R/S   Year number followed
by annual energy costs
for that year. Then,
program will halt with
the energy budget for
the entire simulation
on display.

4.   For a new simulation, go to step 2

Data Registers

00	Length of simulation	08	Miles per year, vehicle 2
01	Gallons water per week		
02	Water temperature	09	Miles per gallon, vehicle 2
03	Water fuel costs		
04	Fuel cost per gallon, vehicle 1	10	Inflation per year, hot water fuel
		11	Inflation per year, home heating fuel
05	Miles per year, vehicle 1	12	Inflation per year, gasoline
		13	Counter for years
06	Miles per gallon, vehicle 2	14	Current year energy costs
		15	Home heating costs
07	Fuel cost per gallon, vehicle 2	16	Total energy costs for entire simulation period

217

LOC	CODE	KEY	COMMENTS	LOC	CODE	KEY	COMMENTS
000	58	FIX		050	91	R/S	
001	02	02		051	55	÷	
002	42	STO		052	01	1	
003	15	15		053	00	0	
004	01	1		054	00	0	
005	42	STO		055	95	=	
006	13	13		056	42	STO	
007	91	R/S		057	12	12	
008	42	STO		058	91	R/S	
009	01	01		059	42	STO	
010	91	R/S		060	00	00	
011	42	STO	Locations	061	43	RCL	Calculate
012	02	02	000-058	062	15	15	home heating
013	91	R/S	for data	063	42	STO	costs
014	42	STO	entry and	064	14	14	
015	03	03	storage	065	43	RCL	
016	91	R/S		066	02	02	
017	42	STO		067	75	-	
018	04	04		068	05	5	
019	91	R/S		069	05	5	
020	42	STO		070	65	×	
021	05	05		071	08	8	
022	91	R/S		072	65	×	
023	42	STO		073	43	RCL	
024	06	06		074	01	01	
025	91	R/S		075	65	×	
026	42	STO		076	05	5	Calculate
027	07	07		077	02	2	hot water
028	91	R/S		078	95	=	costs
029	42	STO		079	87	IFF	
030	08	08		080	01	01	
031	91	R/S		081	34	⌈X	
032	42	STO		082	55	÷	
033	09	09		083	04	4	
034	91	R/S		084	06	6	
035	55	÷		085	00	0	
036	01	1		086	00	0	
037	00	0		087	00	0	
038	00	0		088	00	0	
039	95	=		089	76	LBL	
040	42	STO		090	44	SUM	
041	10	10		091	65	×	
042	91	R/S		092	43	RCL	
043	55	÷		093	03	03	
044	01	1		094	95	=	
045	00	0		095	44	SUM	
046	00	0		096	14	14	
047	95	=		097	42	STO	
048	42	STO		098	03	03	
049	11	11		099	43	RCL	

218

LOC	CODE	KEY	COMMENTS	LOC	CODE	KEY	COMMENTS
100	05	05		148	15	15	
101	55	÷		149	65	×	
102	43	RCL	Gasoline	150	43	RCL	
103	06	06	costs,	151	11	11	Calculate
104	65	×	vehicle	152	95	=	increase for
105	43	RCL	one	153	44	SUM	home heating
106	04	04		154	14	14	fuel
107	95	=		155	44	SUM	
108	44	SUM		156	15	15	
109	14	14		157	43	RCL	
110	42	STD		158	03	03	
111	04	04		159	65	×	
112	43	RCL		160	43	RCL	Calculate
113	08	08		161	10	10	increase for
114	55	÷		162	95	=	hot water
115	43	RCL		163	44	SUM	fuel
116	09	09	Gasoline	164	14	14	
117	65	×	costs,	165	44	SUM	
118	43	RCL	vehicle	166	03	03	
119	07	07	two	167	43	RCL	
120	95	=		168	04	04	
121	44	SUM		169	65	×	Calculate
122	14	14		170	43	RCL	increase for
123	42	STD		171	12	12	gasoline
124	07	07		172	95	=	
125	76	LBL		173	44	SUM	
126	33	X²		174	04	04	
127	43	RCL	Display year	175	44	SUM	
128	13	13		176	14	14	
129	66	PAU		177	01	1	
130	66	PAU		178	44	SUM	Increment
131	66	PAU		179	13	13	counter
132	43	RCL		180	61	GTD	
133	14	14		181	33	X²	
134	44	SUM	Display	182	76	LBL	
135	16	16	current year	183	45	Y×	Display total
136	66	PAU	energy costs	184	43	RCL	costs
137	66	PAU		185	16	16	
138	66	PAU		186	91	R/S	
139	22	INV		187	76	LBL	
140	97	DSZ	Check for end	188	34	ГX	Net Btu/kwh.
141	00	00	of program	189	55	÷	for electric
142	45	Y×		190	02	2	hot water
143	43	RCL		191	06	6	
144	07	07	Combine	192	06	6	
145	44	SUM	gasoline	193	03	3	
146	04	04	costs	194	61	GTD	
147	43	RCL		195	44	SUM	

219

Energy Reserves

Our standard of living in the United States, and in the world, depends heavily on fossil fuels. As more energy is needed for industry, agriculture, transportation, and business, we find ourselves in an energy crisis. Without an adequate and continuing supply of fossil fuels, the United States and the world will come to an abrupt stop.

Assume that the known recoverable reserves and the annual production of the fossil fuels petroleum, natural gas, and coal are those shown in Table 3-7.

TABLE 3-7   Energy Reserves of the World and the United States

	Petroleum (Metric Tons)		Natural Gas (Cubic Meters)		Coal (Metric Tons)	
	Recoverable Reserves	Annual Production	Recoverable Reserves	Annual Production	Recoverable Reserves	Annual Production
World	8.74×10^{10}	2.98×10^{9}	7.30×10^{13}	1.47×10^{12}	5.21×10^{11}	3.11×10^{9}
United States	3.59×10^{9}	4.30×10^{8}	5.49×10^{12}	5.77×10^{11}	1.55×10^{11}	5.16×10^{8}

How long will the known fossil fuel reserves last, assuming there is a constant annual percentage increase in usage?

Solution

The formula for compound interest with interest compounded yearly can be used in the solution of this problem. This formula is:

$$An = p(1 + \frac{r}{100})^n$$

Where: An = total amount at end of n years

p = principal

r = rate

Write a program to determine the number of years that the energy sources of petroleum, natural gas, and coal will last if the rate of increase is 0%, 2%, 5%, and 10%.

User Instructions

Step	Procedure		Press	Display
1.	Enter program			
2.	Initialize		*CMs RST	
3.	Enter rate, r	r	R/S	r
4.	Enter annual production, p (use scientific notation)	p	R/S	p
5.	Enter reserves, R	R	R/S	n
	Program will stop and display number of years fuel will last			
6.	For a new case, go to step 2			

220

Data Registers

01 r

02 p

03 n

04 Sn

Output

TABLE 3-8 Number of Years World Energy Reserves Will Last with Increasing Use

| | | Years | |
Rate of Increase (%)	Petroleum	Natural Gas	Coal
0	30	50	168
2	23	35	74
5	18	25	45
10	14	18	30

TABLE 3-9 Number of Years United States Energy Reserves Will Last with Increasing Use

| | | Years | |
Rate of Increase (%)	Petroleum	Natural Gas	Coal
0	9	10	301
2	8	9	98
5	7	8	56
10	6	7	36

Energy Reserves

LOC	CODE	KEY	COMMENTS	LOC	CODE	KEY	COMMENTS
000	42	STO	Enter and	018	02	02	
001	01	01	store r	019	65	×	
002	91	R/S	Enter and	020	53	(	
003	42	STO	store p	021	01	1	
004	02	02		022	85	+	Calculate and
005	91	R/S	Enter and	023	43	RCL	display An
006	32	X⫪T	store R	024	01	01	
007	22	INV	Set display	025	55	÷	
008	52	EE	format	026	01	1	
009	01	1		027	00	0	
010	66	PAU	Set n = 1,	028	00	0	
011	66	PAU	store, and	029	54	)	
012	66	PAU	display	030	45	Y×	
013	42	STO		031	43	RCL	
014	03	03		032	03	03	
015	76	LBL		033	03	3	
016	11	A		034	95	=	
017	43	RCL		035	66	PAU	

LOC	CODE	KEY	COMMENTS	LOC	CODE	KEY	COMMENTS
036	66	PAU		048	03	03	
037	66	PAU		049	66	PAU	
038	44	SUM	Add An to Sn	050	66	PAU	
039	04	04		051	66	PAU	Display n
040	43	RCL		052	66	PAU	
041	04	04		053	11	A	Transfer
042	77	GE		054	76	LBL	
043	12	B	Compare Sn	055	12	B	
044	01	1	to R	056	43	RCL	Display n
045	44	SUM		057	03	03	
046	03	03		058	91	R/S	
047	43	RCL					

Inflation What will the cost of a new car be in the year 2000, assuming it now costs $8000 and that there will be a: (1) 6% annual inflation rate? (2) 10% annual inflation rate? (3) 15% annual inflation rate?

Solution

$$An = p(1 + \frac{r}{100})^n$$

An = total amount at the end of n years

p = principal

r = rate

Using the above formula, write a program to determine the cost of the car in periods of ten years from 1980 to 2090.

User Instructions

Step	Procedure	Press	Display
1.	Enter program		
2.	Initialize	*CMs *FIX 2 RST	
3.	Enter rate, r, as a whole number	r R/S	r
4.	Enter principal, p	p	
5.	Run program	R/S	n
			An
6.	For a new case, go to step 2		

Data Registers

01 r

02 p

222 03 n

Output

Table 3-10 indicates the cost of a car for several selected years when the annual rate of inflation is 6%, 10%, and 15%.

TABLE 3-10   Future Costs of an $8000 Car Resulting from Inflation

| | | Cost | |
Number of Years	At 6% Inflation	At 10% Inflation	At 15% Inflation
10	14,326.78	20,749.94	32,364.46
20	25,657.08	53,820.00	130,932.30
30	45,947.93	139,595.22	529,694.18
40	82,285.74	362,074.04	2,142,908.37
50	147,361.23	939,126.82	8,669,259.53
60	263,901.53	2,435,853.12	35,071,989.97
70	472,607.44	6,317,975.65	141,885,760.30
80	846,367.95	16,387,201.72	574,007,035.20
90	1,515,716.09	42,504,180.89	2,322,178,602.00
100	2,714,416.67	110,244,898.70	9,394,507,606.00

Inflation

LOC	CODE	KEY	COMMENTS	LOC	CODE	KEY	COMMENTS
000	42	STO	Enter and	026	02	02	
001	01	01	store r	027	65	×	
002	91	R/S		028	53	(	
003	42	STO	Enter and	029	01	1	
004	02	02	store p	030	85	+	
005	01	1		031	43	RCL	Calculate An
006	00	0		032	01	01	
007	00	0		033	55	÷	
008	32	X:T	Initialize	034	01	1	
009	00	0		035	00	0	
010	42	STO		036	00	0	
011	03	03		037	54	)	
012	76	LBL		038	45	Yˣ	
013	11	A		039	43	RCL	
014	43	RCL		040	03	03	
015	03	03		041	95	=	
016	85	+	Increment n	042	66	PAU	
017	01	1	and display	043	66	PAU	Display An
018	00	0		044	66	PAU	
019	95	=		045	66	PAU	
020	42	STO		046	43	RCL	
021	03	03		047	03	03	Test for end
022	66	PAU		048	22	INV	of program
023	66	PAU		049	67	EQ	
024	66	PAU		050	11	A	
025	43	RCL		051	91	R/S	Halt

Appendixes

Appendix 1: Compatibility of Programs with TI Calculator Models

	TI-57	*TI-58*	*TI-59*
Changing Operations	Yes*	Yes	Yes
Four Consecutive Integers	Yes	Yes	Yes
Three-Digit Number	No	Yes	Yes
Integer Oddity	Yes	Yes	Yes
The Fibonacci Sequence	Yes*	Yes	Yes
Fibonacci Number Patterns	Yes	Yes	Yes
When Will We Meet Again?	No	Yes	Yes
Day of the Week	Yes	Yes	Yes
Sequence of Figurate Numbers	Yes	Yes	Yes
The Twelve Days of Christmas	Yes	Yes	Yes
Square-Triangular Numbers	Yes	Yes	Yes
Triangular Number Puzzle	No	Yes	Yes
Prime Factorization	Yes*	Yes	Yes
Prime Number Formulas	No	Yes	Yes

	TI–57	TI–58	TI–59
How Far Apart Are Adjacent Primes?	No	Yes	Yes
The Monkey and the Coconuts	Yes	Yes	Yes
The Book Problem	Yes	Yes	Yes
The Carpenter's Error	No	Yes	Yes
My Apartment	Yes*	Yes	Yes
The Birthday Problem	No	Yes	Yes
Bubble Gum Cards	Yes	Yes	Yes
The Wine Taster	No	Yes	Yes
Jack and Jill	No	Yes	Yes
Jelly Beans	Yes	Yes	Yes
The Arabian Prince	Yes	Yes	Yes
Kristin's Knockouts	Yes	Yes	Yes
Flight Fare	No	Yes	Yes
Squares and Rectangles	Yes	Yes	Yes
The Painted Box	No	Yes	Yes
Pythagorean Triplets	Yes	Yes	Yes
Integral 60° and 120° Triangles	No	Yes	Yes
The Red Square	Yes	Yes	Yes
Football	No	No	Yes
Sequence	No	Yes	Yes
Mystery Number	No	Yes	Yes
Calculaser	No	No	Yes
Race Car Driver	Yes	Yes	Yes
Random Numbers	No	Yes	Yes
Pseudorandom Numbers	No	Yes	Yes
Dice Simulation	No	Yes	Yes
Spinner Simulation	No	Yes	Yes
Dieting: Calories or Pounds	No	Yes	Yes
Cell Growth	No	Yes	Yes
Mammalian Life Spans	Yes	Yes	Yes
Metabolic Rates	No	Yes	Yes
Habit Formation	No	Yes	Yes
Aging through Space	No	Yes	Yes
How Far Is the Storm?	Yes	Yes	Yes
Compute Your Radiation Dose	No	No	Yes
Where Is Your Horizon?	Yes	Yes	Yes
Acid/Base Determination	No	Yes	Yes
General Gas Laws	No	Yes	Yes
Temperature Scales	No	Yes	Yes

	TI–57	TI–58	TI–59
Automobile Miles per Gallon	No	No	Yes
Improved Gas Mileage	Yes	Yes	Yes
Impact of Price Increase	Yes	Yes	Yes
Home Heat Simulations	No	Yes	Yes
Personal Energy Budget	No	Yes	Yes
Energy Reserves	Yes	Yes	Yes
Inflation	Yes	Yes	Yes

*Program will fit if the number of pause statements is reduced.

Appendix II: Correlation of Selected Printer Listings and Keyboard Keys

Printer Listing	*Keyboard Keys*
EQ	2nd $x = t$
GE	2nd $x \geqslant t$
IEQ	INV 2nd $x = t$
IGE	INV 2nd $x \geqslant t$
IFF	2nd If flg
IIFF	INV 2nd If flg
PAU	Pause
PGM	2nd Pgm
P/R	2nd P→R
RC*	RCL 2nd Ind
RTN	INV SBR
SM*	SUM 2nd Ind
ST*	STO 2nd Ind
STF	2nd St flg

501846